Charles and Emma

The Darwins' Leap of Faith

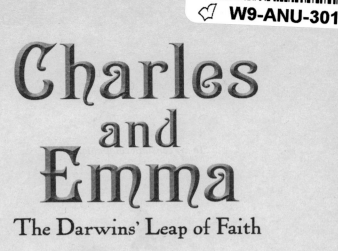

DEBORAH HEILIGMAN

SCHOLASTIC INC.
New York Toronto London Auckland
Sydney Mexico City New Delhi Hong Kong

To my constant companion

ISBN 978-0-545-44873-4

12 11 10 9 8 7 6 5 4 3 2   14 15 16 17/0

Printed in the U.S.A.   40

First Scholastic printing, January 2012

Designed by Elynn Cohen

Contents

Foreword		1
Chapter 1	Better Than a Dog	5
Chapter 2	Rat Catching	17
Chapter 3	Conceal Your Doubts	22
Chapter 4	Where Doors and Windows Stand Open	29
Chapter 5	Little Miss Slip-Slop	36
Chapter 6	The Next World	42
Chapter 7	The Sensation of Fear	47
Chapter 8	A Leap	55
Chapter 9	A Busy Man	60
Chapter 10	Melancholy Thoughts	68
Chapter 11	A Whirl of Noise and Motion	75
Chapter 12	Heavy Baggage, Blazing Fires	83
Chapter 13	Definition of Happiness	90
Chapter 14	Pregnant Thoughts	96
Chapter 15	Little Animalcules	101

Chapter 16	Down in the Country	109
Chapter 17	Sudden Deaths	116
Chapter 18	Barnacles and Babies	126
Chapter 19	Doing Custards	133
Chapter 20	A Fretful Child	137
Chapter 21	God Only Knows the Issue	143
Chapter 22	A Dear and Good Child	150
Chapter 23	Against the Rules	158
Chapter 24	Terrible Suffering	166
Chapter 25	The Origins of *The Origin*	174
Chapter 26	Dependent on Each Other in So Complex a Manner	180
Chapter 27	What the Lord Hath Delivered	187
Chapter 28	Feeling, Not Reasoning	195
Chapter 29	Such a Noise	202
Chapter 30	Mere Trickery	212
Chapter 31	Warmth to the End	217
Chapter 32	Happy Is the Man	225
Chapter 33	Unasked Questions	228
Epilogue	So Much to Worship	234
Acknowledgments		237
Family Tree		240
Source Notes		242
Selected Bibliography		260
Index		263

Foreword

The story of Charles Darwin has never been told this way before.

Authors by the hundreds have written about Darwin's genius and the way his ideas transformed the world. Scholars by the thousands have described the adventures that made him famous: first, his voyage around the world as a young naturalist aboard the HMS *Beagle* and, second, his discovery of the vast, novel, and strange intellectual territory that he mapped in his masterpiece, *The Origin of Species*.

Those two stories are among our civilization's most celebrated eureka moments. But as far as I know, this is the first book to focus on the adventure that began when Darwin, home from his voyage, took out a piece of scrap paper and made himself a quirky, funny, very candid list of the pros and cons of settling down.

Charles Darwin's search for a woman to marry led him almost immediately to a private eureka moment, when he visited his aunt and uncle at Maer Hall, in Staffordshire, and sat down by a fire in the library to have a little chat (they called it "a goose") with his cousin Emma Wedgwood.

In that time and place, marriage between cousins was not at all unusual, and everyone thought Charles and Emma were a good match. There was only one problem, one obstacle to their happiness: Emma was religious. She cared deeply about her Christian faith. When Charles confessed to her the revolutionary ideas that he was scribbling in his secret notebooks, she felt frightened. Emma thought they would be parted by death forever, go separate ways in eternity, because she would go to heaven and Charles would go to hell.

How Charles and Emma struggled with this dilemma and made a successful marriage of science and religion is the story told in this book. Reading it helps us understand in the most vivid, intimate, and personal way how shocking Darwin's ideas were for the people of his time, including some of the people who were closest to him. It helps us see why he felt he had to keep his ideas to himself for so long, writing SECRET on the covers of the journals and notebooks in which he scribbled furiously during the months and years after the voyage of the *Beagle*. The ideas in Charles's notebooks seemed revolutionary and dangerous, not only to many of the people around him in nineteenth-century England but to the woman he loved more than anyone in the world. We can understand better why he spent twenty years refining and polishing his theory before he dared, with dread and misgivings, to publish *The Origin of Species*.

So often the scientific and the religious views of life are seen as two separate worlds. As enemies. And in a sense you might say that Charles and Emma Darwin were each sleeping with the enemy. But they were not enemies. They were the best of friends, and their story is an inspiration. They had ten children. They lost three. One of those deaths was so tragic and terrible that Charles and Emma could hardly bear to talk about it for the rest of their lives. The problem of faith and religion and the afterlife in some ways only grew larger as they confronted those tragedies and faced the chasm at the end of life. And yet together they triumphed.

Darwin's revolutionary ideas have become so established now that biologists cannot imagine life without them. But those same ideas still have the power to frighten and disturb many devout people. The ability of Charles and Emma to go beyond those differences—to love each other in spite of them—is an inspiring story for our time.

Because the love story of Charles and Emma has not been told before at full length, even old Darwin fans will find much here to enjoy. Consider the last paragraph of *The Origin of Species*, one of the most famous passages in science. There Darwin sums up his whole view of life by talking about an entangled bank. I never knew until I read this book that this was a bank that Charles and Emma often saw on their walks from Down House, their home in the country. Charles and Emma were entangled in their love and science, just as mind, heart, and spirit are entangled in each one of us.

Reading *Charles and Emma*, one feels that their love story was one of the most significant adventures and greatest masterpieces of Darwin's life.

—JONATHAN WEINER
Pulitzer prize-winning
author of *The Beak of the Finch*

In her presence he found his happiness,
and through her, his life.
—FRANCIS DARWIN

Chapter 1

Better Than a Dog

Why, the shape of his head is quite altered.
—DR. ROBERT DARWIN, IN 1836,
AFTER CHARLES'S FIVE-YEAR VOYAGE

In the summer of 1838, in his rented rooms on Great Marlborough Street, London, Charles Darwin drew a line down the middle of a piece of scrap paper. He had been back in England for almost two years, after a monumental voyage around the world. He was in his late twenties. It was time to decide. Across the top of the left-hand side, he wrote *Marry*. On the right he wrote *Not Marry*. And in the middle: *This is the Question*.

It was easy for Charles to think of things to write under *Not Marry*.

"Freedom to go where one liked," he began. Charles loved to travel. His voyage had lasted almost five years; he had been the naturalist on the HMS *Beagle*, a British surveying ship. He was horribly seasick while on board, but he spent as much time as he could on land, exploring on horseback and on foot, and collecting thousands of specimens, from corals in the Cocos-Keeling Islands of the Indian Ocean to beetles in Australia to a fox in Chiloé Island, Chile. He now lived in London with his servant from the *Beagle*, Syms Covington, "Fiddler and Boy to the Poop Cabin." Charles had taught Syms to shoot and skin birds and to help him list and catalogue the specimens. Now Charles and Syms were surrounded by neatly stacked wooden crates, casks, and barrels filled with many of their treasures from Patagonia, Brazil, Chile, and Tierra del Fuego: fossil bones, skins, shells, fish preserved in spirits of wine, mammalia in spirits of wine, insects, reptiles and birds in spirits of wine, plants, rocks, carcasses of dead animals, and beetles. What if Charles wanted to go on another adventure and collect more specimens? How could he do that if he got married?

Next, under *Not Marry* he wrote: "—choice of Society & little of it.—Conversation of clever men at clubs—"

On Great Marlborough Street, Charles lived just a few doors away from his older brother, Erasmus, and he was spending much of his time with Eras and his circle of intellectual friends, which included the historian and writer Thomas Carlyle and his wife, Jane; the writer Harriet Martineau; and the Darwins' first cousin, Hensleigh Wedgwood. They discussed the huge changes in England brought on by industrialization. When Charles had left for his voyage, there were a few trains; now the railroad zigzagged all over the country, reaching places only horse-drawn carriages had gone before. The growing number of mills and factories changed the landscape as well; towns and cities were expanding, as was the division between rich and poor. The rich benefited from the new industry and from Great Britain's burgeoning empire. The poor suffered in the squalor that Charles Dickens was capturing so well in his serialized novels. Erasmus and his circle debated the Poor Laws, which were shunting the destitute into workhouses; they discussed the need for social reform.

There were divisions in religion in nineteenth-century England, too. Religious zealots and religious dissenters were making noise while members of the Church of England and Unitarians like the Darwins also quietly questioned their faith. Freethinking liberals, Eras and his circle were respected members of the British upper classes, and Charles found it easy—and stimulating—to be with them. Because they were open-minded and liberal, Charles knew he could broach with them some of the radical scientific thoughts he was beginning to have. This was what mattered to him. Not going to dinner parties, teas, and other torturous social occasions where people inundated him with seemingly endless questions about his travels.

Not that all of his social occasions were torturous. Charles was spending time with—and being courted by—three sisters in one family. The Horner girls were clever young women, well-read and educated, with promising intellectual futures. They even shared his interest in natural history, geology, and zoology. Their oldest sister, Mary, was already married to a new friend of his, Charles Lyell, a prominent geologist. Mr. Horner approved of Charles Darwin as a son-in-law and hoped for a match. "I have not seen anyone for a long time with a greater store of accurate knowledge," he wrote to Mary. Erasmus teased Charles, calling Mrs. Horner "Mother-in-law." So the marriage question was not hypothetical.

And Charles Darwin *was* a good catch. He was a tall man, about six feet, thickset—big but not fat. He was athletic and fit from his adventures on the voyage. He dressed conservatively in the styles of the day: tailcoat, fine linen shirt with standing collar, and tall hat. He had gray eyes, a ruddy complexion, and a pleasant face, though he did not like his nose, which he felt was too big and bulbous. He was from an upstanding, wealthy family; he had much to talk about, and he had a promising future. His reputation had, as they say, preceded him. While he was traveling, Charles had sent back thousands of his specimens to his old Cambridge professor, John Stevens Henslow. Some of these specimens had begun to make him famous in the natural history world before he had even returned to England, including a rare fossil head of a giant ground sloth he had found in Argentina "in horizontal position in the cemented gravel; the upper jaw & molars exposed," as Charles had written in his first geological specimen notebook. The remarkable fossil sloth head had been presented at a meeting of the British Association of the Advancement of Science in Cambridge.

But if he were to marry one of the Horner girls, or anyone else, he could see the obligations ahead, whereas if he remained single, he would be freer to pursue his science.

He added to the *Not Marry* side of his list, "Not forced to visit relatives, & to bend in every trifle." He liked his brother, his sisters, his cousins the Wedgwoods. But what if he didn't like his wife's relatives? There was so much compromising you had to do if you were married. He could see it in his friends, many of whom had gotten married while he was away.

Walking down the street one day not long after he had gotten back, he had seen his cousin Hensleigh carrying a child in one hand and a round box in the other. Hensleigh had married a cousin from the other side of his family in 1832, the year Charles left on the voyage. (First cousins often married at this time, especially in the upper classes.) Now Hensleigh had two children, and Charles shuddered at the thought of all the juggling a young father had to do. Did he want the responsibility? His reaction to this scene was so strong that it made the rounds of the family gossip: Emma Wedgwood, Hensleigh's sister, wrote to her sister-in-law with amusement how struck Charles was by Hensleigh's juggling.

Not surprising, therefore, that Charles continued his *Not Marry* list with "—to have the expense & anxiety of children— perhaps quarrelling." It wasn't just the time and distraction that worried him; although he was frugal, he doubted he would ever make enough money by collecting beetles and writing about coral. Lack of money always led to fights, that he knew. And could he stand the anxiety and worry of having children? Cholera, a deadly disease, had just reached England for the first time, and there were epidemics of typhus, typhoid fever, and scarlet fever. Children got sick, children died. So there would be worry about health along with worry about money. And it all would take so much time. That was the crux of the issue. He wrote and underlined twice "Loss of time."

Charles needed as many hours a day as he could have to do his work. First of all, he had to solicit more experienced naturalists to help him analyze his specimens. Charles had so many kinds of specimens; he was not an expert on every bird, bone, and bug. He had already given out his rare *Megatherium* bones and his finches and mockingbirds from the Galapagos Islands. But he had more of his collections to distribute to experts, and he had to urge them, coax them, to tell him what they thought. What did he have? Had he found new species? What significance did his finds have, if any?

As a single man with no family responsibilities, he could

meet with these experts, go to scientific meetings, and visit museums and libraries whenever he wanted to. He didn't have to worry about a wife or her relatives dictating how his time should be spent.

Charles felt strongly that he had no time to waste. Near the end of his voyage, he had heard from one of his sisters that Henslow and another old professor of his, Adam Sedgwick, were both very interested in the bones he had sent back. Sedgwick declared his collection "above all praise" and said that Charles would have "a great name among the Naturalists of Europe." Charles found this terribly gratifying and knew that with those endorsements he would continue to work hard on natural history. He wrote, "A man who dares to waste one hour of time has not discovered the value of life."

Before the voyage, Charles had been a typical natural history collector. In nineteenth-century England, everyone from country parsons to teenage girls collected butterflies, flowers, even stuffed birds and fossil bones. Looking at God's wondrous handiwork was a worthwhile avocation, and in some cases, vocation. Collectors tried to amass and describe as many of God's species as possible and hoped to find new crabs, moths, finches, or ferns. And if you were lucky, the new species you discovered would be named after you—Charles had a few named after him, including a South American ostrichlike bird, the *Rhea darwinii*, and a frog that lived in Chile and Argentina, *Rhinoderma darwinii*.

Although he was pleased to have such an extensive collection, Charles was thinking about something bigger when he looked at his fossils. He was thinking about the origins of life. While on the voyage, reading Charles Lyell's *Principles of Geology* and looking at desert islands, rugged cliffs, and volcanoes, Charles knew that Lyell was right: Earth was not formed in

4004 B.C. as Archbishop James Ussher had calculated in 1658. This date had been incorporated into an authorized Bible in 1701, and many people still believed it was a fact. But Charles was certain that the earth was formed much longer ago than that and *was still being formed.* Once he realized that the earth was changing, that the story of creation in the Bible was not literally true, Charles's mind was opened to the possibility of a different kind of creation in the animal and plant kingdoms. Looking at the specimens he had collected, Charles realized that species were forming and changing all the time, too. The idea of evolution, or transmutation, as it was then called, had been debated and refuted for years. But toward the end of his voyage, and now back in England, as he looked at bird specimens from the Galapagos Islands, Charles had the beginnings of a new theory to explain transmutation. He felt sure that if he could work it through, he would change the way the world thought about creation. He desperately wanted and needed to work it through. He had started the great project already, and he was consumed by it, giving it hours and hours every day.

He was making copious notes in small leather notebooks filled with high-quality paper made from linen rags. Each notebook was labeled with a letter. He had opened the first one, a brown leather notebook with a metal clasp, in July 1837. On the cream-colored pages, he had begun to jot down his secret and revolutionary thoughts about the origin of new species. Examining specimens he had collected, Charles was finding evidence that went against the prevailing concept of creation, which was that God had created all the species of birds, bees, and beetles at once and that there were no new ones since the first creation. Some people argued that fossils existed because God, displeased with his creations, had engineered a few worldwide catastrophes that had destroyed all the existent species and then had started creation all over again. But Charles had a very different idea, and he was accumulating pages and pages of observations, thoughts, ideas, and questions, filling up more and more notebooks, each with a different focus and marked with a different letter. He had many questions, from the everyday: "Owls. transport mice alive?" to the pointed: "How easily does Wolf & Dog cross?" How could he answer all of them if he succumbed to the mundane responsibilities of married life? He would have to spend his time hurrying down the street with a box in one arm and a baby in the other. There was so much to write on the *Not Marry* side of the page!

He continued, "Cannot read in the Evenings—fatness & idleness—Anxiety & responsibility—less money for books &c if many children forced to gain one's bread."

And yet, even on this side of the paper, he conceded "(But then it is very bad for ones health to work too much)."

Back to the negatives. "Perhaps my wife won't like London; then the sentence is banishment & degradation into indolent, idle fool."

Charles wasn't completely sure he liked London himself. The city was noisy and dirty, the weather murky, the air often polluted with a yellow smog from the new factories and from all the fireplaces burning dirty coal. He often longed for the countryside near Wales where he grew up. But he thought that living in the country might make him lazy, which would be terrible for his work. He absolutely did not want to be either idle or a fool. On the other hand, you could stay in London and still be idle. Erasmus was; he was no fool, but he had neither a wife nor a career. Charles looked at him and knew that was not what he wanted.

So. That's where he ended his list of reasons not to marry.

Under *Marry*, Charles began: "Children—(if it please God)." He did enjoy other people's children. He played with them, and he observed them. He wrote in one of his secret notebooks "Children have an uncommon pleasure in hiding themselves & skulking about in shrubbery. When other people are about: this is analogous to young pigs hiding themselves."

Looking at his friends' and cousins' children he thought not only of pigs but also of "savages," as the English called native people. During his voyage around the world, his encounters with natives had been startling and enlightening. On the *Beagle* there were three people from Tierra del Fuego who had lived for a while in England. They had been "civilized" in that they now wore British clothes and had adopted British manners. But when Charles and his shipmates first arrived in Tierra del Fuego, a group of natives perched on an overhang above the sea "sprang up, and waving their tattered cloaks sent forth a loud and sonorous shout." They wore little clothing. Some of them, even full-grown women, were completely naked. Their hair was tangled, but many of the people had dramatically painted faces, with a bright red bar from ear to ear, white-chalked eyelids, streaks of black charcoal. As different as they looked, they were able to communicate with the English travelers and could imitate anything. One native man had learned new dance steps, which impressed Charles. Spending time with these people had made Charles think of ways that pigs, children, primitive peoples, Englishmen all were related. This was a clue to his secret theory.

But now, thinking about children, he was thinking also as a man and a potential father. It would be nice to have his own little piggies skulking about in the bushes.

Charles definitely liked to be surrounded by people. He

had good friends and was close to his sisters and his brother. Having a wife would be really nice. He continued on the *Marry* side, "constant companion (& friend in old age) who will feel interested in one—"

He hoped his wife would live a long time, unlike his mother, who had died painfully, probably of an infection, when Charles was only eight. His father, an experienced and extremely successful doctor, had not been able to save her. Her death devastated Dr. Darwin, though Charles himself hardly remembered her. He hoped he would find someone who would be interested in him, definitely, but he also wanted someone he could love. He wrote "object to be beloved & played with."

And then: "better than a dog anyhow."

Sometimes Charles thought dogs were easier than people. He had loved dogs since he was a boy, and they loved him. When Charles had just gotten back from the voyage, he found it difficult at first to resume where he had left off with his sisters and his father. He had changed, and they didn't seem to be able to adjust to that. But when he went out into the yard and whistled, his dog (who was surly to everyone else but adored him) rushed out to walk with him, as if their last walk had been the day before, not five years earlier. Why couldn't people be more like dogs? he wondered—and wished. But a dog can't do everything, and so a wife *would* be better than a dog anyhow.

He listed more positives: "Home, & someone to take care of house—Charms of music & female chit-chat.—These things good for one's health.—but—"

There it was again—"terrible loss of time." Too much music, too much chitchat. Not enough time to do his work. Again he looked at his brother, Erasmus. Even though he was a bachelor, Eras spent much of his time with women—mostly other men's wives—taking them on errands in his carriage, going to dinners. But then he returned them to their husbands. Harriet Martineau wasn't married, and there was gossip about Harriet and Erasmus. But Eras seemed determined to remain single. His father and sisters wanted to fix him up with their cousin Emma Wedgwood, mostly to stop the gossip, but so far nothing had happened there. Erasmus was in control of his own life, as Charles could be if he stayed a bachelor, too. Yet—

"My God, it is intolerable to think of spending ones whole life, like a neuter bee, working, working, & nothing after all.—No, no won't do.—Imagine living all one's day solitarily in smoky dirty London House."

Alone in his smoky, dirty London house, Charles thought about love and romance and what went with it. He read poems by the romantics William Wordsworth and Samuel Taylor Coleridge—"Where true Love burns Desire is Love's pure flame. . . ." He filled his notebooks with the scientific aspects of love, with questions about breeding and heredity. So far most of his questions were about animals, but in his notebook marked "B," Charles wrote in brown ink on pages with faint green rules, "In Man it has been said, there is instinct for opposites to like each other." Perhaps he and his wife would be opposites, but close.

"Only picture to yourself a nice soft wife on a sofa with good fire, & books & music perhaps—"

And heading off to bed later.

He ended his list under *Marry*, "Compare this version with the dingy reality of Grt. Marlbro' St."—his life on Great Marlborough Street, where he went to bed alone.

The lists on the left and right side of the page looked

about the same length. But Charles felt that he had found more reasons to marry than not. He wrote on the left side, squeezed at the bottom, the answer to his question: "Marry— Marry—Marry Q.E.D."

QED: *quod erat demonstrandum*, Latin for "which was to be demonstrated or proved." He had proven to himself that he should get married. On paper at least. But he had one other fear, a fear that he could not bring himself to write down. The issue was too big. He would have to talk to his father.

Chapter 2

Rat Catching

I do not believe that anyone could have shown more zeal
for the most holy cause than I did for shooting birds.
—CHARLES, ON HIS CHILDHOOD PASSION

To talk to his father, Charles set out for home. Home was the Mount, a large, square brick house in Shrewsbury, a quiet market town in the county of Shropshire about 150 miles northwest of London. Even with the expanded railroad, the trip from London to Shrewsbury was a long one; it had to be made by train and carriage. The journey would take Charles all day, about twelve hours.

The Mount was typical of Georgian architecture from the previous century. The house had regular, strict proportions, which was how Charles's father liked things. Charles's father, Dr. Robert Darwin, was a huge man—over three hundred pounds, with a huge personality and reputation to match. People from all over Shropshire came to him for advice—both medical and financial, for he was a successful physician and a keen businessman. He had invested his and his wife's money well. Charles's mother, Susanna, was the daughter of Josiah Wedgwood, who had founded the famous and profitable Wedgwood pottery company.

The house was set at the bend of a river, and there were beautiful gardens out back. It was the home of a wealthy family, with maids and other servants to boil water, empty chamber pots, light the gaslights and oil lamps, keep the fires going to make the house warm(ish), prepare the meals, do the laundry (by hand), and in general run the house, just as they had when Charles was growing up.

Charles was born at the Mount on February 12, 1809 (the very same day a baby named Abraham Lincoln was born across the Atlantic Ocean in a log cabin in Kentucky). Charles—or Bobby, as he was called as a baby—was the fifth of six children. He and Erasmus were the only boys. There were four girls, including Catherine, who was born not quite two years after Charles.

Because Susanna had died when Charles was so young, it was Robert Darwin who was the main adult presence in the household—and a presence he was. From the time Charles was little, Dr. Darwin would hold forth for hours at a time at the dinner table and in the parlor afterward with his children and any company as captive audiences. He expounded his ideas about medicine, human nature, politics, and business. Though he loved his children, he did not give them much freedom of thought: He was certain that his views were the right views. In only one area did he allow them some amount of leeway, and that was in religion. He raised the children as Unitarians. Unitarianism was a lenient Christian faith at the center of social reform in England. It was not very demanding about the specifics of belief. Charles's grandfather, Erasmus

Darwin, had made fun of Unitarianism, saying it was a "feather-bed to catch a falling Christian." Dr. Darwin liked to quote that saying, too. But being a Unitarian was good for many reasons. Unitarians did not stand out in society as heretics, but the faith was easy to live with if you felt uncomfortable with a more serious, stricter branch of Christianity.

Susanna Wedgwood had been a bright and lively woman, and Dr. Darwin had been very much in love with her. But she was sickly before she died, so Charles and Catherine were raised and taught by the older girls: Marianne, Caroline, and Susan. Charles was very close to his older sisters, and looked to them as mothers. And he always adored and looked up to his big brother, Erasmus. But growing up he liked to spend much of his time alone. He took long walks by himself around the Shropshire countryside, thinking.

One day he was walking on a public footpath at the top of some old ruins around Shrewsbury. He was so caught up in his thoughts that he walked right off the footpath and fell down seven or eight feet. He remembered years later that "the number of thoughts which passed through my mind during this very short, but sudden and wholly unexpected fall, was astonishing."

Charles could entertain himself for hours just by thinking, or by observing birds, or watching sticks and leaves float down a stream. He made notes as he watched the birds, writing down what they did, how they behaved. And like many young boys, he was a collector. He collected shells, seals, coins, and minerals. He studied them and organized them by kind—in the tradition of natural historians. As he got older, his great love was hunting and shooting. Later in life he shuddered at how many animals he had killed. But at the time he quivered with joy and excitement before picking up a gun.

Soon after Susanna died, Dr. Darwin sent Charles to a boarding school that was just a mile from the Mount. Since school was so close and since he was not happy there—they didn't teach him much, or what they did try to teach him he wasn't interested in learning—Charles went home often and usually had to run to school before classes started or before the buildings were locked up at night. When he wasn't sure he would get there on time, he'd pray earnestly to God to help him. Much later he remembered that if he got to school on time, he attributed his success "to the prayers and not to my quick running, and marveled how generally I was aided." In spite of his father's nonbelief, Charles gave God the credit.

In high school, Charles was still not a good student. Yet outside of school, in a little shed at home, Charles loved to do chemistry experiments with Erasmus. He did them so often that his school friends nicknamed him Gas. But science was not considered a valuable use of any young man's time, and his headmaster admonished him for not paying more attention to his math or his Latin.

Dr. Darwin decided to take Charles out of high school since he wasn't making much use of it anyway. Erasmus, who was twenty-one, was going to Edinburgh, Scotland, to study medicine; Charles could tag along. Both boys were bright, and it seemed obvious to Dr. Darwin that they should follow him in his profession. So at only sixteen, Charles went straight to medical school.

In Edinburgh, some of the professors and students loved natural history, and Charles learned from them. He spent time with Erasmus, went to scientific talks, joined clubs, and got to know a freed slave named John Edmonstone, who taught him how to stuff birds. This would become quite handy later on, and he enjoyed Edmonstone's company very much. But he didn't like his medical school classes. He watched two operations, both of which he ran away from before they were finished. One of them was an amputation on a child; the child screamed in pain, for there was no anesthesia. Charles listened to the poor child's screams and saw all that blood and decided he could never go into medicine. He hated the sight of blood for the rest of his life.

When Dr. Darwin heard that Charles wanted to leave school, he wrote to him in anger, "You care for nothing but shooting, dogs, and rat-catching, and you will be a disgrace to yourself and all your family. "

Erasmus did not become a doctor either. Dr. Darwin, it seems, was not always right. But now, in the summer of 1838, Charles still wanted to get his father's advice about marriage. He arrived at the Mount determined to talk to his father about the problem that was so big he hadn't put it on his *Not Marry* list.

Chapter 3

Conceal Your Doubts

*Man in his arrogance thinks himself a great work, worthy
the interposition of a deity. More humble and I believe
true to consider him created from animals.*
—CHARLES, "C" NOTEBOOK, 1838

Dr. Darwin had seen everything in his medical practice. He
was not surprised by much. So now, in the summer of 1838,
when Charles told him that he wanted to get married but was
afraid about a few things, Dr. Darwin was ready to help.

First Charles told his father that he was worried he
wouldn't be able to support a family with his current plan of
pursuing science. Dr. Darwin knew Charles was going to have
his first book published, an account of his voyage on the *Beagle*, and it was clear that he had a promising scientific career.

But, Charles's father told him, even without any income
from his work, he would be fine. With family money from the
doctor's practice and wise investments, Charles would have
enough to support himself and a family quite nicely while he
pursued natural history and wrote books.

This was a huge relief to Charles. But there was still a major concern holding him back. A problem so big that even Charles, who wrote down all of his thoughts, couldn't put it on paper. This problem was as big as it got.

The problem was God.

Charles hadn't always thought about God or religion as a problem. In fact, after he had given up the idea of medicine, both Charles and his father thought he was going to be a country parson. Even though Dr. Darwin was not a religious man himself, having a son who was in the church was not an anathema to him. Being a country parson was an honorable profession for a British gentleman, and one that left a good amount of time for pursuing other activities, such as collecting. So ten years earlier, Charles had left Edinburgh and had gone off to study theology at Christ's College, Cambridge.

While at university, Charles read theology, not just on assignment but also for pleasure. He especially enjoyed the works of William Paley. He read Paley's *A View of the Evidences of Christianity*, his *The Principles of Moral and Political Philosophy,* and his *Natural Theology*. Paley wrote about natural history, arguing that if you examined specimens carefully, you could see how beautifully they were created, how perfect they were in their adaptations. This to Paley was evidence of the existence of God and proof that God was the creator of all species. Charles thought these arguments were well-written, coherent, and logical. He did not, at that point, question Paley's premises about God's role in creation. He later said that he had learned from Paley how to construct an argument.

But at the same time that he devoured Paley and theology, Charles was devouring natural history and collecting specimens, especially beetles. One day he was walking around Cambridge, foraging for beetles to study. He had a beetle in one hand, and when he found a second, he put it in his other hand. But then he saw a different kind of beetle on a tree. He wanted all three. He put the second one in his mouth and picked up the third. "Alas," he wrote later, the one in his mouth "ejected some intensely acrid fluid, which burnt my tongue so that I was forced to spit the beetle out." He lost that one and dropped the third beetle, too. It was a lesson for him: Bugs don't always do what you want them to, and not all beetles want to be caught.

While at university, Charles became close friends with a botany professor, John Stevens Henslow. They would spend hours together, walking around picking up plants and insects. Charles became known as "the man who walks with Henslow."

Although Charles graduated from Cambridge with no great academic distinction, because of his connection to Henslow he was offered the position of naturalist on the *Beagle*. He really wanted to go. He would spend two years as a companion to the captain, a man named Robert FitzRoy. And he would be able to see the world—collecting specimens along the way. It was a dream come true. But since it was not a paid position (in fact, he would have to pay his own way), he needed not only his father's permission, he needed his money.

Dr. Darwin thought the trip was a bad idea. He told Charles it was "a wild scheme," one that would be disreputable to his future career as a clergyman. The doctor did not think the trip would be useful in any way for his son's future. Furthermore, his father said, settling down after such an adventure would be too difficult. Dr. Darwin told Charles to say no to the voyage. But he also said that if Charles could find a respectable person who disagreed, he would reconsider.

After that conversation, Charles had gone to visit his mother's brother, Josiah Wedgwood, at his house, Maer Hall.

Maer was only a day's carriage ride from the Mount, and when he was a child, Charles and his Wedgwood cousins visited back and forth often. Charles was especially close to his uncle Josiah, whom he found to be a good contrast to his father. Although Uncle Jos was quiet and reserved, not animated and talkative like Dr. Darwin, he was much more open-minded. On this visit Charles told Uncle Jos, Aunt Bessy, and his cousins about the possibility of the voyage and about his father's objections. They all thought he should definitely go. Uncle Jos agreed to try to convince Dr. Darwin that Charles should be able to take advantage of this opportunity. Charles wrote to his father, "I have given Uncle Jos what I fervently trust is an accurate and full list of your objections, and he is kind enough to give his opinions on all." Charles asked his father to look at the list and Uncle Josiah's answers and then to please give him a yes or a no. If it were to remain a no, Charles assured him, "I will never mention the subject again."

Uncle Jos found he could answer most of Dr. Darwin's objections easily. He wrote, "I should not think it would be in any degree disreputable to his character as a Clergyman. I should on the contrary think the offer honourable to him; and the pursuit of Natural History, though certainly not professional, is very suitable to a clergyman." He did not think it would be a wild scheme, as Charles "would have definite objects upon which to employ himself, and might acquire and strengthen habits of application, and I should think would be as likely to do so as in any way in which he is likely to pass the next two years at home."

Uncle Jos agreed that the voyage would probably not directly prepare him for a career as a clergyman, but argued that it would help him grow as a man, affording him "such an opportunity of seeing men and things as happens to few."

Uncle Jos and Charles sent the letter to Dr. Darwin early in the morning, and then Charles went out shooting in the woods near Maer Hall. After a few hours, Uncle Jos sent Charles a message saying that he was going to the Mount to talk to the doctor directly. Charles put down his gun and went with him. When they arrived at Shrewsbury, Dr. Darwin told them that he had been convinced. He gave Charles his consent. He also gave him a generous purse and the assurance that he could always write home and ask for more money. Charles needed to, and did. Often. The voyage that was meant to be two years lasted almost five.

As Dr. Darwin had predicted, the voyage did not prepare him for a life as a vicar. While he traveled, however, Charles did go to church quite regularly, both to the services that his captain led and on shore whenever he got the chance. Some of the crew made fun of him for how religious he seemed. And his first publication, in 1836—with his captain— was a letter in the *South African Christian Recorder* arguing for increased funding for Christian missionaries.

But natural history became his true passion and now, after the voyage, in 1838, Charles was having serious doubts about God and Jesus, about the Revelation, about heaven and hell. He wasn't an atheist, but he had begun to reject God's role in creation. At the same time that he was making his *Marry, Not Marry* list and writing in his notebooks about transmutation of species, he was reading and writing about religion and talking to his friends about his beliefs. He did not believe that God created the earth and all its creatures in six days. He felt certain just as the earth's geography was changing, so were new species being created all the time, and God did not have a role in that creation.

He also began to have doubts that Christianity was *the* religion. Why should he believe it was the only right way? He felt that the Hebrew scripture's history of the world was false, that there was no Tower of Babel, no rainbow as a sign from God after a big flood. The Bible was no more to be trusted than any other religion's holy book. He also began to disbelieve the Old Testament idea of a wrathful God, a revengeful tyrant. He found it hard to believe anything in the Bible was literally true—including the Gospels. If the Gospels were not true, then where did that leave belief in Jesus as savior? How could Christianity be Divine Revelation? How could Christianity be the one true religion? He was not dismissing God altogether, nor was he dismissing Christianity. But his doubts were strong, and growing.

He knew that these doubts and his revolutionary thoughts about transmutation and the creation of species would stand in his way of finding a wife. Most women were believers and wanted their husbands to be believers, too.

On this visit home, Charles confessed all to his father and asked for his counsel. Dr. Darwin had no problem with his son's religious doubts. He shared them. But he did have very strong advice for him: When you find the woman you want to marry, don't tell her! The doctor had seen many marriages in his medical practice, and he told Charles that he had known "extreme misery thus caused with married persons. Things went on pretty well until the wife or husband became out of health, and then some women suffered miserably by doubting about the salvation of their husbands." And then, Dr. Darwin concluded, the husbands suffered, too.

The doctor encouraged his son to take the plunge. He thought Charles would be happy being married. He also told him that children were healthier if they were born to younger parents and Charles wasn't getting any younger; he was nearing thirty. So the doctor gave Charles another piece of advice: hurry up.

But don't forget, Dr. Darwin warned his son, "Conceal your doubts!"

Chapter 4

Where Doors and Windows Stand Open

*Emma's handwriting ... was, like herself, firm,
calm, and transparently clear.*
—HENRIETTA DARWIN LITCHFIELD

*Excuse this scrawl but I have such a Pen and besides
never could write like any thing but what I am.... Burn
this as soon as read—or tremble at my fury and revenge.*
—FANNY OWEN IN A LETTER TO CHARLES, JANUARY 1828

A few weeks later, in the summer of 1838, Charles decided to make another trip. He wanted to visit Uncle Josiah and Aunt Bessy and his cousins at Maer Hall. Late July was a good time to get out of murky, hot, dirty London, and Charles loved the Staffordshire countryside around Maer, which "was very pleasant for walking or riding." He also loved the atmosphere of peaceful hospitality at the Wedgwoods' home. At Maer "life was perfectly free." He looked forward to the summer evenings when "there was much very agreeable conversation ... the whole family used often to sit on the steps of the old portico with the flower-garden in front, and with the steep wooded bank opposite the house reflected in the lake, with here and there a fish rising or a water-bird paddling about."

Charles's Wedgwood cousins had been brought up with few, if any, rules and the encouragement to think freely. Whereas Uncle Jos could seem stern, he was a much more accepting person than Charles's father, and a more relaxed parent. Both Uncle Jos and his wife, Bessy, thought everyone— boys and girls, men and women—should have their own opinions and be able to express them. Back in 1819, a family friend who had visited Maer wrote in her journal "I never saw anything pleasanter than the ways of going on of this family, and one reason is the freedom of speech upon every subject; there is no difference in politics or principles of any kind that makes it treason to speak one's mind openly, and they all do it. There is a simplicity of good sense about them, that no one ever dreams of not differing upon any subject where they feel inclined. . . . There is no bitterness in discussing opinions." The children "have freedom in their actions in this house as well as in their principles. Doors and windows stand open, you are nowhere in confinement; you may do as you like; you are surrounded by books that all look most tempting to read; you will always find some pleasant topic of conversation, or may start one, as all things are talked of in the general family. All this sounds and is delightful."

Charles was already good friends with one of the Wedgwood children, Hensleigh, the juggler of children and boxes. And a few months earlier, Charles had spent some time with another cousin, Emma, who was just nine months older than he was. He had seen her late that spring when she and his sister Catherine stopped in London on their way to and from a trip they took together to Paris. On their way back, Hensleigh and his wife had a dinner party for them and invited Charles, Erasmus, and Thomas and Jane Carlyle.

As her daughter later described her, Emma was pretty, with gray eyes, a clear complexion, a nice high forehead, a firm chin, a straight nose, and beautiful long, thick brown hair. She wore gold spectacles. She was of medium height, had nice shoulders and pretty hands and arms. She didn't care much for fashion or dressing up (her aunts often chided her about her clothes), but she was graceful and carried herself well. Like her father, she could be reserved; she was unflappable and good-natured. She was very smart, and extremely well-read, but she wasn't after intellectual pursuits in the same way the Horner girls were. She was content to stay home and help her sister Elizabeth take care of their aging parents.

Perhaps Charles would find his "constant companion" at Maer. He had decided he wasn't that interested in marrying any of the Horner girls. They were too much for him—too literary and intellectual, too clever in spades. It made sense to stay in the family, anyway. And maybe a woman who had grown up in such a free and liberal household as the Wedgwoods' would be understanding about his religious doubts, if he could not manage to conceal them. Of the five Wedgwood girls, there were only two single ones left living at Maer Hall. One was Elizabeth, a tiny woman with a curved spine. She was sixteen years older than Charles. The other was Emma. Was she the right wife for him?

Emma had definitely noticed Charles on that London visit. At dinner in her brother Hensleigh's dining room, she thought Charles lively, funny, and smart. Although she had already turned down a handful of marriage proposals and was not looking for a husband, Charles made an impression on her. But she didn't think he liked her especially. "I was not the least sure of his feelings," she later said, "as he is so affectionate, and so fond of Maer and all of us, and demonstrative in his manners, that I did not think it meant anything."

A few years back there had been talk about matching up Charles with another Wedgwood cousin, Emma's sister Fanny. Caroline Darwin thought Fanny would be a good wife. She was neat and orderly, just like Charles. She was also a good contrast to another Fanny who had all but broken Charles's heart—Fanny Owen.

Fanny Owen had grown up near Charles's home—a few hours away by galloping horse. Charles visited her often during his college years, when he came home from Cambridge during school holidays. Fanny Owen was petite and dark-haired; she was engaging, flirtatious, passionate, and maybe a bit wild. As his sisters Catherine and Caroline wrote Charles about her in 1826, "Fanny Owen has quite the preference to Sarah [her sister] among all the gentlemen, as she must have every where; there is something so very engaging and delightful about her."

Both Charles and Fanny Owen loved to go shooting, and they spent many happy hours in the woods near her house. Charles was impressed with how charming she looked when she fired one of his guns. He loved it that she showed no sign of pain even though the kick of the gun made her shoulder black and blue. The two of them walked through the gardens in the summer sun, picking and eating strawberries. Though it seemed unlikely that they would marry—she was much more interested in society and dancing than he was, and she had many other suitors—Charles was definitely in love.

One vacation Charles spent a whole week with her.

Afterward his lips were so sore, presumably from kissing, that when he got home Dr. Darwin gave him small doses of arsenic to relieve the pain. But Fanny spent time with her other beaux, and Charles had another love, too—beetles. Over the next few years Charles struggled with which love came first—beetles or Fanny. Fanny was not pleased with the competition.

And it was serious competition, for Charles was passionate about those beetles.

By the time he had graduated from Cambridge, he realized that like the beetle that burnt his tongue, Fanny might not want to be caught either. Her letters had grown much cooler; she was pulling away from him. Then right before he left for Falmouth, where he was to depart for his voyage around the world, Charles and Fanny Owen saw each other again and rekindled their romance. As Charles suffered through a two-month-long delay of the *Beagle*'s launch, he wondered if he should have proposed to her. When she heard that he was waiting around in Falmouth for the boat to sail, she sent him a letter asking him to "write me one last adieu if you have a spare half hour before you sail . . . you cannot imagine how I have *missed* you already at the Forest." Charles folded her letter nice and small and took it with him on the voyage. He did not propose.

A few months into his trip, when he collected his mail at a port of call in Rio de Janeiro, he read a letter from his sister Catherine. She informed him that Fanny Owen had married someone else. He was stunned. Although he hadn't written to her yet, and probably had already decided not to marry her, the shock of her marrying someone else so soon was unsettling to him. When he wrote to his sister Caroline, he made light of the news. "It may be all very delightful to those concerned but as I like unmarried women better than those in the blessed state, I vote it a bore. . . ." But by the end of that letter, he confessed his dismay. "I am at a loss what to think or say."

He got over it fairly quickly, though, preoccupied with his adventures and his collections. Besides, he knew that Fanny would not have cared at all about that giant sloth head he had found in Punta Alta. He and Fanny would not have been a good match. It would have been a disaster. But she had been his first love and five years later when he got back from his voyage, he thought about her again. He even went so far as to send her flowers. He heard from the family grapevine that his gift left her speechless. She was miserable; her marriage was loveless.

Now, in July 1838, as he headed toward Maer, he knew that the woman he married would have to be one who would not fight his passion for beetles and beaks of finches. He had loved natural history since he was a boy; he wrote late in life, "my love of natural science has been steady and ardent." He didn't want a wife who would fight him for attention; but he also couldn't bear the thought of an unhappy marriage. Maybe it would all work out with Emma—if she didn't mind his nose, and if he managed to conceal his religious doubts.

When Charles arrived at the beautiful stone house of Maer, Emma and Elizabeth were preparing for a charity bazaar. Charles helped them choose dishes and knickknacks, and clean them for sale. But he thought most of the things were quite ugly. He teased them and told them he did not think they would make much money selling such horrid items. He refused to buy anything unless the honor of his family demanded he do so. The Wedgwood women were not offended. They enjoyed him very much for his charm and high spirits as well as for his forthrightness and openness.

One evening during the visit, Charles pulled Emma into the library—where she had spent many hours reading history, philosophy, French, and her favorite novels (she loved Jane Austen). Charles and Emma had an intimate talk, a "goose," as they called it, by the fire. A man and a woman alone by the fire was a sure sign of something. They talked quietly for a long time, but Charles did not bring up the subject of marriage.

Emma felt that if they saw more of each other, Charles would really like her. But she had no idea that he was thinking about proposing to her. Unlike the young women in the novels of Jane Austen, Emma Wedgwood was not mooning over Charles or plotting for a marriage. No one else was plotting on her behalf, either. Back when she had received those four or five marriage proposals, she had gotten "quite weary of it." One of the men who proposed, a curate who lived near Maer, was so upset when she turned him down that he walked Elizabeth around and around the pond in tears, asking what Emma thought was wrong with him. He was just not good enough to tear Emma away from her life at Maer. Nor were the others. It would take a special man to pry Emma away from home.

Chapter 5

Little Miss Slip-Slop

I love Maer much too well not to be glad
always when I come home.
—Fanny Wedgwood, from Geneva,
to her mother, January 1827

When he got back to London, Charles received a note from Emma, reporting on the success of the bazaar. He answered her, "My dear Emma, Many thanks for the news of the Bazaar, and for Elizabeth's purchases. . . . I am glad to hear there were some few uglier things at the Bazaar than those you took." In newly industrialized England, riding the trains was an adventure and an unpredictable thing, so he reported on his trip. "I was altogether disappointed with the railroad—it was so rough and so much plague with the many changes."

And then he let his heart show a little. "This Marlborough St is a forlorn place.—We have no ducks here, much less geese, and as for that sentimental fat goose we ate over the Library fire,—the like of it seldom turns up.—I feel the same spiteful joy at hearing you have had no other geese."

He continued, "Pray remember I consider myself invited to Maer, the next time I come down into the country.—in fact, I think I have been so often that I have a kind of vested right, so see me you will, and we will have another goose."

But what did he mean when he said that their "goose" was so nice, of the kind that seldom turn up? Was he telling her something? Emma didn't think so. She figured she and Charles would go on for years, having geese by the fire and staying friends. That was fine with her. She was content to stay at Maer Hall with Elizabeth, playing the piano, reading, doing needlework, and taking care of their beloved mother, who was bed-ridden and very ill.

Emma had been born into the carefree, happy, supportive Wedgwood family on May 2, 1808. She was the youngest. She had four brothers and three sisters (a fourth older sister had died as a baby)—Elizabeth, Josiah, Charlotte, Harry, Frank, Hensleigh, and Fanny. She was closest to Fanny, who was only two years older than she was. They were inseparable, spending almost every moment together from the time Emma was born. The family often spoke of them as if they were one person. They called them the Dovelies or Miss Salt and Miss Pepper.

But Emma and Fanny were quite different. Fanny was short and not thought to be as pretty as Emma, though she was "most radiant in her person and brilliant in her colouring," according to their Aunt Jessie. We can imagine rosy cheeks and bright eyes. She was a quiet, gentle, and good person, organized and industrious. She made lists all the time: lists of temperatures, words in different languages, sights seen on travels, chores to be done. Her father called her his little secretary; her mother's nickname for her was Mrs. Pedigree. As she got older, people in the family thought she'd be a good match for her cousin Charles, also an organizer, a collector, and a list maker.

On the other hand, Emma's nickname was Little Miss Slip-Slop. She was disorganized, and a slob. But she was brilliant, learned easily, and when she liked something, she put her all into it. At only five, she started reading a favorite classic of the day, John Milton's epic poem *Paradise Lost*. Telling the story later, some relatives said she read the whole thing, others said she started it and asked her mother to finish reading it to her. Either way, it certainly was not typical reading material for so young a child.

Paradise Lost begins:

> *Of Man's first disobedience, and the fruit*
> *Of that forbidden tree whose mortal taste*
> *Brought death into the World, and all our woe,*
> *With loss of Eden. . . .*

Paradise Lost is the story of Adam and Eve's disobedience and expulsion from the Garden of Eden. It explores fate, sin, heaven, and hell. (Charles also loved *Paradise Lost*—when he was older. He took a pocket-sized edition with him on his voyage and carried it in his jacket whenever he went ashore.)

Emma's large extended family loved both of "the little girls" (as they were called into their twenties), but Emma was a favorite. She was lively and high-spirited, yet had a serenity and a good nature that never seemed to get ruffled. She did not put up with nonsense, though, and she called things as she saw them. At ten, Emma wrote to her brother about a family she and Fanny were staying with: "I like the Coloes very except the youngest Louis who bothers one very much."

Both girls read voraciously, pulling book after book off the Maer library shelves. And, in the few hours of the morning set aside for lessons, they learned French, Italian, and German.

Emma was good at everything she took up—languages, archery, skating, needlework, horseback riding—but her great talent was music. She played the piano, and although she didn't work very hard at it—she played for only about an hour a day—she was so good that when she was older, she took lessons from the famous pianist and composer Frédéric Chopin. Her daughter Etty later said that Emma's piano playing clearly reflected her character: She played with a fine, crisp touch, with intelligence and simplicity. She put vigor and spirit into her playing, but not sentimental passion. Emma didn't like sentimentality.

When they were little, Emma was sure that Fanny was a better person than she. Fanny was inherently Good. Emma brooded over her own flaws, in contrast to what she considered Fanny's moral superiority. One time an older cousin brought three brooches for Fanny, Emma, and another young cousin. Fanny had first choice, and Emma watched as she chose the least pretty pin. Emma's turn came next, and rather than leave the prettiest pin for her cousin, as her older sister had done, she took it for herself. She felt badly about this and regretted it her whole life.

But Fanny adored Emma, too. After taking care of the Dovelies for a while, one of their great-aunts wrote to their mother:

> I marvel at the strength of the girls' spirits as much as I do at the perfection of their tempers. I feel now very sure that not only not a cross word ever passes between them, but that an irritable feeling never arises. Fanny, to be sure, is calmness itself, but the vivacity of Emma's feelings, without perfectly knowing her, would make me expect that Fanny's reproofs, which she often gives with an elder sister air, would ruffle her a little; but I have never seen that

expressive face take the shadow of an angry look, and I do think her love for Fanny is the prettiest thing I ever saw.

The aunt went on to say that Emma's character was shaped by her closeness to Fanny.

I ascribe much of Emma's joyous nature to have been secured, if not caused, by Fanny's yielding disposition; had the other met with a cross or an opposing sister there was every chance that with her ardent feelings, her temper had become irritable. Now she is made the happiest being that ever was looked on, and so much affection in her nature as will secure her from selfishness.

Fanny was not only generous, she was also more religious than Emma. Although both girls taught in the little village Sunday school, Fanny took it more seriously, as she did her confirmation at sixteen. Emma was more interested in parties and plays. Right after her confirmation, Emma and her Darwin cousins celebrated with a party at Maer. They put on a play, *The Merry Wives of Windsor,* and had so much fun that Emma's mother complained they kept her "in such a whirl of noise, and ins and outs, that I have not found any leisure."

The sisters enjoyed traveling, and when they were nineteen and twenty-one, they went to Geneva, Switzerland, and spent eight months with their favorite aunt, Jessie, and her eccentric Italian husband, J. C. de Sismondi. Aunt Jessie and Sismondi were deeply in love and had no children, so they showered their love and attention on the Dovelies. They introduced them into society and took them to fancy parties. After one ball, Emma wrote home to Elizabeth:

The whole Theatre was quite full and it looked very pretty. We were to dance with whoever asked us. The first man I danced with was very disagreeable and vulgar, which put me rather in despair for the rest of the ball; however the rest of my partners were very tidy, so I liked it very well. I had the good luck to dance with one or two Englishmen. . . . When I was afraid any particularly horrid-looking man was going to ask me to dance I began such a very earnest conversation with Fanny that they could not interrupt me. . . .

When it was time for the girls to leave Geneva, their father arrived to escort them home, bringing along Caroline Darwin for company. Afterward, Caroline wrote them a letter that she began "My dear Fanny and Emma," and then she added in parentheses, "I know you like being classed together, and as Charlotte and Eliz. to this day speak of you both as if you were but *one*, I shall follow their example." The sisters, different as could be, *were* as one, and happily so.

All in all, what Jane Austen says about Emma Woodhouse in the opening paragraph of her novel *Emma* could have been said about Emma Wedgwood:

Emma Woodhouse, handsome, clever, and rich, with a comfortable home and happy disposition seemed to unite some of the best blessings of existence; and had lived nearly twenty-one years in the world with very little to distress and vex her.

Emma Wedgwood had lived until she was twenty-*four* with nothing at all to distress her. But in the summer of 1832, everything changed for the Dovelies.

Chapter 6

The Next World

*The sorrows and distresses of life ... soften and humanize
the heart, to awaken social sympathy, to generate
all the Christian virtues.*
—Thomas Robert Malthus, *An Essay on
the Principle of Population*, 1798

At twenty-four and twenty-six, Emma and Fanny lived at home with their parents and their older sister Elizabeth. That August, in 1832, while Jos and Bessy were away, Fanny got sick.

At first nobody at Maer thought it was anything to be worried about. And Elizabeth and Emma were both experienced at taking care of sick people. Elizabeth was thirty-six. She had spent years nursing the poor in the village. Emma was often her assistant. So they thought nothing of caring for Fanny themselves, even though it could not have been easy with no running water or flush toilets.

Uncharacteristically, Emma took precise notes of what happened. "On Monday 13th August 1832," she wrote, "my dear Fanny complained of uneasiness in the bowels. Eliz gave her calomel and jalap but she would come and sit at the dinner table to save appearances as she said. The pain continued all night."

They didn't know what was wrong with her—she may have had cholera, or it may have been another kind of intestinal illness. There were cholera outbreaks all over England—from Liverpool in the north down to Oxford and even into East London. People throughout the country were scared it would spread, including the Wedgwoods' neighbors in Staffordshire. The symptoms of cholera were severe vomiting and diarrhea, leading to dehydration, weakness, and often death.

In the nineteenth century, the treatment of an intestinal disease focused on purging the system through vomiting and moving the bowels. Those nursing the sick also tried to keep the patient comfortable, which wasn't very easy, with all of that purging. They also gave fluids, although the dire effect of dehydration was not well known.

Elizabeth "fomented her" (applied hot packs) and tried to give an injection, but it didn't work. The injection was probably liquid ammonia or saline. Concerned that Fanny was not improving, Emma and Elizabeth sent for the apothecary, a Mr. B., who "ordered fomentation with poppy heads," Emma noted. The heat from the compress, probably more than the traces of opium from the poppy seeds, helped and "the pain gradually went off." Then Emma put twenty leeches on Fanny, which they hoped would suck the disease out with the blood.

Soon Fanny seemed to be getting better. Emma wrote, "Saturday . . . she had a peaceful day and slept a good deal. She asked to have Charlotte's letter read to her. I slept in the room with her and only had to help her up once or twice. Early on Sunday morning she was low and Eliz gave her some hot drink. She revived during the day."

The next evening, she "took an injection which gave her violent pain and after that she was restless and uneasy; told Elizabeth to sponge her face twice and her back and chest. At 4 o'clock sent for Mr. B. He found her sinking when he came and gave her brandy and she was thoroughly warmed."

Months later, while on his voyage, Charles received a letter from his sister Caroline. Charles read that his cousin Fanny Wedgwood, who had been suggested as a possible wife for him, had

> seemed very ill for two days with vomitings and pain and then appeared to get better, so much so that not one of the family had an idea she was in danger. 7 days after she became unwell, Elizabeth sat up with her at night as she (Fanny) was too restless to sleep; towards morning she seemed cold and more uncomfortable & they sent for the apothecary … from some misunderstanding none of the family had an idea her danger was so immediate.

No doubt in hindsight Caroline wondered why they hadn't sent for a doctor, perhaps their father, Dr. Darwin? An apothecary was the least-skilled medical person; why not go for the best? They could afford to pay a doctor. But they just did not realize how seriously ill Fanny was. Even Dr. Darwin, or any doctor, might not have been able to help much.

At Maer Emma recorded in her notes, "At 9 came the fatal attack and in 5 minutes we lost our gentle, sweet Fanny, the most without selfishness of anybody I ever saw and her loss has left a blank which will never be filled up."

Emma's other half was gone.

In Caroline's letter, Charles read about the family's grief. "Uncle Jos was terribly over come & Aunt Bessy it was some time before Elizabeth could make her understand what had happened," Caroline wrote. "Father says mortification must have taken place in her bowels." And Caroline saw, as everyone did, how terrible Fanny's death would be for Emma, the other Dovely. She wrote, "The loss to Emma will be very great, hardly ever having been separated, all her associations of her pleasures & youth so intimately connected with her."

For Emma it was a terrible, wrenching loss, and one that she had not anticipated at all. It had come so quickly that it was, in a profound sense, unbelievable. But Emma found a way to cope. In Jane Austen novels, a death often precipitates the loss of a fortune, which propels the heroine to seek a husband. In this case the death propelled our heroine to seek something else. She wrote a note to herself, on a scrap of paper that she never showed anyone (her daughter Henrietta found it after her death). "Oh Lord," Emma wrote, "help me to become more like her, and grant that I may join with Thee never to part again. I trust that my Fanny's sweet image will never pass from my mind. Let me always keep it in my mind as a motive for holiness. What exquisite happiness it will be to be with her again, to tell her how I loved her who has joined with me in almost every enjoyment of my life."

Emma resolved to become good like Fanny and religious like Fanny so that she would join her in heaven. To Aunt Jessie, Emma wrote, "I feel a sad blank at the thoughts of having lost my sweet, gentle companion who has been so closely joined with me ever since we were born, but I try to keep my mind fixed upon the hope of being with her again, never to part again."

Emma needed to believe that she would see Fanny again one day. She told Aunt Jessie, "Such a separation as this seems to make the next world feel such a reality—it seems to bring it so much nearer to one's mind and gives one such a desire to be found worthy of being with her."

Charles Darwin would later say, looking back at his own childhood and at the great differences between him and his brother, Erasmus, that he was inclined to agree with a cousin of his that "education and environment produce only a small effect on the mind of anyone, and that most of our qualities are innate." Even so, it is unquestionable that Fanny's life and then her death affected Emma profoundly. It cemented a faith in God and eternity that could have dwindled otherwise. Emma Wedgwood now firmly believed in a heaven and a hell. She believed that if you were a good Christian you would go to heaven. And if you weren't you would go to hell.

Chapter 7

The Sensation
of Fear

*My experience of English lovers is that if they mean
anything, they come straight to the point and make it evident.
But if not, they are as friendly as they can be, without
the least idea of anything more.*
—MAUD DU PUY DARWIN, WIFE OF GEORGE DARWIN, JUNE 1887

On the voyage, Charles had been vigorous and brave. He withstood horrible seasickness, weathered harsh conditions, witnessed a battle in Bahía Blanca, Argentina, and experienced an earthquake in Valdivia, Chile. "There was no difficulty in standing upright, but the motion made me almost giddy," he wrote about the earthquake. But now, back in London in 1838, he truly was scared. The thought of marriage and of Emma terrified him and gave him serious headaches. He knew she was religious, and he was consumed by the fear that his secret idea would go against her beliefs.

Charles had been spending hours at the London Zoo watching Jenny, an orangutan. The zoo had recently acquired her; she was the first orangutan the zoo had, and was one of the first apes in England. On an unseasonably warm March day, Charles had observed Jenny in her cage in the giraffe house. The keeper showed Jenny an apple but, teasing, didn't give it to her. Then, Charles wrote to one of his sisters, Jenny "threw herself on her back, kicked & cried, precisely like a naughty child."

Watching Jenny, Charles asked himself questions: How much was an ape like a child? How similar were people and animals? Does an orangutan have the same emotions we do? If so, how closely are we humans related to animals? He kept going back to the zoo to watch Jenny. That autumn he wrote in a new notebook, one marked "Expression" and labeled "N," that "children understand before they can talk, so do many animals.—analogy probably false, may lead to something."

He was careful not to jump to conclusions, but he saw what he saw: "Jenny was amusing herself—, by getting out ears of corn with her teeth from the straw, & just like child not knowing what to do with them, came several times & opened my hand, & put them in—like child."

Like a child. What would it mean about God's creation if apes and humans were related? In the religious worldview, there was a hierarchy of living things, from the lowliest of the low, animals like lice or slugs, to fish and birds and cats and apes, up to human beings, who were at the top—but not as high up as angels. Charles was beginning to think that people were more closely related to orangutans than to angels, if angels existed at all. *Like a child.* People and apes must be related, and if so, they must have a common ancestor. But how did the common ancestor change to create humans and apes? If species do change, as Charles felt certain they did, how was that happening? What was the mechanism that drove this change?

Charles, like Emma, was a voracious reader, and as he read in a wide range of subjects, from philosophy and theology to history and political theory, he was reading with a purpose—to understand the natural world and, most specifically, the origin of species.

On September 28, 1838, two months after his visit to Maer, Charles opened another notebook (he wrote in many at once). This one was red leather, with a "D" on the front. In gray ink, on pages edged in green, he wrote about something he'd read. *An Essay on the Principle of Population* was written by the economist Thomas Robert Malthus in 1798. Malthus's essay was about society, and about people, most especially about how poor people succumb in an environment where there are limited resources. He argued that without disease, famine, and poverty, the human population would grow too fast. People need food; people need sex. If there is more population growth than the food supply can accommodate, something must and will happen to reduce the population.

People still discussed and argued about what Malthus had to say, especially about the problems of poverty. Were workhouses the answer, as Malthus said? Should the poor be given charity, or should they be left to fend for themselves? The novelist Charles Dickens felt Malthus depicted poor people as less than human; in novels such as *Oliver Twist*, he sought to remedy that, making poor people well-rounded main characters. Charles, Erasmus, and their London friends discussed these problems over dinner. What might Malthus's ideas mean—for better or for worse—to society?

But Charles was even more interested in what Malthus's theory might mean for nature and for the origin of species. As Charles read the essay, he thought more about animals and plants than about people. He believed there was a direct analogy, a way into the species problem. Reading Malthus and thinking about the natural world, Charles realized that nature was not happy and peaceful, as Paley had described in his natural theology books. The lion did not lie down with the lamb. Life in nature was a struggle, just as in the crowded, poverty-ridden neighborhoods of London. In human society there were not enough jobs for the growing numbers of people; in nature—on a desert island or on top of a mountain—there was also a struggle for existence when there was not enough food for the growing number of birds, beasts, or bugs. Charles reasoned that if too many individuals of a species are born in the same place and try to live off a limited supply of food, there is a fight for survival. The weaker ones die. The ones that are strongest, best adapted to the conditions of the area and most able to get the food, survive. Those who survive pass on their traits to their offspring. This was true of cockroaches, sheep, bees, and beetles.

And birds.

While on his voyage, Charles had usually been careful to label every bird, every fossil, every plant. He would write down where he found it and what he thought (or knew) it was. But leaving the Galapagos Islands, he uncharacteristically had thrown birds from different islands into one bag. He regretted this later when he realized that the mockingbirds and the finches would have been wonderful evidence for his theory. On the journey home, he thought about how the mockingbirds from the Galapagos Islands of San Cristóbal and Isabela looked the same, but the ones from Floreana and Santiago seemed different. And each kind was found only on its own island. Were they just varieties, or were they evidence of new species? Had the birds been blown over from the coast of South America and then diverged as they lived and died, generation after generation, on the islands? he wondered. And if they had, what did that mean about the creation of new species?

When he got back to England, he had given his mockingbird and finch specimens to John Gould, an ornithologist. Gould was especially excited about the finches: There seemed to be more than a dozen species of finches never seen anywhere else before. Gould told Charles that he had brought back birds that seemed to live only in the Galapagos. Charles's inkling was confirmed: Species were not stable. They were not created in one fell swoop by God, never to change, as the Bible said and most people believed.

As Charles looked at the beaks of the finches, he began to see evidence of the fight for survival that precipitated the change. He began to see that beaks adapted to the kinds of seeds available on the island. Big beaks could crack open big, hard seeds; small beaks were better for hard-to-get-at seeds. This was not God's design; it was design brought about by the need for food. His birds and Malthus's theory had given him the mechanism for the transmutation of species.

In his notebooks, Charles began to write about his idea of how it all happened. He thought about how traits get passed down, over and over again. He surmised that traits that are passed on change and adapt according to what is needed for survival. These changes—very small ones—add up over time to make bigger changes. These bigger changes result in the creation of new species. He called his idea "modification by natural selection." He knew he had to study his idea in minute and exacting detail, in an organized and disciplined way. But he now had "a theory by which to work." Observing Jenny, reading Malthus, thinking about the finches, he put it all together.

He was beyond excited. He now knew for sure that this theory was going to be the governing force of the rest of his life.

But what about Emma?

His theory essentially eliminated God's role in the process of creation. What would Emma think? He knew he was flirting with materialism, the philosophical doctrine that says that there are no spiritual or divine forces in nature, only matter. If Emma knew, would she want him to be flirting with her? In one of his notebooks he wrote, "Oh you materialist!" There was no denying—to himself—what he was becoming.

This juxtaposition of his heart and mind gave him not only headaches but weird dreams. One night he had an anxiety attack that woke him up. Not to be deterred, he used himself as a specimen, just like Jenny, and made observations.

"Fear must be simple instinctive feeling," he wrote in his "M" notebook, a dark red leather one marked "private" inside because he was filling it with thoughts about emotions and mental issues—his own and those of his family and his friends. "I have awakened in the night being slightly unwell & felt so much afraid though my reason was laughing & told me there was nothing, & tried to seize hold of objects to be frightened at."

He watched himself carefully and in the dim light recorded, "The sensation of fear is accompanied by troubled beating of heart, sweat, trembling of muscles." He asked himself how his fear related to what happened in the jungle to an animal scared by a predator: "are not these effects of violent running away," he scribbled.

Looking back at early man, perhaps, or at his ape cousins, he saw that running away was what you did instinctively when you were afraid; retreating was the usual effect of fear. He could relate to the instinct to run away. Wouldn't it be easier to run than to confront the object of your fear? But what if you could not run fast enough to get away? Could an orangutan outrun a lion? What were the other options? You could play dead: "the state of collapse may be imitation of death, which many animals put on." Should he play dead with Emma? Just forget the idea of marrying her? Or of marrying at all?

He was anxious not because he thought he was wrong about the origin of species, but because he felt sure he was right. He knew what he had to say would be shocking to Emma and others who believed that God was the creator of all species. And he knew that if he confessed that he thought God was not part of the equation, he would hurt people close to him, especially the woman with whom he wanted to share his life.

"Conceal your doubts!" his father had said. He just couldn't. Not completely. He could not lie. But maybe he didn't have to tell everything he was thinking. He wrote to himself, in his notebook, just after his anxiety attack, that he would "avoid stating how far, I believe, in Materialism." He didn't have to tell the whole thing. Yet.

He wrote down his thoughts about marriage again, this time focusing not on the "if" but on the "when." "If one does not marry soon, one misses so much good pure happiness—" of caressing his wife, of feeling that flush of passion. But what about adventure? If he married soon, "I never should know French,—or see the Continent,—or go to America, or go up in a Balloon, or take solitary trip in Wales. . . ." But again he came to the same conclusion: "Never mind my boy—Cheer up—One cannot live this solitary life, with groggy old age, friendless and cold and childless staring one in one's face, already beginning to wrinkle. Never mind, trust to chance—"

* * *

Finally he couldn't take it any longer. He couldn't stop thinking about Emma. On November 9, he, along with Hensleigh
and Hensleigh's wife, who was also named Fanny, got on the
train toward Staffordshire. Charles was scared that Emma
wouldn't accept him—not just because of the religion question, but also because of his ugly nose. He had almost been
rejected for his nose once before; the captain of the *Beagle*,
Robert FitzRoy, was a believer in phrenology and physiognomy and thought you could tell someone's character by the
shape of the skull and face. He looked at Charles and worried
that the shape of his nose meant he was lazy. He almost didn't
let him on the ship. But FitzRoy had taken a chance on
Charles, and now Charles had to take a chance. He would ask
Emma and pray she said yes. He felt sick the whole journey to
Maer, and Saturday was torture. Maer was filled with people—
cousins, two elderly aunts—and Charles didn't think he could
summon up the courage to ask her. What if she said no?

But on Sunday morning, Charles got Emma alone by the
library fire for another goose. *The* goose. He finally asked her
to marry him.

Emma was shocked.

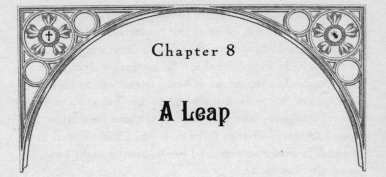

Chapter 8

A Leap

E. says she can perceive sigh, commences as soon
as painful thought crosses mind, before it
can have affected respiration.
—CHARLES DARWIN, "N" NOTEBOOK

When Emma and Charles walked out of the library and back into the hubbub of the family gathering, they both looked dismal. The elderly aunts who were visiting took one look at them and came to the conclusion that Charles had proposed and Emma had refused. No one else in the house seemed to suspect anything at all, and Emma went on with her regular Sunday schedule. She went to the village Sunday school to teach. She had continued teaching there, even with Fanny gone; it was a part of her attempt to live more like Fanny had, more religiously. She had even written her own children's stories to use in the classes.

But when she got to the Sunday school—held in the Maer Hall laundry—and tried to teach the children, she couldn't concentrate. As she put it later to Aunt Jessie, "I went straight into the Sunday School after the important interview, but found I was turning into an idiot and so came away."

Emma had had no idea that Charles was going to propose. She thought they would go on being friendly cousins, maybe close friends, for years. But when he asked her, she knew her answer right away. She had said yes without hesitation. She wanted to marry Charles Darwin. It was Charles's turn to be shocked; he had not expected her to answer right away. He got another headache.

He had chosen Emma, and she had said yes in large part because they had known each other their whole lives. But they didn't really *know* each other. It was a big leap to go from being friendly cousins to being husband and wife. What had they done?

Emma wrote to Aunt Jessie later that she was "too much bewildered all day to feel my happiness." And since there were so many people around, they did not make a big announcement. "We did not tell anybody except Papa and Elizabeth and Catherine."

But when they did tell Josiah, he cried with happiness. He loved Charles and thought he would be a perfect match for Emma, his youngest daughter. He felt Charles was a prize. There were practical reasons for his joy, too. Since they were cousins, the family money would stay within the family, just as it had when Emma's brother Jos had married Charles's sister Catherine. Charles had every reason to hope his father would feel the same way. He would ask his permission the next day. Catherine was delighted, too, of course. She and Emma were friends; they had made that trip to Paris together, stopping in London on the way back. Maybe she had seen the signs back in May during that visit.

Even Elizabeth was happy, for she liked Charles very much. It must have been hard news for her to take, though. She was sure she wouldn't get married. And it meant she would be left at home to take care of their aging father and ill mother. Bessy had been sick for quite a while; she slipped in and out of dementia. But when they told her, and she understood, she was thrilled, too.

Emma reported to Aunt Jessie, "Indeed I was so glad to find that all of them had been wishing for it and settling it. It is a match that every soul has been making for us, so we could not have helped it if we had not liked it ourselves."

And yet Emma and Charles spent the whole day feeling rather miserable at the shock of their engagement; they were both astonished at the suddenness of their decision. They didn't tell anyone else in the house until the evening, when they went into Hensleigh's bedroom.

As they gathered, Emma learned that Hensleigh's wife Fanny had suspected what had occurred. They had a "large party talking it over till very late." Hensleigh—he of the box and child—had given Charles serious pause about getting married. But now Charles would be joining him in the juggling of domestic life. Back in London, he talked with Hensleigh about science and religion, working out his thoughts about transmutation of species, about God, and about natural selection. Hensleigh, like Emma, was a theist. But he was also a scholar. He was a philologist, looking at how language evolves over time.

Late into the night, Emma was "seized with hunger." The servants were asleep, but, as she wrote to Aunt Jessie, "Hensleigh went down to forage in the kitchen and found a loaf and 2 lb. butter and a carving knife, which made us an elegant refection."

They ate bread and butter to celebrate their engagement.

Charles wrote in his diary on November 11, 1838, "The day of days." The next day Charles and Emma had a few little talks, which put them both a bit more at ease. Then Charles and Catherine went back to Shrewsbury so he could ask his father's permission as well.

Having finally proposed and been accepted was a huge relief to Charles. After all those tumultuous months, filled with turbulent thoughts, anxiety attacks, and headaches, it was finally settled. He would marry. His wife would, he hoped, sit next to him on the sofa, take care of him, and anchor him.

When he was traveling around the world on the *Beagle*, Charles was wretchedly seasick almost every day he was on board the ship. He lived for the times he could get off the rolling, rocky seas and onto solid land. Emma might not be passionate like his old girlfriend, Fanny Owen, was; she might not be sophisticated the way the Horner girls were, but she was brilliant and she was open-minded and she was unflappable. She could be his solid land in the tumultuous seas of his heretical thoughts.

At Shrewsbury, Dr. Darwin couldn't have been happier with Charles's choice. He wrote to his brother-in-law Jos that the marriage gave him great happiness. For days he walked around the Mount telling Charles that he, too, had "drawn a prize!" just as Josiah said Emma had.

Everyone in the extended circle of family and friends was thrilled. Letters flew back and forth praising the match. One friend wrote, "It is very like a marriage of Miss Austen's, can I say more!" But the plot was very different. In Jane Austen's novels there are star-crossed lovers who have impediments thrown in their way—by their parents, society, or their own doubts. There are issues of class, suitability, or inheritance.

There is much buildup to the engagement, and then the book ends quickly with a happy wedding.

With Charles and Emma, there was very little buildup, very little—if any—flirting before the engagement. There was no denial, no star-crossed agony leading to their engagement. It was afterward that things began to heat up.

It was that day, by the fire, that their story really began. In the library at Maer, they had made a leap, though not over class lines or parental objections. They had made a leap to marry even though they had one big difference between them that could stand in the way of their happiness. For Charles had not heeded his father's advice: He had not concealed his religious doubts.

Chapter 9

A Busy Man

I hardly expected such good fortune would turn up for me.
—CHARLES DARWIN TO CHARLES LYELL, NOVEMBER 12, 1838

*You will be forming theories about me & if I am cross or
out of temper you will only consider 'What does
that prove.' Which will be a very grand &
philosophical way of considering it.*
—EMMA TO CHARLES, JANUARY 23, 1839

As soon as Charles got to Shrewsbury, he wrote to his friend Charles Lyell, the geologist, in London. Lyell probably read the letter the next day, for the mail in England was quite efficient. The post was picked up and delivered more than once a day—a few times, in fact, depending on where you were— and it arrived at its destination later that day or the next. Sometimes the mailman would wait until you wrote a response to a letter just received. In two years, the British post would become the penny post, which meant that a letter would cost a penny per half ounce no matter where it was going in England. But now, in 1838, it was more expensive to send a letter outside of London, though that didn't matter to Emma or even to frugal Charles. It was the only way to communicate. Letter writing was one of the centers of social life in nineteenth-century England, along with visiting relatives and friends and going to or giving parties.

In London Lyell read, "I have the very good, and shortly since very unexpected fortune, of going to be married. The lady is my cousin, Miss Emma Wedgwood, the sister of Hensleigh Wedgwood, and of the elder brother who married my sister, so we are connected by manifold ties, besides on my part by the most sincere love and hearty gratitude to her for accepting such a one as myself."

Charles had two reasons for writing to Lyell right away. One was to tell his friend the good news. The other was to tell him that he was marrying Emma and not a Horner girl, so Lyell would tell his wife's family before Charles got back to London. It might be less awkward for Charles when he ran into Mr. Horner, or the "Mother-in-law," if they had time to get used to the idea that he was no longer available.

The Horners did not react positively to the engagement of Charles Darwin to Emma Wedgwood (and for good reason!). But they were the only ones. All over the countryside in Shropshire and Staffordshire, in London, as well as in Geneva, where Aunt Jessie lived, family and friends were exulting in the news.

Emma's beautiful older sister Charlotte, whom Charles had had a crush on when he was younger, wrote to her future brother-in-law, "How truly & warmly I rejoice in this marriage. Nothing else could have happened to give me so much pleasure—it seems as if it was the only thing to wish for. As

much as it is possible to rely upon the happiness of any two
people I feel a reliance on yours & Emma's."

Even Poor Old Ras, as Charles called his brother,
expressed his excitement and his vicarious happiness. He
wrote to Charles, "It is a marriage which will give almost as
much pleasure to the rest of the world as it does to your-
selves—the best auspices I should think for any marriage."

There were, indeed, many reasons to have auspicious hopes
for the marriage. In Geneva, Aunt Jessie wrote to her niece:

> Everything I have ever heard of C. Darwin I have particu-
> larly liked, and have long wished for what has now taken
> place, that he would woo and win you. I love him all the
> better that he unites to all his other qualifications that most
> rare one of knowing how well to chuse a wife, a friend,
> companion, mother of his children, all of which men in
> general never think of. . . . I know I shall love him.

Aunt Jessie was a devotee of palm reading, one of the
"minor superstitions" that was in vogue, along with séances,
phrenology, and physiognomy. She continued in her letter, "I
knew you would be a Mrs. Darwin from your hands."

But Aunt Jessie didn't quite have the whole picture from
Emma's letter. Jessie had known her fiancé very well, and she
was madly in love with him. So even though some of her family hadn't approved that she was marrying an Italian, not
someone from their British social circle, her engagement was
a time of social whirlwind and happiness. She and Sismondi
hadn't had to get to know each other. It was different for
Charles and Emma; for them, the engagement was a time for
discovery. There were things to talk about and work through,
what kind of life they'd like, where they'd live—and then there
was the religion question.

Through letters and visits, Charles started to say things to Emma that he had been too nervous to say before. Although there was the risk of a broken engagement, it was unlikely. Emma was already in love and wanted to know what Charles thought about everything. His openness was something she prized. She wrote to Aunt Jessie, "He is the most open, transparent man I ever saw, and every word expresses his real thoughts. He is particularly affectionate and very nice to his father and sisters, and perfectly sweet tempered."

And Charles knew he had made the right decision; he was in love with Emma and he told her so. On the Wednesday after their engagement he wrote to her from Shrewsbury to say that "there was never anyone so lucky as I have been, or so good as you. . . . I have thought how little I expressed how much I owe to you; and often as I think this, I vow to try to make myself good enough somewhat to deserve you."

Ever organized and practical, he went on to ask her to think about the decisions they would have to make—mostly where they would live. He asked her to make sure a fire was lit in the library when he returned to Maer on Saturday so they could sit next to the warmth and have "some quiet talk together."

Charles was worried that Emma would find life with him dull, since she was so used to the many lively family gatherings and parties at Maer. He loved Maer, too: "My life has been very happy and very fortunate, and many of my pleasantest remembrances are mingled up with scenes at Maer, and now it is crowned." But he confessed to her that he had a great deal of work to do that preoccupied his mind. He had his boxes of specimens to analyze, and he had questions, thoughts, and ideas exploding inside of him. He was still worried about some items on the *Don't Marry* side of his list, especially "loss of time." Emma for her part was worried about, among other things, plays; Charles didn't like them very much, and she would miss them if they never went to the theater.

Charles couldn't hide his excitement at their marriage, and he was already impatient. He could not wait until they would be together always. "Like a child that has something it loves beyond measure, I long to dwell on the words *my own dear Emma*."

He begged her not to show the letters to anyone; he said he wanted to feel like it was just the two of them, sitting side by side. "My own dear Emma, I kiss the hands with all humbleness and gratitude, which have so filled up for me the cup of happiness—It is my most earnest wish I may make myself worthy of you. . . . Most affectionately yours, Chas. Darwin."

Charles knew that Emma was torn about leaving Maer, and leaving her sister Elizabeth alone to care for her sick parents. Josiah was now ill, too. Emma put herself in Elizabeth's place and realized that she probably would not have rejoiced if it had been her sister who was leaving. She felt guilty and wanted to push the wedding off a little bit to help ease the transition for all the Wedgwoods.

But Charles couldn't wait, and he couldn't help himself. After he signed his name, he wrote, "Remember life is short, and two months is the sixth part of the year, and that year, the first, from which for my part, things shall hereafter date." He told her he would leave the timing up to her but that he would be in agony "until I am part of you—Dearest Emma, good-bye."

After another visit to Maer, and more talks by the fire, Charles went back to London. He found it impossible to concentrate on work, though he did try. All he wanted to do was find a house for them. On November 23, 1838, he wrote to Emma, "I positively can do nothing, & have done nothing this whole week, but think of you & our future life.—you may then, well imagine how I enjoy seeing your handwriting.... It is a very high enjoyment to me, as I cannot talk to you, & feel your presence by having your own dear hand within mine."

He *was* able to write in his notebooks, especially to explore his own emotions and feelings. In his "M" notebook, where he had written about his pre-proposal anxiety attack, he now analyzed jealousy. Where did those horrible feelings come from? Again thinking of man as a part of the animal kingdom, he realized that "Jealousy probably originally entirely sexual." A man, an ape, a blue-footed booby tries to attract a female to mate with. He becomes jealous if there is competition and he fails "to drive away rival."

And in another private notebook, his "N" notebook, bound in rust-colored leather, he analyzed his body and new sensations he was having from those geese by the fire, which likely were no longer just intimate *talks*. "Sexual desire makes saliva to flow," he wrote, and added later, "yes, certainly."

He had a "curious association" thinking about his new-found romantic life. He thought of watching a family dog, Nina, "licking her chops." Though kissing Emma had to be better than kissing a dog, anyhow, he could not help but make the connection to people kissing. He wrote, "ones tendency to kiss, & almost to bite, that which one sexually loves is proba-bly connected with flow of saliva, & hence with action of mouth & jaws." He made another human-animal connection: "Lascivious women are described as biting: so do stallions always."

He continued, "No doubt man has great tendency to exert

all senses, when thus stimulated." And he read up on the subject and quoted a certain Professor Bell, who said there was a connection between smell and sexual desire and the feelings one gets when listening to beautiful music: Charles thought that listening to music could be rapturous, religious even.

Thinking about love and sexual desire, he returned to a favorite theme—how are we humans like animals? He thought about dogs, how mother dogs licked their puppies partly to clean them, but also to show affection. "This habit probably originated in the females carefully licking their puppies—the dearest object of their love—for the sake of cleansing them. . . .Thus, the habit will have become associated with the emotion of love."

No wonder Emma's friend Ellen Tollet wrote to her, "You two will be quite too happy together, and I hope you will have a chimney that smokes, or something of that sort to prevent your becoming quite intoxicated."

Charles *was* getting carried away, intoxicated. His intense feelings were offset by tentativeness, though. He felt shy: "Shyness is certainly very much connected with thinking of oneself . . . blushing is connected with sexual, because each sex thinks more of what another thinks of him, than of any one of his own sex." Here was a difference with his animal cousins: Animals do not blush. But "sensitive people apt to blush."

He wrote, "Blushing is intimately concerned with thinking of ones appearance,—does the thought drive blood to surface exposed, face of man, face, neck—upper bosom in woman: like erection." The women Charles had seen in England had little exposed, but gowns, especially dressy ones, could have low-cut necklines, exposing the upper bosom.

He talked to his father the doctor. Dr. Darwin might have told him that when the time arrived he could extinguish the lamps because, Charles wrote, "No surer way to blush, than particularly to wish not to do so. How directly personal remark will make any one blush.—Is there not some saying about a person even blushing in the dark. . . . A person who blushes in the dark is proverbially a most modest person."

Charles thought about Emma all the time. He read and reread her letters, three, four, five times.

Meanwhile back at Maer, referring to all the scientific work she thought her future husband was doing, Emma had written to Aunt Jessie, "I am so glad he is a busy man."

Chapter 10

Melancholy Thoughts

*My reason tells me that honest & conscientious
doubts cannot be a sin, but I feel it would be
a painful void between us.*
—EMMA TO CHARLES, NOVEMBER 1838

As he prepared for their upcoming marriage, Charles had certain things on his mind. Emma had others. She was back at Maer getting new clothes because her aunts told her she had to present herself better once she was married. Aunt Jessie wrote that Emma should always be "dressed in good taste; do not despise those little cares which give everyone more pleasing looks, because you know you have married a man who is above caring for such little things. No man is above caring for them."

So Emma thought about and prepared a new wardrobe for her new life. And she relished the time with her family; it would be hard for her to leave them. "I bless the railroad every day of my life, and Charles is so fond of Maer that I am sure he

will always be ready to steam down whenever he can. So that
we shall always be within reach of home," she wrote, reassuring
herself. During this time before the wedding, she visited
with her friends, wrote letters to Charles, and looked forward
to letters from him.

She expressed no regret about her decision to marry him,
and when Charles visited Maer, she felt happy and in love. Yet
when he left, she felt depressed. She worried about the big
subject that was in the way of their happiness. For in those
talks by the fire he had not concealed his doubts about God,
miracles, and creation. He had told her at least part of what he
was thinking about the origin of species, and he admitted that
he was not a believer as she was.

At Maer without Charles, his charm, his wit, his very presence
to remind her of all she loved about him, the problem of
their religious differences loomed large. Emma wrote to him,
"When I am with you I think all melancholy thoughts keep
out of my head but since you are gone some sad ones have
forced themselves in, of fear that our opinions on the most
important subject should differ widely."

She was glad he had told her of his doubts, even though
his father had advised him not to say anything. (He had confessed
that, too.) The fact that he was open with her gave her
hope for their future. She wrote, "I thank you from my heart
for your openness with me & I should dread the feeling that
you were concealing your opinions from the fear of giving
me pain."

But as she contemplated leaving her home to start a life
with him, she was scared. In fact, she was more than scared;
she was in pain. Although she knew that honest and conscientious
doubts could not be a sin, and she told him so, she had
to be honest with him about her fears, too. She wrote, "It is

perhaps foolish of me to say this much but my own dear Charley we now do belong to each other & I cannot help being open with you." She worried that their difference of faith would be a terrible void between them. She was not willing to give up her belief in an afterlife; to do so would relinquish hope that she would see her sister Fanny again. Perhaps she could convince him to find another route to faith, one that did not require belief in Genesis.

"Will you do me a favour?" she asked. "Yes I'm sure you will," she answered herself. She knew that Charles cared as much about their happiness as she did; she knew, also, that Charles was not someone who wanted to upset her or anyone else. She asked him to read Jesus' farewell discourse to his disciples, which begins at the end of the thirteenth chapter of John. "It is so full of love to them & devotion & every beautiful feeling. It is the part of the New Testament I love best."

According to the book of John, before he was betrayed by Judas, Jesus washed his disciples' feet. He tells them, "If I then, your Lord and Master, have washed your feet; ye also ought to wash one another's feet." Jesus wanted his disciples, and all of his followers, to love their neighbors enough to even wash their dirty feet. Emma found this love beautiful.

"This is a whim of mine it would give me great pleasure, though I can hardly tell why," Emma wrote to Charles. But they both knew why she wanted him to read that chapter: She desperately wanted Charles to believe in Jesus so he would go to heaven with her.

Jesus tells his disciples that if they follow his teachings, "Whither I go, thou canst not follow me now; but thou shall follow me afterward." But "if a man abide not in me, he is cast forth as a branch, and is withered; and men gather them, and cast them into the fire, and they are burned." Emma could not bear the thought of spending eternity without Charles, of Charles burning in hell. She did not want him to give her his opinion; she asked him just to read it, and then she changed the subject to her new wardrobe. "The plaid gown arrived safely yesterday & is unanimously pronounced to be very handsome & not at all too dashing."

Emma knew Charles was a good man, an honest and moral one. He was affectionate and kind to his family and to animals. He was vehemently antislavery, as was their Wedgwood grandfather, Josiah, who had campaigned against slavery from 1787 until his death in 1795. Josiah Wedgwood's pottery factory had made a medallion that was the emblem of the antislavery movement. It had a black basalt relief figure of an African slave in chains, bent down on one knee. In a semicircle around it were the words "Am I not a man and a brother?" Josiah's factory reproduced many copies of the figure on brooches and seals, too. He sent some of the medallions across the Atlantic to Benjamin Franklin, for use in his American antislavery campaign. Slavery had been outlawed in Britain in 1807, but it still caused contention among some of the British upper class.

During Charles's voyage, at a stop at Bahia in Brazil, he had gotten into a heated argument with Captain FitzRoy over slavery. FitzRoy defended slavery, stating that some slaves were happy because their masters were good to them. The proof was that when those slaves were asked if they wanted to be freed, they said no. In front of their masters. Charles hated confrontation and controversy, but he could not hold his tongue about this. He told his captain that it was impossible for slaves to answer truthfully in front of their masters, and that it was impossible to be happy without having any control over your own life, without hope of change. FitzRoy had

almost thrown Charles off the ship for disagreeing with him.
Charles wrote about this incident in his account of the voyage, which would be published soon after his marriage to
Emma. He wrote, "These deeds are done and palliated by
men, who profess to love their neighbours as themselves, who
believe in God, and pray that his Will be done on earth! It
makes one's blood boil, yet heart tremble, to think that we
Englishmen and our American descendants, with their boast-
ful cry of liberty, have been and are so guilty."

Emma knew Charles really thought things through and
that he struggled with his doubts about faith. She knew that
belief in God was not something he was just tossing out the
way the maids at Maer tossed out the dirty water. So she
prayed for him just as Jesus prayed for his disciples in
John 17:3: "And this is life eternal, that they might know the
only true God, and Jesus Christ, whom thou has sent." She
loved Charles and was about to tie herself to him. But how
could she give her all to him as she wanted to do, so that they
belonged completely to each other, bound in love, if she
couldn't be sure that they would be together in heaven, as she
would be with Fanny and, she hoped, as she would be one day
with all her loved ones? Emma's mother was slipping away,
too. Once brilliant and vibrant, Bessy was spending more and
more time in a fog. Emma knew she soon would lose her
completely. She could let her go without too much pain since
she knew she would see her again in heaven. But what about
Charles?

Emma was not asking Charles to believe in everything as it
was written in the Bible. She did not believe that every part of
the Bible was literally true either. She was just asking Charles
to accept the love of Jesus, whom she saw as the kind, sweet,
loving son of God.

Charles apparently did as she wished: He read Jesus' farewell discourse. But the letter he wrote to her afterward is lost. Her reply survived: "I am sitting with Mamma instead of going to church. I shall find it much pleasanter to have a little talk with you than to listen to Allen's temperance sermon." (John Allen Wedgwood was Emma's cousin on her mother's side, and the vicar of Maer.) She continued, "Thank you dear Charles for complying with my fancy. To see you are in earnest on the subject will be my greatest comfort & that I am sure you are. I believe I agree with every word you say, & it pleased me that you shd have felt inclined to enter a little more on the subject."

So what did he say? How did he reassure her? He had friends who were deeply religious. His old mentor Henslow, for one. Charles himself had not given up on God entirely. He remembered standing in the Brazilian rain forest while on his voyage and being stirred by its beauty, moved to think of a higher power. He had written in his *Journal of Researches*, the account of his voyage, which he was preparing to be published, that "it is not possible to give an adequate idea of the higher feelings of wonder, admiration, and devotion which fill and elevate the mind."

But that feeling of devotion would not be enough to satisfy most people. Most people around Charles believed that God had not only created all the species of animals at once, but that he had also created the social structure of their world. The church was an integral part of British society, and it dictated the rules of the class-ordered society that they all lived in. Some people did see the problems with the British class system, and many people knew that something did have to be done to help the poor, but the upper classes wanted desperately to hold on to their position at the top of the society.

And they felt that the people in the lower classes, the servants who cooked the meals, scrubbed the floors, washed the clothes, and emptied the chamber pots at Maer and the Mount were doing what they were meant to be doing. With God at the top, British society was neat and ordered. Everyone knew his (or her) place.

For Charles to go against God and religion was to go against the established social structure. If his theory became well known, and popular, it could topple British society on its head. If God had not ordained the hierarchy everyone lived by, then England could tumble into chaos. And Charles—a polite man, a conservative in the sense that he did want to conserve the British way of life, a man who did not want to hurt any-one—certainly did not want to be responsible for chaos.

As for Emma, she did not know why Charles had to reject God. While she and her family always questioned the status quo, she didn't think you had to deny the existence of God. And she desperately wished Charles wouldn't either. Although she did feel somewhat relieved because he had read Jesus's farewell to his disciples, she was still concerned about the void between them.

For Charles, marrying Emma made his religious doubts real and tangible. As real as the person who would be lying in the bed next to him.

Chapter 11

A Whirl of Noise
and Motion

*I quite agree with you in the happiness
of having plenty to do.*
—EMMA TO HER UNCLE J. C. DE SISMONDI, DECEMBER 1838

Day after day, at the end of a morning spent deep in thought—it was late November and he was now able to get a little work done—Charles would come out of 36 Great Marlborough Street into the yellow autumn fog. "I have seen no one for these two days," he wrote to Emma, "and what can a man have to say who works all morning in describing hawks and owls, and then rushes out and walks in a bewildered manner up one street and down another, looking out for the words 'To let.'" Up and down Regent Street, Oxford Street, and Cavendish Place. Maybe he would find a home near where Lyell and the former Mary Horner lived on Harley Street; or maybe he would find a house in Chelsea, where Thomas and Jane Carlyle had moved a few years earlier. To the east was Russell Square, and to the north was the area around the new university, University College London, which was known as the godless university, where great men were thinking great thoughts—but were not being trained, as at Cambridge and Oxford, for the church.

Everywhere he walked in London he had to avoid horse manure (one hundred tons left each day) and mud, and the street sweepers who swept it all away, as well as the hansom cabs and personal horse-drawn carriages—barouches, landaus, broughams, and curricles—rolling through the streets. He endured the "whirl of noise and motion," as Dickens characterized London in his then-current serial, *The Life and Adventures of Nicholas Nickleby*, which everyone was gobbling up in *Bentley's Miscellany*, a literary magazine.

Charles was desperate to find a house. After talking it over, he and Emma had agreed that they would begin their lives together in London, for Charles still had much to do in the city. As secretary of the Geological Society, he listened to debates about the significance of fossils. Many of the geologists argued against an evolutionary theory that one of his old Edinburgh professors, Robert Grant, proposed. Grant's theory mostly came from one that had been suggested by a Frenchman named Jean-Baptiste Lamarck late in the previous century. Charles agreed with much of what Lamarck had to say, especially that the environment in which an animal lives causes it to change. And he enjoyed listening to the debates. But he knew that he had more to contribute and would have even more to contribute if he could get more analysis of his specimens—those that were already out with experts and those that still needed to get to other specialists. To do this, he had to be in London, especially so he could use his considerable charm to convince the experts to hurry up.

Maybe later Charles and Emma would move out to the

country, for the ease and quiet. But for now they would stay in town, and they needed to find a place to live—his rooms on Great Marlborough Street were not big enough for Charles, Emma, a butler, a cook, a maid, and all the beetles, fossils, and shells. He moaned to Emma in a letter, "Houses are very scarce and the landlords are all gone mad, they ask such prices. Erasmus takes it to heart even more than I do, and declares I ought to end all my letters to you, 'yours inconsolably.'"

In the mornings he was not only writing about hawks and owls, he was also pouring out his ideas about religion and faith, and about morality and conscience. His thoughts spilled into his notebooks, and out of them, onto scraps of paper, and onto stationery from the Athenaeum Club, where he took most of his dinners. He wondered if morality was innate, not learned or taught. He scribbled, "I suspect conscience, an hereditary compound passion. Like avarice." If people were, in essence, naturally moral, what was the need for religion, really? Don't we all have the right moral instincts? In his "N" notebook, he observed, "It does not hurt the conscience of a Boy to swear, though reason may tell him not, but it does hurt his conscience, if he has been cowardly, or has injured another bad, vindictive.—or lied &c &c." The acts we do that hurt others seem wrong to us. Why? Are we born knowing right from wrong, or do we have to learn it?

He had grown up with the Ten Commandments—including "Thou shalt not bear false witness"—and with the injunction to love your neighbor as yourself. But soon after his mother died, he had told a classmate that you could grow different-colored flowers by watering them with colored water and that his mother had taught him how to figure out the name of a plant by looking inside its blossom. Charles had made this all up and felt terrible about his lie later. Though maybe he shouldn't have—his classmate went on to become a well-known lichenologist and botanist, and he said that Charles had roused his attention and curiosity.

Charles thought back to his boyish lies and misdeeds. He once picked fruit from one of his father's trees and hid it in the bushes. Then he ran in "breathless haste" and "spread the news" that he had discovered a hoard of stolen fruit. He also stole fruit to eat and to give away to some poor people who lived nearby. Once he killed a bird with a stone, and he still felt bad about that, too. He felt ashamed about all of this and confessed these incidents in his autobiography, which he wrote as an old man.

Charles thought about arguments for belief—Emma's and other people's. He pondered his own reactions to those arguments. He read other people's ideas, not only those of Malthus, but also of Adam Smith, who had written in the previous century about free-market economics and capitalism. Charles read scholars and theologians who wrote about religion and philosophy. He talked to his friends, to Erasmus and to Hensleigh. They questioned just as he did. He thought of his mentor, John Stevens Henslow, who was a scientist and was also religious, as was Charles Lyell. He thought about Captain FitzRoy, who had married a religious woman and was now a Bible literalist—he thought every word in the Bible was true. Thomas Carlyle thought about these questions, too, and he wrote what would become a motto of the Victorian era: The dilemma was that they were becoming "destitute of faith, yet terrified of skepticism."

Charles was skeptical, and was scared to take it public. He wasn't ready to shake up the world. He had to think of Emma's feelings. In his private notes, Charles wrote that people do believe in things that can't be proved. Belief was not about reason, he concluded: "Belief allied to instinct."

He made notes to himself about the strong emotions that make one think about God and heaven. "The emotions of terror & wonder so often concomitant with sublime." He realized that it makes people feel good and powerful to feel a part of God, a part of the sublime. It is on that feeling of sublimity, even greater than one feels when standing atop a mountain and looking at a glorious view, that religions are based. Charles had sublime feelings listening to Handel's *Messiah*. But nothing, not his mother's death, not his feelings of awe in a Brazilian rain forest, had given him a faith in the afterlife the way Fanny's death had done for Emma.

He also went over the ideas of Malthus again and again. He thought about the similarities between people and animals, especially people at war. "When two races of men meet, they act precisely like two species of animals," he wrote. "They fight, eat each other, bring diseases to each other &c, but then comes the more deadly struggle." What was at stake in nature was the survival of an entire species. Not only the survival of an entire species, but also the creation of new species. The thought made him wild with excitement.

But he did not let the emotion overcome him; he looked at facts. And he looked at how people changed animal species. He looked at dog breeders, who created new breeds by selecting for traits they wanted. They bred dogs for foxhunting, for duck hunting, for bringing down bulls, and for squeezing into tight places to catch rats and other vermin. He looked at dogs crossed with wolves and with foxes; he looked at Persian greyhounds, Italian greyhounds, setters, and spaniels. He looked at how quickly new breeds were made. The same thing happens in nature, he realized, without human intervention. "It is a beautiful part of my theory that domesticated races . . . are made by precisely the same means as species." In nature, without human intervention, the changes took longer. But he felt nature did it with more perfection. (Late in the twentieth century, scientists would show that species can change quickly in nature—in guppies, in bacteria, and, most poetically, in the finches of the Galapagos Islands, which were key to Charles's theory.)

And the more he looked at animals and people, the more he came to believe we are all related. He watched a dog and a horse and a man yawn and wrote that it "makes me feel how much all animals are built on one structure." Not because God had made everything from a pattern, as some people thought, but because we all evolved from the same pattern.

His work was going better than the house hunting. When he complained to Emma, she wrote that she would come to help. "I quite approve of your plan of furnishing a bit of the house first & getting into it how we can & then furnishing at our leisure," she wrote. And she knew he needed some of her guidance. "I think it would be quite insulting to take the house in Bedford Place just opposite the Horneritas," she wrote to him. Charles had made amends, somewhat, with the Horner girls and their parents, but it would be too awkward to run into them all the time on the block where they lived.

Emma left Maer and arrived in London by train. She stayed with Hensleigh and Fanny, and spent days walking up and down the streets with Charles looking for a home.

Neither of them cared too much about how a house looked. They were more concerned with price—it should be affordable—and that it have the number of rooms they needed, including a study for Charles, as well as quarters for servants. They also wanted a decent-sized yard. Finding a piece of land in London wasn't easy. "Some London houses," Dickens wrote in Nicholas Nickleby, "have a melancholy little plot of ground behind them, usually fenced in by four high whitewashed walls, and frowned upon by stacks of chimneys: in which there withers on, from year to year, a crippled tree. . . . People sometimes call these dark yards 'gardens;' . . . No man thinks of walking in this desolate place." But Charles really needed to walk and to pace in order to think things through, and they had both grown up in the country and loved green and flowers and trees, so they made a good-sized garden a priority.

Finally, on Gower Street, near University College, Charles and Emma found a house that would do. It wasn't perfect—it was garishly decorated—but it had the right number of rooms and a decent yard that they would be able to see when they sat in the back of the house. Emma wrote to Aunt Jessie and Sismondi that the house had "a front drawing-room with three windows, and a back one, rather smaller, with a cheerful look-out on a set of little gardens, which will be of great value to us in summer to take a mouthful of fresh air; and that will be our sitting-room for quietness' sake. It is furnished, but rather ugly."

The house was tall and skinny, like all the houses around it. It had four floors; a cook and other servants could stay in the attic and in the basement. Its blue walls clashed with the yellow curtains. Blue and yellow reminded them of a parrot; they dubbed it Macaw Cottage. By the end of December, Charles wrote triumphantly to Emma, who was back at Maer, "Gower Street is ours, yellow curtains and all."

Besides the awful curtains, there was a dead dog decomposing in the garden. After the dog was removed, Charles would move in and get things ready for Emma's arrival. He couldn't wait.

"But why does joy, & OTHER EMOTION make grown up people cry.—What is emotion?" Charles wrote in his "N" notebook, looking at himself. And then, "A man shivers, from fear, sublimity, sexual ardour.—a man cries from grief, joy & sublimity."

To Emma he wrote, "I long for the day when we shall enter the house together. How glorious it will be to see you seated by the fire of our own house."

Chapter 12

Heavy Baggage, Blazing Fires

*I take so much pleasure in the house, I declare I am just
like a great over-grown child with a new toy; but then, not like
a real child, I long to have a co-partner and possessor.*
—CHARLES TO EMMA, JANUARY 20, 1839

Charles got out of bed early on December 30, 1838, unable to sleep. He could move into Macaw Cottage in just two days. He had planned to have a quiet day of work, but by eleven o'clock in the morning, he realized that was not going to happen. He rang for Syms Covington.

"I am very sorry to spoil your Sunday," he told his manservant, "but begin packing up I must, as I cannot rest."

"Pack up, Sir, what for?" asked Covington, his eyes wide with astonishment.

"As if it was the first notice he had received of my flitting," Charles reported to Emma.

Syms Covington, who had been working for Charles ever since the *Beagle*, would not be staying on after the marriage.

He was off to Australia, with Charles's blessing and help. But now he worked with Charles, arranging the specimens and packing them for the move. Charles sorted "a multitude of papers"—including his notes on scraps of paper, envelopes, and Athenaeum stationery, and his readings. He had piles of scientific papers he had read or was planning to read; books he needed to get to, which he listed in his notebooks: Buffon on varieties of domesticated animals and Smellie and Flemming on the philosophy of zoology; Bevan on the honeybee, Paxton on the culture of dahlias; Cuvier on instinct. He had his secret notebooks to move with him, to keep close by, and he had field notebooks from the voyage, notebooks that listed all of his specimens and where he got them, the fossil vertebrates and invertebrates, plant fossils, stuffed birds, mammal fossils, mammals, and fish.

The next day, Charles and Syms began to pack in earnest: the books, clothes, linens, pots and pans, all the specimens. By three thirty on January 1, they had filled two large horse-drawn vans with "goods, well and carefully packed." Charles was moving into Macaw Cottage with an abundance of baggage, much of it heavy. He wrote to Emma, "I was astounded, and so was Erasmus, at the bulk of my luggage, and the porters were even more so at the weight of those containing my Geological Specimens."

Charles and Syms carried by hand "some few dozen drawers of shells," so the shells wouldn't shatter. By six o'clock they were in the house and by eight they had a meal of eggs, bacon, and tea. Charles felt "supremely comfortable."

There were so many specimens everywhere that the house looked like a museum. Over the next few days, the two men moved as many crates of specimens as they could into one of the front attic rooms, and Charles dubbed it the Museum. He wanted the rest of the house to be a home for Emma; he did not want the science to take over completely.

Charles exulted in his new home. It was only a hundred yards from Regent's Park, where he and Emma could go walking together. And now that the dead dog was gone, he assured her, "The little garden is worth its weight in gold." It was very narrow, but it was ninety feet long, big enough for Charles to pace in every day. He spent the next days working, setting up the house as best he could, hiring a cook and other servants—consulting with Emma and his sisters and Fanny. He also started receiving wedding gifts. One puzzled him: "My good old friend Herbert sent me a very nice little note, with a massive silver weapon, which he called a Forficula (the Latin for an earwig) and which I thought was to catch hold of soles and flounders." But Erasmus, who knew these things, told him it was for asparagus. Harriet Martineau sent some of her own books to help start their library, and Henslow brought Charles a silver candlestick. Mrs. Henslow offered to give him advice on household matters.

In between setting up, he found time to make some notebook jottings, too. Once again he analyzed Specimen Number One, Charles Darwin. "What passes in a man's mind. When he says he loves a person—do not the features pass before him marked, with the habitual express emotions, which make us love him, or her.—it is blind feeling, something like sexual feelings...." What else influences love, he wondered. Is it affected by other emotions? He thought of Emma and was eager, lonely, and frustrated.

His frustration grew when he read a letter from Emma postponing the wedding five days. "You will have a few days more time on your hands than you expect my dear Charley as the marriage must be fixed for the 29th instead of the 24th (I always said *about* the 24th) I am afraid you will be rather vexed at this but I hope you will have the Drs maxim that I *must always* be in the right properly impressed on your mind." She *was* right about one thing—it did vex him.

For her part, Emma was vexed when he referred to the house as "his," not "ours," and she told him so. She also told him that she did not approve of Lyell's idea that he and Charles should dine every evening at the Athenaeum Club, leaving the wives at home alone. Apparently Henslow told him he should take many solitary walks, too. Emma was not eager to move to London and be left alone all the time: "I must say looks as if you meant to give in a good deal, to Mr Lyells plan of the Athenaeum. If you follow Mr Henslows advice about walking & Mr Lyells precepts about dining I shall see quite . . . little of you. . . . These excellent steady old friends of yours have a good deal to answer for in corrupting your mind."

Charles had no intention of leaving Emma alone; he wanted to be with her as much as she wanted to be with him. Even though he reassured her, Emma still was not happy with Lyell, and especially not with the way he treated his wife, who just sat quietly and did not say much. Emma decided not to read his book, as she had been planning to do.

Emma was not one to sit by quietly and not say much. "By the way now we seem to be clearing old scores," she wrote to Charles, "they told me at Shrewsbury that you had the audacity to call me 'little baggage'! but I won't believe it till I hear it with my own ears, (& then I advise you to take care *of your* own ears)."

Charles, for his part, also wanted to come clean. He warned her about what she was really in for with this man devoted to his specimens and his thoughts. After a lovely visit to Maer a few weeks before the wedding, he told Emma that she would have to humanize him. Five years on the voyage and the last two spent working so hard had made him too much of a brute, and he hoped that Emma would "soon teach me there is greater happiness than building theories and accumulating facts in silence and solitude."

Charles was so preoccupied with his thoughts that he forgot to show up for a dinner he had been invited to attend. Maybe it was his instinct for survival—the dinner was at the Horners' house. The family waited around the table for him while he sat happily alone at the Athenaeum, reading and eating his dinner as he had taken to doing. "I made a very stupid mistake yesterday," he wrote to Emma. "I utterly forgot the invitation & kept the whole party waiting whilst I was quietly at dinner here.—I had to send a very humble note this morning, & backed it by calling, and had a very pleasant sit."

It wasn't just work that preoccupied him; it was the thought of Emma:—"My own dear future wife." The letters flew back and forth, daily or even twice a day. Emma, uncharacteristically for her, was also romantic and sentimental. She was almost embarrassed by her enthusiasm. "I am rather ashamed of writing to you so soon again but if I disguise my writing in the direction I am in hopes the post master at Newcastle will think it is somebody else." She wrote with candor, letting Charles see who she really was, just as he was doing with her: "Today the Miss Northens are coming very early & I shall have to do a prodigious quantity of friendship with Ellen who adores me extremely & will want to know all about every thing & my chief aim will be to tell her nothing about any thing. I shall treat her like your sisters do the Owens pretend to be very open & carefully never tell anything."

And although (perhaps because) she found it difficult to talk about religion in person, Emma once again wrote to Charles. On January 23, less than a week before the wedding, she wrote about her concerns.

You need not fear my own dear Charles that I shall not be quite as happy as you are & I shall always look upon the event of the 29th as a most happy one on my part though perhaps not so great or so good as you do. There is only one subject in the world that ever gives me a moments uneasiness & I believe I think about that very little when I am with you & I do hope that though our opinions may not agree upon all points of religion we may sympathize a good deal in our feelings on the subject. I believe my chief danger will be that I shall lead so happy comfortable & amusing a life that I shall be careless & good for nothing & think of nothing serious in this world or the next.

This world or the next. She wasn't letting go.

On the day they had originally set for the wedding, January 24, 1839, Charles was elected a Fellow of the Royal Society, which was a rather important milestone in his career, but he didn't even mention it in a letter to Emma. Instead he told her that he had had a bad headache for two days and two nights. He was afraid he wouldn't be well enough to get married, but the train to Shrewsbury "quite cured me." He arrived at the Mount to get ready for the wedding, and wrote to her at Maer. She had asked him to, afraid that it would be the last letter she ever got from him, for once they were married they did not expect to be spending time apart. "The house is in such a bustle," Charles told her, "that I do not know what I write. I have got the ring, which is the most important piece of news I have to tell."

Finally, on Tuesday, January 29, Charles, with the ring, and Emma in a green silk dress, went to the church at Maer. Emma was thirty, Charles would turn thirty in two weeks. Neither one liked pomp and ceremony, so the service was quick and attended only by a few members of their close family. Emma's mother, Bessy, was too sick to leave her bed, and Erasmus did not even come in from London. Charles's sister Caroline and Emma's brother Josiah were there, but their infant was very ill, which set a pall over the whole day.

The group went back to Maer Hall, where Emma quickly changed out of her fancy clothes, and the two newlyweds said their farewells. Emma tried to say good-bye to her mother, but Bessy was still asleep. This was actually a great relief to Emma, who had been worried that her mother was lying there feeling terrible for missing the ceremony.

With a packed lunch in hand, Emma and Charles took the train back to London. "We ate our sandwiches with grateful hearts for all the care that was taken of us, and the bottle of water was the greatest comfort," Emma reported in a letter to her mother.

As Charles had arranged, when they got home to Gower Street, the fires were blazing in welcome.

Chapter 13

Definition of Happiness

*A thousand thanks to you, dearest Emma, for your delightful
letter which from the cheerful happy tone of it drew tears of
pleasure from my old eyes. I am truly thankful to find you
so happy, and still more so that you are sensible of it,
and I pray heaven that this may only be the
beginning of a life full of peace and tranquility.*
—BESSY WEDGWOOD TO EMMA, FEBRUARY 1839

In Jane Austen's novel *Pride and Prejudice*, Charlotte Lucas tells
her friend Elizabeth Bennet that it is better to go into a marriage blind to the other person's faults. "Happiness in marriage
is entirely a matter of chance. If the dispositions of the parties
are ever so well known to each other, or ever so similar
beforehand, it does not advance their felicity in the least."
Charles and Emma had gotten to know each other through
letters and visits, but like any couple, they would only really
get to know each other by living together.

But happiness in marriage, as Austen's heroine Elizabeth

Bennet knows, is not only a matter of chance. It's also a matter of love, and a matter of determination on both sides. And willingness to compromise. "It is better to know as little as possible of the defects of the person with whom you are to pass your life," Charlotte Lucas continues in her speech to Elizabeth Bennet. After a short time with Emma, Charles knew he was going to have to make a serious compromise. Little Miss Slip-Slop had grown up into Big Mrs. Slip-Slop. Unlike Charles, she was not careful to put things back where she got them; the freethinking atmosphere at Maer had not inculcated order into her as the strict atmosphere at the Mount had into Charles. Their new home was not going to be as neat and organized as Charles liked. But Emma was worth it; so, as his daughter Henrietta wrote much later, he "made up his mind to give up all his natural taste for tidiness." He decided he "would not allow himself to feel annoyed by her calm disregard for such details." He would keep his study neat and orderly, but the rest of the house would be how Emma wanted.

In their first few days together, they mostly stayed in—it was snowing. But they also did some shopping for furniture, dishes, and clothes, including a morning gown for Emma. It was "a sort of clarety-brown satin," she wrote to Elizabeth, and she felt it was "very unobjectionable." They borrowed some novels from the library, starting a lifelong tradition of reading together—usually Emma read to Charles while he rested from his work. Charles liked novels with happy endings, and he once wrote, "I often bless all novelists. A surprising number have been read aloud to me . . . and I like all if moderately good, and if they do not end unhappily—against which a law ought to be passed. A novel, according to my taste, does not come into the first class unless it contains some person whom one can thoroughly love, and if it be a pretty woman all the better."

Charles and Emma both took setting up house seriously. For once, Charles did not mind spending money. But he did start recording every pound he spent in a pocket account book and would continue that practice for the rest of his life. He wrote that they started with £573 in the bank and £36 cash in hand. They spent money on medicine, a coffeepot, a pickle pot, stationery with their new address (12 Upper Gower Street) printed on it, a haircut for Charles, shaving soap, beer, biscuits, a table for the pantry, wages for the servants, fares for hackney coaches, and tickets for the opera. Charles also bought a going-away present for Syms Covington.

Soon they ventured out and "went slopping through the melted snow," as Emma wrote to Elizabeth, to pick out a pianoforte that was to be a present from Emma's father. Both Emma and Charles were so thrilled at the prospect of having the beautiful mahogany grand—Emma for herself, Charles because he knew it would make her happy—that when they were walking on Gower Street a few days later and saw a pianoforte van, Charles shouted out to see if it was going to number 12. It was. They put the piano in the small back room, where, even though it was cramped, they spent most of their time, for it looked out on their garden. This room seemed more like the country and therefore more like home than any other part of the house.

Emma gave Charles "a large dose of music every evening," as she said, and even though he could never remember a tune and was probably tone deaf, he enjoyed her playing very much. ("Charms of music and female chit-chat," as he had written on the *Marry* side of his list.) In that first week they also gave their first dinner party, as sort of practice, for Hensleigh and Fanny and Erasmus. Erasmus was condescending at first; he said the dinner was just like those he gave. But, as

Emma reported home, "when the plum-pudding appeared he knocked under, and confessed himself conquered very humbly."

Charles had written in one of his notebooks, "Definition of happiness the number of pleasant ideas passing through mind in given time." Now he found happiness not just in his mind; he found it in real life.

But sad news arrived during this happy time. Caroline and Jos's baby had died. Emma was quite shocked, though Charles had known it was coming from the way his sister described the baby's appearance and symptoms. At that time many infants died—as many as one in four or five, depending on social class and living conditions. To lose a baby was not unusual, but it was, of course, very sad. Caroline, who had married late, was devastated. Elizabeth wrote to an aunt, "the thoughts of this precious child and the preparations for it have occupied her in an intense way." The death had an effect on everyone in the family, including Charles and Emma, who were hoping to have their own baby soon.

For the newlyweds there was much to absorb and to get used to, going from single to married, and without a honeymoon for a transition. (Neither one of them wanted to take a trip.) Emma wrote to her mother that Charles wasn't quite used to her "honours yet." He picked up a letter addressed to her and "could not conceive who Mrs. C. Darwin could mean."

But time and shared experiences got them used to being husband and wife. One day, as they were out walking near the Athenaeum Club, they saw Leonard Horner—father of the Horner girls. He looked like he was trying to avoid them. "Charles said his face, trying to pretend not to see us, was the most comical thing he ever saw." Later that evening, Charles

received a note from Mr. Horner. Apparently his report of seeing the newly married Charles Darwin with his bride made a
big impact on the Horneritas. Together Charles and Emma
imagined the scene.

Emma even got Charles to go to church with her. She kept
hoping he'd find a way to have faith. Erasmus's friend Harriet
Martineau had a brother, James, who was a Unitarian theolo-
gian. James Martineau preached that the gospels could trans-
form an individual into a believer just through their beauty,
not through strict, traditional belief in every word of the
Bible. That's what Emma hoped would happen with Charles.
If only he would take the gospels to heart. Yet perhaps going
to church wasn't good for him. She wrote to her sister Charlotte, "My Charles has been very unwell since Sunday. We
went to church at King's College and found the church not
warmed, and not more than half-a-dozen people in it, and he
was so very cold that I believe it was that which has made him
so unwell."

So the dance of a married couple had begun. She played
the piano for him, and though he had a tin ear, he listened
with enjoyment and love. He put up with her sloppiness; she
understood his need for long hours at work. She agreed to go
to fewer parties and dinners since he did not like them. He
went to the theater with her, and to church.

Fanny wrote to a friend that the couple was settling in to
married life well. "Emma is looking very pretty and unanx-
ious, and I suppose there are not many two people happier
than she and Charles."

Emma kept notes in a little date-book diary, as she had for
years. She did not write at length—just small notations about
the weather and about household events: "Erasmus drank tea"
and "Wrote to Mamma" and "Wrote to Elizabeth," "Church at

King's college," "Fanny and Hensleigh here," "Dined Dr. Holland's," and "Party at Lyell's." Charles took Emma to one of his old favorite haunts, which Emma recorded in her diary only as an enthusiastic, "Zoo!"

In April she made the little note "Charles Journal." Charles's first book was to be published that summer—his account of the voyage on the *Beagle*. It was part of a multivolume set called *Narrative of the Surveying Voyages of HMS* Adventure *and* Beagle *Between the years 1826 and 1836*. The other volumes were written by Captain FitzRoy. Darwin's part would be called, first, *Journal and Remarks*. It later became known simply as *The Voyage of the* Beagle. He had kept a 770-page diary while on the voyage; the book was culled from that. When the page proofs arrived, he was nervous about how his book would be accepted.

In spite of his happiness, Charles was not well physically. He suffered from stomach problems, fatigue, and at times, nervousness, as well as headaches. Emma had had headaches, too, since she was a teenager. She kept track of his symptoms as well as her own in her diary. She also made note of her menstrual cycle.

And on August 15, Emma wrote, "halfway now I think from symptoms."

Chapter 14

Pregnant Thoughts

*I should be most unhappy if I thought
we did not belong to each other forever.*
—EMMA TO CHARLES, AROUND FEBRUARY 1839

Emma was pregnant. They had both hoped for a baby, and they were thrilled, but pregnancy was dangerous in the nineteenth century. About one in every two hundred women died in childbirth. As Emma knew well from her sister Fanny's early death, one never knew when her time would come. Or her husband's. Women were at greater risk because of pregnancy and childbirth, but Charles's health continued to worsen, and they didn't know what was wrong with him. Were his stomach upsets, heart palpitations, fatigue, and bouts of giddiness symptoms of something that might be fatal? What if Charles died soon? What if Emma did not survive this pregnancy and childbirth? Would they meet again in heaven? The question of what happens after death had a new urgency for Emma.

Meanwhile as Charles worked hard, not only on his geology, but also on his ideas about the transmutation of species, the more he learned, the more skeptical he became about religion. Every morning he left Emma sleeping comfortably in their bed, to go "write about coral formations," as he wrote to his sister Caroline. He worked until about ten, and then had breakfast with Emma. Afterward they sat together, and Charles watched "the clock as the hand travels sadly too fast to half past eleven—Then to my study & work till 2 o'clock luncheon time." They spent afternoons together at home often, with Emma doing needlework in Charles's study. Sometimes they did errands in town together, but Charles also went off to scientific meetings or to talk to an expert about his specimens. In the evenings, Emma read to Charles and played piano for him. And "then bedtime makes a charming close to the day," wrote Charles. He told Caroline that Emma was "essentially going on well & undeniably growing."

But the gulf Emma felt between them pained her. While she tended to the running of the house, hiring and firing cooks and other servants, planning meals that might help settle Charles's stomach, while her body cradled and nourished their developing child, Charles was in his study with his specimens, writing in his notebooks, and honing his arguments. Emma wondered if he was keeping himself open to the possibility of God. She took out a piece of paper and while he worked, she began once again to set down her thoughts about religion.

She wrote that she knew he was "acting conscientiously & sincerely & sincerely wishing, & trying to learn the truth." He could not be wrong in pursuing his science, she said. But Emma had grave doubts that science was the answer to everything. She knew that Charles prized openness and honesty as she did and she hoped "that my own dearest will indulge me."

She worried that he was so busy with his science that he wouldn't look elsewhere for answers. "Your mind & time are full of the most interesting subjects & thoughts of the most absorbing kind, viz following up your own discoveries—but which make it very difficult for you to avoid casting out as interruptions other sorts of thoughts which have no relation to what you are pursuing or to be able to give your whole attention to both sides of the question."

Emma knew that Charles did look at every side of a question. He had even shown her his *Marry, Not Marry* list and other notes he had written about the marriage question. So she asked him to look at the religious side again. She told him she thought he was unduly influenced by other people, especially his older brother, Erasmus, "whose understanding you have such a very high opinion of & whom you have so much affection for, having gone before you." Emma knew Erasmus had what she considered heretical thoughts. Since he had paved the way, it made it easier for Charles to go down this path without fear. But Emma thought these kinds of doubts should scare Charles; they scared her. She asked him to take the time and effort to move away from Erasmus and the other doubters and to look at the other side. "It seems to me also that the line of your pursuits may have led you to view chiefly the difficulties on one side, & that you have not had time to consider & study the chain of difficulties on the other, but I believe you do not consider your opinion as formed."

Not everything can be proven, Emma reasoned, but that does not mean something that cannot be proven is wrong. Belief comes from a different place than science. Charles had written about this very idea in his notebooks before the wedding—"Belief allied to instinct." Emma prayed for him: "May not the habit in scientific pursuits of believing nothing till it is proved, influence your mind too much in other things which cannot be proved in the same way, & which if true are likely to be above our comprehension." We humans cannot prove everything; we cannot understand everything, Emma told her husband. Yet that was just what he was trying to do, in his study.

"I should say also that there is a danger in giving up revelation," she wrote. Don't forget what Jesus did for us and for the rest of the world, she begged him. She did not mean to say that she was right and he was wrong; she had, after all, grown up in the freethinking atmosphere of Maer, where all sides were openly discussed. "I do not know whether this is arguing as if one side were true & the other false, which I meant to avoid, but I think not." She was asking him to leave the door open.

Just as Dr. Darwin had predicted would happen, she was in agony over her husband's lack of faith. As Charles's father had warned, "Things went on pretty well until the wife or husband became out of health, and then some women suffered miserably by doubting about the salvation of their husbands." Emma told Charles that he should pray, that she now realized that acting morally was not enough. She wrote, "I do not quite agree with you in what you once said—that luckily there were no doubts as to how one ought to act. I think prayer is an instance to the contrary, in one case it is a positive duty & perhaps not in the other. But I dare say you meant in actions which concern others & then I agree with you almost if not quite."

Again Emma asked him not to answer, but to think about her letter; "It is a satisfaction to me to write it." She asked him to have patience with her about this issue. And with tenderness she wrote, "Don't think that it is not my affair & that it does not much signify to me. Every thing that concerns you concerns me & I should be most unhappy if I thought we did not belong to each other forever."

She ended her letter with love, and thanked him for all the affection he gave her. His love, she told him, "makes the happiness of my life more & more every day."

Charles read the letter and cried. He was as in love with her as he could be; he wanted so much to make her happy. Alone in his study, he was committed to his theory of natural selection, the theory that would leave God out of creation. But he was committed to Emma, too, and so as he examined lily hybrids and dog breeds, as he worked out a new theory about how coral islands had evolved, he also agonized over the religion question and over the effect his work was having, and would have, on her. He felt—literally—sick to his stomach.

Yet even with the emotional pain it caused him, Charles thought Emma's letter was beautiful. "Every thing that concerns you concerns me" went both ways. He kept the letter safely preserved always. Sometime later he wrote at the edge of it:

When I am dead, know
that many times, I
have kissed and cryed
over this. C.D.

Chapter 15

Little Animalcules

The baby performed his first smile to-day, a great event.
—EMMA TO AUNT JESSIE, FEBRUARY 7, 1840

The summer of 1839 was one of anticipation—happy and anxious. Emma and Charles anticipated the arrival of their first child, and Charles anticipated the reaction to his first book. They both felt sick much of the time, too. Emma suffered from morning sickness and other discomforts of pregnancy; Charles had headaches and was often nauseated.

They went to the country to get some fresh air and visit their families. At the Mount "Charles got some of his father's good doctoring," Elizabeth wrote to Aunt Jessie. Although he had been quite healthy and robust on the voyage—save for the seasickness and a few bouts with illness—Elizabeth blamed his ill health on that long trip. She told her aunt that he "is much better again, but I suppose he is feeling the effect of too much exertion in every way during his voyage and must be careful not to work his head too hard now." But Charles would not put work aside unless he had to.

At Maer Hall, he proudly gave Elizabeth a copy of his book, his first literary child, as he called the *Journal*. She wrote her aunt that "his journal is come out at last along with two other thick volumes . . . but I have not had time to read it yet."

Charles was eager for her to read it; he was eager for everyone to read his book. He had also given copies to Erasmus, Uncle Josiah, Henslow, Lyell, and Hensleigh. But he was, of course, most concerned about how critics and the reading public would react. When he received his author's copies he saw that FitzRoy had added a volume with a religious polemic arguing against Charles's geological findings—that the earth was formed gradually and was still being formed. After reading Charles's section in the page proofs of the book, FitzRoy quickly had written a chapter called "A Very Few Remarks with Reference to the Deluge," in which he argued for the biblical account of creation and the flood. Charles was furious at his captain, and Lyell agreed with him. Charles told his sister Caroline that Lyell said "it beat all other nonsense he has ever read on the subject."

Charles knew he owed a considerable amount of his success to FitzRoy. The captain not only took a chance by choosing him as his companion on the voyage, he also had supported him as he collected his specimens, and even helped him send back some of them at the Crown's expense. But given this latest development, Charles said he didn't think he could see much of his old captain anymore.

On the home front, other than illness, all was going well. Emma and Charles were close, content, and devotedly in love. After a visit, Elizabeth wrote to Aunt Jessie that Emma was "so entirely happy in her lot, with the most affectionate husband possible, upon whom none of her pleasant qualities are thrown away, who delights in her music and admires her dress." Elizabeth was so taken with this that she told Aunt Jessie she was going to start dressing better herself. She made a plan to go to London to visit Hensleigh and Fanny, who had moved to Gower Street, four doors away from Emma and Charles.

When Charles started getting reactions to his book from reviewers as well as from people he knew, he relaxed. As it turned out, almost everyone liked the *Journal of Researches* and many loved it—his expert friends *and* reviewers in journals and papers. Charles had a natural flair for writing—his charming, funny, and modest voice shone through—and he painted the scenes of his travels so well that his readers felt as if they were right there, looking at the cliffs and mountains, the coasts and the plains, the flora and the fauna. One reviewer called him a "first-rate landscape-painter with a pen." Charles put himself in the first paragraph, as if to extend a hand and say, Come, walk with me. Describing his first stop, Porto Praya on St. Jago (now Santiago), an island in the Cape Verde Islands, he wrote, "The scene, as beheld through the hazy atmosphere of this climate, is one of great interest; if, indeed, a person, fresh from the sea, and who has just walked, for the first time, in a grove of cocoa-nut trees, can be a judge of any thing but his own happiness." It was extremely unusual for an Englishman to have such an adventure, to explore far-away lands, and now in his book Charles took his readers with him on the adventure. In the first pages, he introduced them to a land quite different from the green English countryside. He wrote of St. Jago, "The island would generally be considered as very uninteresting; but to anyone accustomed only to an English landscape, the novel prospect of an utterly sterile land possesses a grandeur which more vegetation might spoil. A single green leaf can scarcely be discovered over wide tracts of the lava plains; yet flocks of goats, together with a few cows, contrive to exist."

The publication of the *Journal* made his name among England's reading public. Scientists were impressed with his work as well. He had spent as much time on land as possible and threw himself into the collecting, making every moment and every step into new territory count. He had much to report in his book, including his fossil discoveries, and discoveries of previously unknown species. But he didn't report everything. He didn't report that as he reviewed some of his finds on the journey home, he began, tentatively, to explore the idea of the transmutation of species.

In the book, he wrote, "In the thirteen species of ground-finches, a nearly perfect gradation may be traced, from a beak extraordinarily thick, to one so fine, that it may be compared to that of a warbler. I very much suspect, that certain members of the series are confined to different islands. . . ." In a later edition, he would go on to say more, but just a little bit more, about how "one species had been taken and modified for different ends." He was hinting here, in print, about the transmutation of species, about how new species were created, by adapting to their surroundings, by the means of natural selection. But he was just hinting.

FitzRoy's volumes did not get as positive a reception as Charles's, so the publisher released Darwin's volume as a separate book without telling him or compensating him financially. The new single volume by Charles Darwin, the humble and articulate guide, was a huge popular success. It made money for the publisher, and although Charles did not receive any income from it, he was proud of the book. He said later, "The success of this my first literary child always tickles my vanity more than that of any of my other books."

* * *

The last week of December 1839, Emma was ready to give birth. A few days before she was confined (as they called going into labor), Charles got sick again, with bad headaches and an upset stomach. He was terrified of the childbirth, for good reason. He was also terrified of seeing Emma in pain. There was not much he could do to help, and there was no anesthesia to use. He wrote later to his cousin and good friend William Darwin Fox, "What an awful affair a confinement is: it knocked me up almost as much as it did Emma herself."

So when Elizabeth arrived at Gower Street to help her sister with the birth, she had two patients to deal with—Emma and Charles. But Emma's delivery was the priority. William Erasmus Darwin was born on December 27, 1839. Emma and the baby survived. So did Charles. Elizabeth wrote to her parents to tell them the good news. Her mother answered immediately: "It cost me a good cry, but such tears are precious . . . remember my love and blessing to both parents of the welcome stranger, who will, I hope, be as great a comfort to them as their predecessors have been to us." It seems to be the last letter Bessy ever wrote.

William was a joy to Emma and Charles. They called him Mr. Hoddy-Doddy or Doddy. Charles looked upon Doddy not only as a "little prince," as he wrote in a letter to a naturalist friend, but also as "a prodigy of beauty and intellect," as he wrote to his cousin Fox. Emma was, as usual, less sentimental than Charles. She wrote to Aunt Jessie after she regained her strength that she was able to enjoy "my baby, and a very nice looking one it is, I assure you. He has very dark blue eyes and a pretty, small mouth, his nose I will not boast of, but it is very harmless as long as he is a baby." He seemed to have gotten Charles's nose.

Not even that bothered the proud papa. Charles was so thrilled that he put aside his anger and wrote to FitzRoy about the birth of his son. "I find as you always prophesied would be the case being married, a very great happiness. . . . My little animalcule of a son, William Erasmus by name is also very well. He is 8 weeks old tomorrow, and has learnt to smile." Charles also did not lose the opportunity to tell FitzRoy that he was going to keep on working on his scientific theories: "I have nothing to wish for, excepting stronger health to go on with the subjects, to which I have joyfully determined to devote my life."

He continued to work on his book about coral reefs; he continued to make notes in his notebooks, and he continued to review his specimens, both preserved (in spirits of wine) and squalling. How could he not use his first child as a research subject? He watched William to see when he would smile, what he looked like when he cried, when tears formed. He had begun a new notebook right after the baby's birth. "During first week," he wrote, Doddy "yawned, streatched himself just like old person—chiefly upper extremities— hiccupped—sneezes, sucked, surface of warm hand placed to face seemed immediately to give wish of sucking, either instinctive or associated knowledge of warm smooth surface of bosom.—Cried & squalled, but no tears."

To Doddy all of this seemed like good attention—most of the time. When Doddy was about four months old, in the interest of science, Charles tried to scare the baby: "I made in his presence many odd noises and strange grimaces . . . but the noises, if not too loud, as well as the grimaces, were all taken as good jokes; and I attributed this at the time to their being preceded or accompanied by smiles." He got other people into the experimentation, too. "When a few days over six months old, his nurse pretended to cry . . . I saw that his face instantly assumed a melancholy expression, with the corners of the mouth strongly depressed." Doddy had never seen a grown-up person cry, and had rarely seen other children cry. So it seemed to Charles "that an innate feeling must have told him that the pretended crying of his nurse expressed grief" and that he empathized with her.

Charles was not all science by any means: He bathed the baby, kissed him, hugged him, walked him when he cried; he was anything but the stereotypical distant father so often portrayed in Victorian literature. He hated to watch his baby cry. "His sympathy with the grief spoiled his observation," one of his other sons later wrote about him. So his worries about loss of time when he had children were unfounded—he could be a scientist and a father at the same time.

Charles's observations were not just abstract experimentation. Looking at his Doddy was like looking at Jenny. The baby and the orangutan fit right into his theory of the origin of species. As he watched his little guppy, he realized, once again with a shocking and beautiful certainty, that Doddy was related, just as he himself was, to every creature in the animal kingdom. They weren't lined up in a God-made hierarchy, either; they had all descended from the same remote ancestor. Looking at his baby, he was working on a revolution.

He wrote in his "N" notebook, "A child crying. Frowning, pouting, smiling, just as much instinctive as a bull." Just as a newborn calf butts his head, or a young crocodile snaps his jaws, a baby makes his needs known by crinkling his brow, crying, cooing. These things are not learned, but are inherited: "I assume a child pouts who has never seen others pout," he wrote.

He wrote down all his observations and many years later would publish them in *The Expression of the Emotions in Man and*

Animals. But for now, watching the baby helped him formulate his theory. He wrote that it was "extremely difficult to prove that our children instinctively recognize any expression. I attended to this point in my first-born infant . . . and I was convinced that he understood a smile and received pleasure from seeing one, answering it by another, at much too early an age to have learnt anything by experience."

Emma reported to Aunt Jessie, "It is a great advantage to have the power of expressing affection and I am sure he will make his children very fond of him." And children it would be, for four months after writing that letter, Emma was pregnant again.

When their next child was born, on March 2, 1841, it was a girl, Anne Elizabeth. Annie gave Charles ample opportunity for more scientific study. Although Charles was enraptured with Doddy, Annie was a great rival to her brother in his affections. She was from the very beginning a bright and sunny baby, who loved to be held and hugged and kissed. Charles adored her. And when Emma lay in bed with her, the baby reached out to touch her mother. Annie quickly stole her parents' hearts.

Chapter 16

Down in the Country

*A frog jumped near him and he danced and screamed with
horror at the dangerous monster, and I had a bout of kissing
at his open, bellowing mouth to comfort him.*
—CHARLES, DURING A VISIT TO THE MOUNT WITH DODDY

By the spring of 1842, the house on Upper Gower Street was
starting to feel crowded. Annie was no longer a baby; she was
a real little person. Emma wrote to Aunt Jessie, "My little
Annie has taken to walking and talking for the last fortnight."
As usual, she told it like it was: "She is 13 months old and very
healthy, fat and round, but no beauty. Willy is very much
impressed with his own generosity and goodness to her."

The children needed more room to play. The garden,
decent enough for Charles to pace, was too small for romping
around in; now Charles and Emma had to pay for a key to get
into the gardens at Gordon Square, which were enclosed and
a safe place for the children to toddle and run freely. The
house was crowded, not only with Charles's specimens in

spirits of wine and the like, but also with the servants who went along with Charles's live specimens and their nurturing: the children's beloved red-haired Scottish nurse, Brodie, night nurses, other day nurses, the cook, the housemaids, and Joseph Parslow, who had replaced Syms Covington—after the short-lived tenure of a butler who stole the knives.

Both Emma and Charles found that London's whirl of noise, dirt, crowds, and foggy, smoggy air was getting to be too much for them. Emma joked to Aunt Jessie, "The London air has a very bad effect upon our little boy's v's and w's, he says his name is 'Villy Darvin,' and 'Vipe Doddy's . . . own tears away . . .'—my inclination for the country does not diminish."

London seemed to make Emma's headaches worse. Both of them felt better overall during their visits to the country at Maer or the Mount. During a visit to his father the previous summer, Charles had gotten medical advice, as well as a warning about Doddy. To Charles's dismay, Dr. Darwin had pronounced Doddy a delicate child. Charles always wondered if first cousins produced sickly children, and now here was his father confirming that concern. And upon interviewing the servants, Dr. Darwin had discovered that the toddler was being fed half a cup of cream every morning. Charles was chagrined. He told Emma, "I presume you did not know any more than I." The doctor said that was "one of the most injurious things we could have given him." Charles vowed that they should look after their children better and not trust "anything about our children to others." This included religion; they did not name godparents for the children. Although they were not certain yet exactly how they would do it, they knew they wanted to be in charge of their children's religious upbringing.

During that visit to the Mount, Charles had also received

the promise of a loan from his father to buy a house in the country. Although he had some more networking to do in the city and he and Emma were torn about his leaving the scientific center of England, he was not getting out that much because of his ill health. He was spending most of his time inside writing. Emma told Aunt Jessie, "Charles is very busy finishing his book on Coral islands, which he says no human being will ever read, but there is such a rage for geology that I hope better things." After working on it for three years and seven months, he had sent the manuscript to his publisher in January 1842. He felt much relieved at finishing it, and he started to feel better physically.

Now in the spring of 1842, the family made a trip to Maer, where Charles, freed from his coral reefs, started to think again about his species theory. Puzzling over how new species were created, he turned to experts in different fields: He talked to Elizabeth about gardening. He talked to farmers about breeding cattle and sheep. He watched bees pollinate flowers. And as he relaxed with his family around him, he decided to write down his thoughts all in one place. He had left his notebooks back in London, but he had so much in his head anyway. He took out some paper and a soft pencil and wrote down a rough argument for the mutability of species. He called it "descent with modification," and he used the term "natural selection" for the mechanism of change. He began with Part 1: "On Variation Under Domestication, and on the Principles of Selection." He wrote, "An individual organism placed under new conditions [often] sometimes varies in a small degree. . . . Also habits of life develope certain parts. Disuse atrophies." He wrote and then erased, "Most of these slight variations tend to become hereditary."

He did not shy away from problems; he listed them.

"*Difficulties on theory of selection,*" he wrote. "It may be objected such perfect organs as eye and ear, could never be formed." This was where the work was to be done. He would have to provide answers to all the problems he could think of. The sketch was only thirty-five pages long; he knew he would have hundreds more pages when he worked out all the steps and answered all the objections. But just as with his *Marry, Not Marry* list, he left out the problem of religion. He knew that taking God out of the story of creation would cause the biggest objections of all: from Emma, her sister Elizabeth, some of his other cousins, and even his scientific friends Lyell and Henslow. He just did not know how to answer these protests. He still struggled with what he himself believed about God.

He tucked the pages away and, back in London, continued working on the problem of finding a place for his growing family to live. He now was sure he wanted to leave the city. One of his fears, back when he was trying to figure out if he should marry or not, was that moving to the country would make him idle. But working on the species sketch at Maer had gone well; he now knew that he would not be idle in the country. The quiet would, in fact, be good for his work. Erasmus and Lyell were both horrified that he should even consider leaving London, but Charles was determined. He was tired of it all: the yellow fog, the horse dung in the streets, the noise. He needed quiet to think; the children needed space to run. Besides, they definitely needed more room. Emma had gotten pregnant with their third child around the time Charles finished *Coral Reefs*. She was due in September. So the house hunting began in earnest.

Rather than go north to the countryside near where they had grown up, which was too far away from London, Emma and Charles decided they wanted a place that was an easy day's train trip back into the city so Charles could go in if needed but be home at night to sleep. Though he could always stay overnight with Erasmus, he and Emma hated to spend any time apart.

Charles found a house he thought would do in the Kent countryside. It was a Georgian house, not unlike the Mount, in a small village called Down, about sixteen miles from London Bridge. He did not love the house itself; he thought it was rather ugly and looked neither charmingly old nor refreshingly new. But it was in good repair, and there were plenty of rooms and bedrooms. Also it was very much a country house, surrounded by fields and rural walks. He loved the countryside. He did worry that the house was too far away from the train station—the eight and a half miles would take about an hour by horse-drawn carriage. But the train to London would take only about another hour. That was close enough so that Charles could get to London in about two hours and come back the same day. He took Emma to see the house.

It was a gray day when they set out, and Emma had a toothache and a headache. Her reaction was not what Charles had hoped it would be. She did not like the house at all, nor did she like the countryside. The chalky fields did nothing for her; she longed for a landscape like the one around Maer—beautiful, green, and varied. But Charles liked the Chalk District; he loved the landscape of low, rolling hills. And he was taken with the hedges, plants, and flowers, including the purple magnolias up against the house. In the spring there would be pale blue violets and primroses, goldilocks, wood anemones, and white Stellaria. He especially liked the trees. There were some old cherry trees with delicious cherries. There were chestnut trees, walnut trees, lime, mulberry, fir, and a fine old beech tree. There were not many apple trees, but there were quince, pear, and plum trees. He loved all the walking paths around the house—so much bigger than his tiny garden in London. He hoped Emma would ignore the ugliness of the house, the gray day, and her headache, and give it some more thought.

On the ride back to London, Emma started to feel better about the house in Down. She liked a more expensive house in another part of the countryside and wished that Dr. Darwin would give them more money so they could buy a nicer one. But back in foggy, dirty, cramped London, she reconsidered. They could afford Down House. She really wanted to get out of the city. So Down it would be. They decided to use Dr. Darwin's money to buy the house and an additional eighteen acres. They both began to look forward to the calm, quiet life that the country would bring them.

On August 14 Willy cut two teeth, as Emma recorded in her diary; and the next day there were riots in the pottery factories—including Wedgwood Pottery. Workers were striking all over England, fighting wage cuts and demanding the right to vote. Troops marched through London on their way to quell riots in Manchester, passing by 12 Upper Gower Street. Outside the Darwins' home, strikers trying to win support shouted to passersby, "Remember, you are brothers!"

Though Charles and Emma sided with the protesters, they preferred things quiet and calm; neither one liked or wanted to cause any upheaval. It was with the hope of a peaceful and quiet place to live and work that they packed up for the move to Down even as the workers protested around them.

Erasmus did not help with the move this time; he was not needed. He didn't want them to move away; he called their new home "Down-in-the-mouth." Even though it was so close to London, it *was* quiet, very rural, at the edge of the earth,

Eras felt—but that was just what Charles and Emma wanted. It promised a boring social life, too, which was fine with them. They had not been socializing much in London anyway. As Jane Austen's Mr. Darcy says in *Pride and Prejudice*, "In a country neighborhood you move in a very confined and unvarying society." The Darwins would not find many people to visit with in the village of Down—though John Lubbock, an astronomer, banker, and mathematician, was building a house a mile away. Charles and Emma would import friends and relatives. And they would make their life as serene and tranquil as they could.

Not everything in their families was tranquil, though. Dr. Darwin was now in a wheelchair, Bessy was stuck in a fog, and Josiah was sinking from either a stroke or a degenerative neurological disease. Dr. Darwin managed to visit Josiah, but he was so upset by his old friend's terrible condition that he could offer no medical help. He broke into tears.

Aunt Jessie's beloved husband, Sismondi, had died earlier that summer, and just before they moved to Down, Emma got an upsetting letter from her. Jessie was miserable. She could barely go on without her husband. "He so filled every instant of my life, that now my feeling of desolation passes all description." Aunt Jessie wished she could be certain of heaven. "If I could but have . . . firm faith that he has only passed from the visible to the invisible world, and already lives and is waiting for me, oh what happiness that would be."

Emma was sad for her older relatives as she took William and Annie and moved, nine months pregnant with their third child, into Down House on September 14, 1842. Charles joined them a few days later. They were ready to start their new life.

Chapter 17

Sudden Deaths

*I think I have found out (here's presumption!) the simple way
by which species become exquisitely adapted to various ends.*
—Charles to Joseph Hooker, January 11, 1844

On September 22, 1842, just a week after they moved into Down House, Emma wrote in her diary "very feverish, violent headaches" and on September 23, "Mary born." Mary Eleanor looked like Emma's mother, Bessy, which made Emma glad. She hoped the baby would take after her mother not only in looks, but also in personality. Emma worried that each day's post would bring the news that her mother or father had died. A new life to replace the old, fading ones was a blessing, and the new baby should have been a great comfort to Emma. But Mary was weak and sickly.

On October 16, Emma wrote in her little diary, simply, "died."

A few weeks after moving into their new home, they had to bury a baby. Emma bravely wrote to her sister-in-law Fanny,

"Our sorrow is nothing to what it would have been if she had lived longer and suffered more."

Charles was devastated; he had had very little experience with death. His mother had died when he was eight, and all he remembered of her or her death was the body lying on the bed. What had struck him more was the funeral of a soldier he witnessed soon afterward. To the end of his life, he remembered that scene and how it struck him so forcefully. He wrote, "I can still see the horse with the man's empty boots and carbine suspended to the saddle, and the firing over the grave." He had hated funerals ever since. Now, thirty-four years later, Charles had to see his own little baby put into a grave. They buried Mary Eleanor at the Down churchyard cemetery. Emma told Fanny, "Charles is well to-day and the funeral over, which he dreaded very much."

Although both Emma and Charles were struck hard by the death, they found some solace in keeping busy. Emma wrote to Fanny, "I keep very well and strong and am come down-stairs to-day. With our two other dear little things you need not fear that our sorrow will last long, though it will be long indeed before we either of us forget that poor little face."

Charles went back to his notes about geology to work on a book about volcanic islands. This helped to distract him from his grief and his anxieties about his other children. He also threw himself into house renovations, to make the old and ugly house more livable, and even beautiful. He had written to his sister Catherine just before they had moved in, "I feel sure I shall become deeply attached to Down, with a few improvements—It will be very difficult not to be extravagant there." And so it was. Charles took it upon himself to make the house and the grounds so beautiful that Emma would love it as much as she loved Maer. Over the next couple of years,

Charles had the drawing room made bigger and added a
kitchen wing so there would be more room for the growing
number of servants. He moved the lane next to the house farther away, to provide more privacy. He planted flowers like
those at Maer. Emma had always felt that the flowers at Maer
were more beautiful than anywhere else, and Charles wanted
her to feel the same way about the blossoms at Down.

Charles loved the room that he had picked to be his study.
It faced northeast, which meant that it wouldn't be too hot
from direct sun but would be lit by a few rays of sunshine
early in the morning when he started work. He fixed up the
room just the way he wanted it, with wooden shelves built in
an alcove. He used these shelves to file his notes, his notebooks, and pages of books that he tore out. (He didn't always
bother keeping whole books, just the pages he found interesting.) He had a table in the middle of the room where he sat to
look at his specimens through a magnifying glass or simple
microscope, and to read his scientific papers. He sat on a high-
backed chair that he had raised up on an iron frame with
wheels, so he could move around the room. When he wrote,
he put a board across his lap. Since he was often in need of a
privy, he put one in the corner of the room, screened off for
privacy. Behind the curtain he had a chamber pot, bowls,
water, and towels.

Charles added a strip of land about three hundred yards
long on the western boundary of the property. He bought it
from his neighbor John Lubbock. There, Emma and Charles
designed a path after one they both loved at Maer. They
planted it with trees—hazel, alder, birch, and dogwood—as
well as privet hedges and holly bushes. Emma had ivy planted,
and bluebells, anemones, cowslips, and primroses. They made
a path covered with sand from the woods. They called their

path the Sandwalk, and it became Charles's walking and thinking path as well as a place for the children to play.

Charles and Emma both soon became very attached to Down House, and everything about it. When, a few years later, the postal authorities changed the spelling of the town to Downe, the Darwins did not go along. They had moved into Down House, and Down it would remain.

In the autumn of 1842, not long after baby Mary died, Emma's brother Hensleigh fell ill, and Emma invited Fanny to send their oldest children to live at Down House for a couple of months. She would take care of them so Fanny could take care of Hensleigh. The new house now bustled with the activity of five children: Julia Wedgwood, called Snow because she had been born in a snowstorm, age nine; James (called Bro), eight; and Erny, five; plus Doddy, not quite three, and Annie, one and a half.

During this visit Emma discovered that bribery was a good way to get a child to do what you wanted. She overheard one of the nursemaids trying to convince little Erny to put on a warm coat. He refused. Emma intervened. She told him that she would give him a shilling if he wore it now, and would give him a shilling every time he put it on. He put on the coat for the shilling. The next day he put it on again and declared, "I don't want to have that shilling, Aunt Emma; this coat is so nice now I have got it on."

The children said that Emma never used bribery in important moral matters, such as being kind to another person or an animal, but if she wanted a child to put on a coat or shoes, or talk a little more softly at lunch, she had no problem offering a bribe. Emma and Charles were not strict, and they took pains to explain to the children clearly what few rules

there were. There was, therefore, very little willful disobedience. But sometimes, a small bribe was just the thing.

The hustle and bustle of all the children helped Emma
with her grief over the death of her baby, and it distracted her
from worry about her ill parents. Charles's work and the
house renovations comforted him. And Charles and Emma
found consolation in each other. In a few months Emma was
pregnant again.

But by the next summer, when Emma was seven months
pregnant, her fears were realized. Josiah had grown weaker
and in July 1843, he died. Emma went to Maer to be with her
family and that September 25, Henrietta was born. They called
her Etty. There were now three healthy children for Charles
and Emma to love.

Charles missed them terribly when, a few months after
Etty was born, he went to Shrewsbury to see his father and sisters. He wrote to Emma, "I got into a transport over the
thought of Doddy and talked, like an old fool, for nearly an
hour about nothing else. . . . I ended with protest that
although I had done Doddy justice, they were not to suppose
that Annie was not a good little soul—bless her little body.
Absence makes me very much in love with my own dear three
chickens."

But always percolating and demanding his attention was
Charles's species book. In January 1844, he wrote to his friend
Joseph Hooker, a botanist, that he was working on a theory
about the origin of species. "At last gleams of light have come,
& I am almost convinced (quite contrary to opinion I started
with) that species are not (it is like confessing a murder)
immutable."

He most certainly did not want to murder God. But he
felt certain he was right that species were changeable, and

were changing. He continued to make observations and amass facts. As usual when Charles had a question, he went to someone who knew far more about the subject than he. Not just geologists, paleontologists, and ornithologists, but also farmers, breeders, and his hairdresser. He had written in his "D" notebook, "My hairdresser (Willis) says that strength of hair goes with colour. Black being strongest." Was there a hereditary reason for that, he wondered, or for skin color? Would dark skin prevent malaria?

All the observations he made—on himself, his children, the animals and plants around him—were in service to his theory of natural selection. Looking at each organism he studied, he tried to work out how that species had been formed. He always thought, too, about the objections people would raise. And by the next summer, Charles had finished his book *Geological Observations on the Volcanic Islands Visited During the Voyage of HMS* Beagle. So it was with great purpose that, as soon as he sent his volcano book in to his publisher, Charles turned back to the thirty-five-page species draft he had written two summers before at Maer. By early July 1844, he had expanded and rewritten the rough pencil draft. He felt it was good enough to be copied out by someone with a neater hand, so he gave it to the schoolmaster at Down.

When he got it back, seeing his species theory in print—in handwriting other than his own—was scary. His draft did not answer every objection he could think of, and there were probably still more objections he hadn't thought of yet. He knew his ideas were practically blasphemous and so his book had to be as irrefutable as he could make it. He wasn't nearly ready to publish yet.

But what if he died before he felt ready to publish it? It was not unreasonable for him to anticipate his own death—

he had been ill for so long, and the doctors could not figure out what was wrong with him. Had he contracted an illness on the voyage? Did he have some fatal disease? He did not know if his stomach problems and his heart palpitations would lead to his death. He could succumb at any moment— in fact, anyone could.

He had to entrust this draft to someone and give that person instructions on how to publish it in the event of his death. Whom could he trust to make sure it would happen? He didn't turn to Hensleigh, or even to his brother Erasmus, who would not be at all shocked by his theory or have any reluctance to publish it. He turned instead to the one person he had the most faith in, the person he could trust above all others to carry out his wishes.

On July 5, 1844, he wrote, "My. Dear. Emma. I have just finished my sketch of my species theory. If, as I believe that my theory is true & if it be accepted even by one competent judge, it will be a considerable step in science. I therefore write this, in case of my sudden death, as my most solemn & last request . . . that you will devote 400£ to its publication & further will yourself, or through Hensleigh, take trouble in promoting it. . . ." He went on to suggest possible editors for the book—Lyell, or perhaps Henslow.

He rarely sent anything out without Emma reading it first. But how would she respond to his bold theory? In between nursing baby Etty, supervising the kitchen and nursery staffs, taking care of Charles, and playing with the older children, Emma read the draft. She made notes in places where she didn't understand what he was saying, as she often did on his papers.

"Not clear," she wrote a few times, when she thought his language could be more lucid. In two places, where Charles explained how the eye, such a complex organ, had evolved, she challenged his theory. "A great assumption/E.D.," she wrote. And two pages later, "Another bold saying." To believe that the eye had evolved from tiny changes over many years was, to Emma, to make a leap of faith.

Charles had been worried about the eye two summers earlier when he wrote that pencil draft. In fact, he was worried about the formation of the eye and other complex organs even back when he was still living in London. He had written in his "D" notebook, "it will be necessary to show how the first eye is formed." Charles felt that if he could explain the evolution of the eye, he could convince even the harshest skeptic that he was right. Emma was in so many ways the perfect reader. And despite her misgivings about the religious ramifications, Emma not only agreed she would publish this draft in case of his sudden death, she also helped him make it better.

After Emma's reading, he was ready to test it out on a few others. He sent a copy to Joseph Hooker and later to another botanist, in America, Asa Gray. Slowly he started to let his idea out to other trusted friends. He had a unique theory; he knew he was sitting on something big, and original.

But in October of 1844, a book called *Vestiges of the Natural History of Creation* came out. It was published anonymously. The author argued that species were transforming all the time. The author used several of the examples and many of the same arguments as Charles had just done in his draft. The author used Lyell's geological theories, that the earth was constantly changing, and applied it to the living world, just as Charles did. *Vestiges'* argument included fossils, the development of embryos, similarities in anatomy among species, and even behavior, just as Charles did. The book differed in two major ways (other than the anonymity, which Charles would not do): the *Vestiges* author had not figured out evolution by natural selection, the mechanism that Charles believed drove the creation of species. And the *Vestiges* author did do something Charles had not done even in his sketch—the book included mankind and the origin of all life in its scheme. It said that human beings came from orangutans, like Jenny in the zoo. Under the protection of anonymity, the author felt free to go against God.

What upset Charles most about *Vestiges* was the huge public reaction to the book—both positive and negative. Even though it was highly controversial for all the reasons Charles knew that his would be, it sold extremely well. There were three more editions in the first year, and it was published in America almost immediately.

Charles watched as in drawing rooms and scientific clubs all over the British Empire, in newspapers and journals around the English-speaking world, people argued about the book. Not only what it said, but who wrote it. (The author turned out to be a journalist named Robert Chambers, who only confessed to its authorship at the end of his life.)

Hooker was amused by the book, which annoyed Charles to no end. He wrote to his friend, "I have also read the 'Vestiges,' but have been somewhat less amused at it than you appear to have been: the writing and arrangement are certainly admirable, but his geology strikes me as bad, and his zoology far worse." Adam Sedgwick, Charles's old geology professor from Cambridge, declared that *Vestiges* was so uninformed and so inaccurate it could have been written by a woman! Some religious people were furious that it ignored the biblical account of creation and man's expulsion from the Garden of Eden. In general, people who felt England needed a

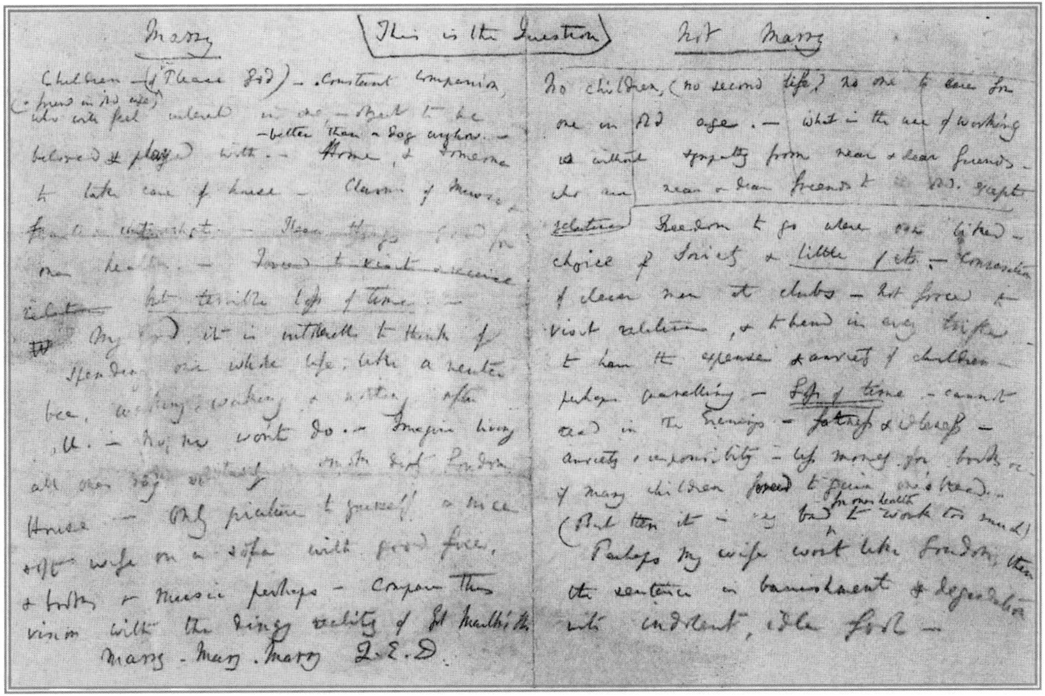
Marry | This is the Question | Not Marry

Children — (if it Please God) — Constant companion, (& friend in old age) who will feel interested in one, — object to be beloved & played with. — better than a dog anyhow. — Home, & someone to take care of house — Charms of music & female chit-chat. — These things good for one's health. — Forced to visit & receive relations but terrible loss of time. —

My God, it is intolerable to think of spending one's whole life, like a neuter bee, working, working, & nothing after all. — No, no won't do. — Imagine living all one's day solitarily in smoky dirty London House. — Only picture to yourself a nice soft wife on a sofa with good fire, & books & music perhaps — Compare this vision with the dingy reality of Grt. Marlbro' St.

Marry — Mary — Marry Q.E.D.

No children, (no second life), no one to care for one in old age. — What is the use of working without sympathy from near & dear friends — who are near & dear friends to the old, except relatives.

Freedom to go where one liked — choice of Society & little of it. — Conversation of clever men at clubs — Not forced to visit relatives, & to bend in every trifle. — to have the expense & anxiety of children — perhaps quarrelling — Loss of time. — cannot read in the Evenings — fatness & idleness — Anxiety & responsibility — less money for books &c — if many children forced to gain one's bread. — (But then it is very bad for one's health to work too much)

Perhaps my wife won't like London; then the sentence is banishment & degradation into indolent, idle fool —

Charles Darwin's list of marriage pros and cons

By permission of the Syndics of Cambridge University Library (f.2r from DAR.210.8)

Portrait of Emma Darwin painted by George Richmond (1840)

Maer Hall, Emma's childhood home (present-day photograph)

Portrait of Charles Darwin painted by George Richmond (1840)

The Mount, Charles's childhood home

Charles and William, 1842
© ENGLISH HERITAGE PHOTO LIBRARY

Annie's grave (present-day photograph)
COURTESY OF JOHN VAN WYHE

Annie, 1849
© ENGLISH HERITAGE PHOTO LIBRARY

Henrietta, c. 1852

Emma and Lenny, c. 1854

George, 1851

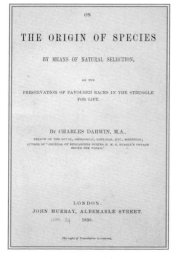

Emma and
Charles Waring,
c. 1857
© ENGLISH HERITAGE
PHOTO LIBRARY

Title page, The Origin of Species,
first edition
© ENGLISH HERITAGE PHOTO LIBRARY

From left to right: Leonard, Henrietta, Horace, Emma,
Elizabeth, Frances, and a visitor at Down House
BY PERMISSION OF THE SYNDICS OF CAMBRIDGE UNIVERSITY LIBRARY (F.9 FROM DAR.219.12)

The Sandwalk

Down House (present-day photograph)

Charles Darwin, 1880
© ENGLISH HERITAGE PHOTO LIBRARY

Darwin's signature on an 1879 letter:
It was unusual for him to sign his full name.
COURTESY OF GEORGE BECCALONI

new social order found *Vestiges* appealing; those who wanted society to remain as it was hated the book.

Charles knew that in order to avoid the criticisms being leveled at *Vestiges*, he would have to build up his argument even more, and gather more examples, more indisputable factual evidence. His own species book had suffered a serious blow, if not a sudden death. He decided to work on a new edition of his *Journal of Researches*, putting in some more hints about his species view. But he had no desire to be the center of a controversy like the one *Vestiges* had started. He would find something else to write about.

Chapter 18

Barnacles and Babies

My chief enjoyment and sole employment throughout life has been scientific work; and the excitement from such work makes me for the time forget, or drives away, my daily discomfort.
—CHARLES, IN HIS *AUTOBIOGRAPHY*

In July 1845, about nine months after Charles read *Vestiges*, George Darwin was born. There were now four children at Down House. And Charles finished the second edition of his first literary child, *The Voyage of the* Beagle, which he sent off to a new publisher, John Murray. Murray would not withhold royalties as his first publisher had, and he would not make Charles pay him to have his books published, as some other publishers did.

At Maer, Bessy was failing, so Emma went home to see her. She went without the children, which was quite unusual, leaving Charles to negotiate his work around them. He kept her apprised of his success (and failure): "In the morning I was baddish, and did hardly any work, and was much overcome by my children. . . ." He reported that the children were romping "in the drawing-room, jumping on everything and butting like young bulls at every chair and sofa, that I am going to have the dining-room fire lighted to-morrow and keep them out of the drawing-room. I declare a month's such wear would spoil everything in the whole drawing-room."

Emma and Charles had been very practical when it came to furnishing their house. The chairs and sofas were to be comfortable, sturdy, and long-lasting. Only after satisfying those requirements did Emma and Charles care what anything might look like. It was a good thing the furniture was sturdy.

In many upper-class Victorian households, the children spent most of their time in the nursery with the nurse or governess or in the kitchen having their meals alone, and were trotted out to say hello to the parents once in a while. At Down the children were not confined to the nursery and the kitchen at all. In fact, a cousin exclaimed after a visit that the only place to be sure *not* to find a child was in the nursery.

And the only place to be sure to find what you were looking for was in Charles's study. Emma had not become more organized or tidy as time went on. This meant that the children were in and out of his study looking for rulers and scissors and scraps of paper to draw on.

Once when Etty was the third or fourth child to run into his study of a morning, Charles gave her "his patient look" and said, "Don't you think you could not come in again, I have been interrupted very often."

The children were sensitive to Charles's needs and routine, but they couldn't help bothering him sometimes. They did try hard to avoid going into his study when they were bleeding and needed a sticking plaster to put over the cut, because they knew Charles hated the sight of blood. Etty later wrote, "I well remember lurking about the passage till he was safe away, and then stealing in for the plaster."

One October day in 1846, in his study, Charles took out one of his last specimens from the voyage. It was a barnacle that he had found on the southern coast of Chile. It was a tiny thing, perhaps the smallest barnacle in the world. Looking at the volcano-shaped creature, he knew what some of his friends had been trying to tell him was correct. To work out his species theory he had to become adept at describing at least one creature in minute detail. Darwin looked at this barnacle under his microscope. Then he looked at other barnacles under his microscope. He was thrilled to see how many small variations there were from barnacle to barnacle, from species to species. He wrote to FitzRoy that he was spending day after day "hard at work dissecting a little animal about the size of a pin's head . . . and I could spend another month, and daily see more beautiful structure."

A century earlier, the Swedish botanist Carl Linnaeus had come up with a system for classifying living beings—from kingdoms (plant and animal) to class (such as mammal), order (Carnivora), family (*Canidae*), genus (*Canis*), and species (*Canis familiaris*, or dog). The system presumed that all species had already been fixed and would not change. Up until this point, if a natural historian saw variation between creatures thought to be of the same species, he ignored it. Charles could not— would not—ignore the variations. He asked other scientists to send him their barnacle collections, and over the next days, weeks, and months he pulled down more bottles of barnacles from his shelves. As he looked at the many minute variations in the *Cirripedia* under his microscope he saw the opposite of the prevailing assumption, and confirmation of his presumption: species were mutable; there was no barrier preventing the creation of new species. And he kept discovering new species of barnacle. Soon the horizontal surfaces in his study were covered with barnacles from all over the earth. By the end of that year, he decided that he would make a detailed study of all the barnacles he could get his hands on.

Even though he continued to suffer from illness ("at present I am suffering from four boils & swellings, one of which hardly allows me the use of my right arm & has stopped all my work & damped all my spirits," he wrote in a letter to Joseph Hooker in April 1847), the next years brought on more barnacles and more babies. In July 1847, another daughter, Elizabeth, was born. The following August, Francis, called Frank, joined the family as the sixth child. Charles did not stop using his children as specimens.

"I asked one of my boys to shout as loudly as he possibly could, and as soon as he began, he firmly contracted his orbicular [eye] muscles." Charles kept making his son yell, and every time he did, he closed his eyes. When Charles asked him why he did that, his son answered that he was not aware he was closing his eyes. So Charles wrote it down to instinct.

These years brought more death, too. Emma's mother, Bessy, had died in March of 1846. Now Dr. Darwin, their last parent, was getting sicker and sicker. Charles hated to leave Down House, but he made the trip up to Shrewsbury to visit his father. He and Emma kept in constant touch, and when she told him about the latest with the children, he wrote back about Annie, "I suppose now and be-hanged to you, you will allow Annie is 'something'. I believe . . . that she is a second Mozart; anyhow she is more than a Mozart considering her Darwin blood." Practically everything he wrote about related to his theory. How did Annie get her musical talent? Certainly not from him, but from Emma. And given the tone-deaf Darwin inheritance she had to overcome, she was clearly a musical genius.

He missed his children dearly as he walked around his old childhood home and its grounds.

> This lovely day makes me pine rather to be with you and the dear little ones on the lawn. Thank Willy and Annie for their very nice notes, which told me a great many things I wished to hear; they are very nicely written. Give them and my dear Etty and Georgy my best love. This place is looking lovely, but yet I could not live here: the sounds of the town, and blackguards talking, and want of privacy, convince me every time I come here that rurality is the main element in one's home.

In November 1848, Charles got word that his father was on his deathbed. Erasmus wanted him to come up to London and go on to Shrewsbury with him. But Charles himself was too sick to go right away. He was also too sad, and too uneasy with death to push himself. Charles would miss his father, the man whose advice he had received (and usually followed) throughout his life. He never spoke of him with anything other than respect and admiration; he said that his father was the wisest man he had ever known. His notebooks were filled with sentences that began, "My father says" and "According to my father." And Dr. Darwin had been supportive of him over the years, both financially and emotionally. Even so, Charles's sisters worried that Charles didn't realize how proud their father had been of him, and they told him so.

But Charles could not move quickly, and Erasmus went on to Shrewsbury without him. Dr. Darwin died, and Charles arrived at the Mount only after the funeral.

Charles's body responded to his father's death, or at least it seemed that way. His illnesses were becoming so bad and so frequent that he sometimes could not work more than twenty minutes at a time without having a pain or discomfort somewhere. Finally, in 1849, the whole family packed up to go to Malvern, where he could get an extensive treatment called a water cure with a doctor named James Gully. The water cure consisted mostly of applying cold water to the outside of the patient's body—with cold showers and baths. The patients were also packed and wrapped in wet sheets. The nurses applied friction, or rubbing. Steam baths were prescribed, too. Charles was concerned that the treatment was delaying his barnacle work, but on May 6 he wrote to Henslow that the water cure was doing him good. "You will be surprised to hear that we all—children, servants, and all—have been here for nearly two months. All last autumn and winter my health grew worse and worse: incessant sickness, tremulous hands, and swimming head. I thought that I was going the way of all flesh." But his illness lessened and he got stronger. At Malvern the regime consisted not only of the water cure but also of plain food and springwater to drink. It was all to be pure air, pure water, pure food.

The doctor also told him to stop using snuff, "the chief solace of life," because it might harm his troublesome digestion. His only complaint was that he couldn't think—he had "the most complete stagnation of mind. I have ceased to think even of barnacles!"

He was feeling so much better that when they got home he continued much of the regimen; he even installed a cold shower outside.

But even with all of this treatment, he did not get appreciably better. Emma spent many nights sitting with him, holding him, comforting him, tending to him, as he suffered from sleeplessness, heart palpitations, and his almost constant digestive upset. During the day she tended to him, too. It was the norm for Charles to be sick.

And for the children, as long as they weren't too horribly ill, it was nice to be sick at Down. Emma and Charles were both loving parents, and illness had kind of a happy aura about it, in part because Charles was always sick, and everyone loved Charles. One of their granddaughters later wrote that "at Down ill health was considered normal." If not normal, at least kind of special. The sick child got the treat of being able to spend the morning in Papa's study, curled up on the sofa while he worked. In the afternoon the sick child got to play many games of backgammon with Papa, or hear stories read by Mama or Papa. The sick child received, above all, extra attention. So it was nice to be sick at Down House. At least just a little sick.

Chapter 19

Doing Custards

*A good, cheerful, and affectionate daughter is the
greatest blessing a man can have, after a good wife.*
—JOSIAH WEDGWOOD TO DR. ROBERT DARWIN UPON
THE ENGAGEMENT OF THEIR CHILDREN, NOVEMBER 1838

Annie often waited outside her father's study until it was
time for his morning walk. She hated to disturb him, but she
was eager to take some turns around the Sandwalk with Papa.
Although Charles walked at a brisk pace, Annie went ahead,
pirouetting in front of him. She called it "doing custards."

From the time she was a baby, Annie was a family favorite.
She was a joyful, happy child, with a bright face and a ready
smile. She loved to play and was a good big sister and older
cousin. The grown-ups loved her, too, for she was open and honest, a much-prized virtue. "Transparent," as Emma had called
Charles a dozen years earlier. Annie's aunt Catherine Darwin said
of her that she was "always so candid and kind-hearted." Aunt
Fanny Wedgwood called her bright and engaging, "so open and

confiding and lovable." Another relative said he "always found her a child whose heart it was easy to reach."

Annie could also read other people easily. Even when she was playing boisterously with her cousins, all Charles had to do was give her a quick look and she would quiet everyone down. She loved to please; Charles could count on her to sneak him a pinch of snuff from the snuffbox, and she watched with pleasure as her father indulged his naughty habit.

Annie took after both Emma and Charles; they felt she was a lovely combination of both of them. She was musical like her mama. But Charles could claim her neatness and propensity for order. Charles noted that from an early age she was neater than her big brother. When she was just over a year old, he watched "how neatly Annie takes hold in proper way of pens, pencils and keys. Willy to present time with equal or greater practice cannot handle anything so neatly as Annie does, often in exact manner of grown-up person." As she got older, she loved to read, like both of her parents, but she had a particular fondness for looking up words in the dictionary and for comparing word by word two editions of the same book. She liked to look up places on the map, and to arrange objects by color.

She was also a good dancer and a good artist. And unlike Emma, Annie liked to dress up and look nice. Charles remembered that one day she dressed up in some of Emma's clothes—a silk gown, cap, shawl, and gloves. Charles thought she looked like a little old woman, "but with her heightened colour, sparkling eyes & bridled smiles, she looked, as I thought, quite charming."

Annie often climbed into Charles's lap or stood behind him and arranged his hair, making it "beautiful," for half an hour at a time. She loved being with her mother, too, and

Emma adored her. When she was little she hated to part with her mother even for a short time. Once, when she was very young, she said, "Oh Mama, what should we do, if you were to die?" And when she was sick, she wanted to be near both of them. Charles said that when Annie was unwell, "her mother lying down beside her seemed to soothe her in a manner quite different from what it would have done to any of our other children."

In the summer of 1850, Annie was nine. Charles described her as very tall for her age, sturdy and strong. She had a firm step. She had long brown hair, dark gray eyes, good white teeth, and a slightly brown complexion. Sometimes when Charles looked at her he thought that in his dear Annie he would have a kind soul tending him in his old age. She would be his solace, his nurse.

Willy was off at boarding school now, for the first time, so Annie was the oldest child at home. They had cousins visiting, and normally Annie would organize games for the younger children. But it was very hot, and she clung to Emma and Charles. At night she cried herself to sleep. She was obviously sick, but she didn't have any clear symptoms that they could point to, and she did have some good days.

Annie and the two other girls, Etty and Elizabeth (nicknamed Betty), had had scarlet fever the year before, but they had all gotten better. Looking back, Charles and Emma realized that Annie had not been herself again after the scarlet fever. Later Emma went back and wrote in her diary on the day marked June 27, 1850, "Annie first failed about this time."

As summer turned to fall, the house was bustling, as usual. In the midst of the bustle, Charles studied his barnacles, and the older girls, Annie and Etty, had their lessons together.

They took lessons from a drawing master and a writing master. Emma taught them, too, and wrote in her diary to keep track of their Latin grammar exercises. Etty, two and a half years younger, was a contrast to the easy-going, cheerful Annie. She was a willful child, with a sharp temper. But the sisters were close, though perhaps not as close as the Dovelies had been.

The other Darwin children were little—George was four, Betty was three, Frank was almost two, and there was, as usual, a baby. Leonard (Lenny) had been born that January—the fourth son and the seventh living child in the family. For the first time, during this, her eighth labor, Emma had had some pain relief for the birth. Chloroform, which had been discovered in 1831, had begun to be used to relieve labor pains a few years earlier. So Charles, who truly hated to see Emma go through the pain of childbirth, had arranged for some to be on hand for the doctor to use when he arrived.

But, as he later wrote to his old professor Henslow, Emma's pains were severe and fast, and he couldn't wait for the doctor to get there: "I was so bold during my wifes confinement which are always rapid, as to administer Chloroform, before the Dr. came & I kept her in a state of insensibility of 1 & ½ hours & she knew nothing from first pain till she heard that the child was born.—It is the grandest & most blessed of discoveries."

It was nice to be able to relieve the pain of one you loved, and Charles and Emma wanted desperately to help Annie feel better.

Chapter 20

A Fretful Child

Her sensitiveness appeared extremely early in life, & showed itself in crying bitterly over any story at all melancholy; or on parting with Emma even for the shortest interval.
—CHARLES, ON ANNIE, 1851

Other than losing Mary Eleanor as an infant, nothing terrible had happened to the Darwin family. They had had the usual bouts with childhood illness, including the recent scarlet fever, but nothing out of the ordinary. Still, Charles could be an anxious and worried father. His own health was so bad, he was afraid he had passed it on to his children. He now worried that Annie had inherited his wretched digestion.

It was hard for Charles to concentrate on work with Annie being listless and weak, so unlike her usual energetic, engaged, cheerful self. He gave her and Etty a canary, hoping it would cheer Annie up. He watched as his daughters played with the bird and taught it how to sing. In the Galapagos, the finches from the different islands were less like each other than birds on the mainland. The birds had evolved because of their island environments. It was those birds that had given him one of his eureka moments about natural selection. He would use them in his argument. But now he focused mainly on the barnacles splayed out in front of him. He was describing them in minute detail, so as to understand the similarities and differences between the different species.

He could not understand or even describe Annie's condition in such detail as he could describe the barnacles. It was frustrating that she didn't have clear symptoms that could point to a particular illness. It could have been consumption or tuberculosis; Erasmus seemed to be a consumptive, always weak and lacking in energy. But he wasn't acutely ill, and no such diagnosis was made with Annie. Since sea bathing was a sort of cure-all for delicate children and invalids, Charles and Emma decided to give that a try. It wasn't as extensive and exhausting as the water cure. But people felt plunging into the ocean was good for the body, promoting good circulation and overall health. And the hope was that sea breezes and fresh air would do Annie good.

So in October, Miss Thorley, their young governess, took Annie and Etty to Ramsgate, which was on the easternmost point of the Kent coast. Ramsgate was a popular seaside town; Queen Victoria had spent holidays there as a child. Being so close to mainland Europe—a short sail to France—it had been a point of embarkation for British troops during the Napoleonic wars earlier in the century. In 1850, as Annie and her entourage arrived, the construction of the Royal Harbour was just being completed.

Two weeks later, Emma and Charles joined them. When they arrived at the train station, Annie greeted them with a bright face and happy step. The family walked on the pier together, and they went into the water twice. It was a nice holiday.

But two days later, Annie developed a fever and a headache. Charles and Emma dragged a mattress into their room so she could sleep with them. A storm hit the next morning, and Charles and the others left for home, while Emma stayed with Annie until she was well enough to travel a few days later.

Back at home, Charles and Emma thought about consulting Dr. Gully, Charles's water cure doctor. Although Charles now was having some success with the treatments, he didn't entirely trust Gully. He was a traditionally trained doctor, but he also believed in things Charles thought were nonsense, such as diagnostic clairvoyance and spiritualism. So they decided to consult Dr. Henry Holland, in London, who had attended Annie's birth and had become their family doctor since Charles's father died. Emma took Annie to London to see Dr. Holland a few times. But he couldn't be of much help.

So Annie spent most of her days with Emma or tucked up on the sofa in her father's study, away from the hustle and bustle of the household: six other children (when Willy was home), their nannies and governesses, all the maids, gardeners, cooks, and other household help. Parslow the butler was kept busy clonking the mud off shoes as the children ran into the house from playing in the Sandwalk, riding ponies from the stable, having games of croquet and ball. There were cats and dogs going in and out, too. But Emma and Charles kept Annie quiet and protected. In the afternoons Charles played backgammon with her, and Emma read aloud to her.

Charles looked through his boxes and found some shells for Annie and Etty to play with—shells he had gathered on his *Beagle* voyage about twenty years earlier. He hadn't managed to interest any experts in them. At least they would go to good use now.

Soon Annie had a bad cough in addition to her lethargy. On December 8, Emma wrote in her diary, "Annie began bark." Since Dr. Holland was not able to help them, Charles relented and wrote to Dr. Gully. Gully prescribed a regime for Annie at home, with plans that she would come to Malvern in the spring if she hadn't gotten better. From January on, she was wrapped in a wet sheet and rubbed vigorously for five minutes every morning, which was supposed to stimulate her nervous system and circulation. Then she was given a "spinal wash," in which a cold, wet towel was rubbed up and down the length of her spine. This was supposed to clear her head and get rid of her lethargy. Every three or four days, she was packed in a damp towel. From February on, she also had a shallow bath and a footbath every morning.

Charles kept careful notes. Some days Annie was "well not quite." Other days she was "well very" or "well almost very" or just "well." And some days she was "poorly." He noted her cries, her coughs, the strength of her pulse, and how well she slept. Ever the good scientist, ever the good parent.

Meanwhile Charles continued to think about religion and faith. He and Emma read and discussed books about theology. They made notations in their family Bible, indicating places where biblical scholars deemed passages inauthentic, added later by unknown authors. For both of them, the question of faith was an ongoing one. Emma took the children to church, though during the Trinity prayer, which proclaimed God as three in one—Father, Son, and Holy Spirit—she turned away from the altar in disagreement. The children followed her lead.

Charles did not go into church with them. He often

walked them there, and then strolled around the village while they prayed. He was friendly with the vicar, and over the years counted a number of vicars as his close friends.

Sometimes he stayed home to read one of his books about theology. A current favorite author was Francis Newman, a Latin professor at University College London. In his books, Newman looked for a new theology that could include science. Working through his doubts, he found ways to believe in God and in an afterlife. Like Charles, he had stopped believing in the literalness of the Bible. But like Emma, Newman believed that you could get to heaven only through accepting Jesus's teachings, by achieving a full sympathy of spirit with God's spirit.

Charles still needed proof. He could not be spiritual based on instinct. He did like much of what Newman had to say, though, and felt some security knowing that someone else not only had doubts but also wrote about them publicly.

Annie turned ten on March 2; Emma gave her a book. She felt well enough to play outside with Willy, who was home from school. They romped around the Sandwalk, and she rode Willy's pony for the first time, with Parslow's guiding hand.

But the respite did not last. A couple of weeks later, the family was hit with influenza. Getting the flu on top of whatever she already had was not good for poor Annie. She stayed in bed with Emma, sick and miserable. Charles lay on the sofa reading another book by Newman, one Erasmus had recommended, *Phases of Faith or Passages from the History of My Creed*. It was a sort of themed autobiography—an account of Newman's own loss of faith and the quest for a new one. To Charles it was powerful and in some ways inspiring. But also upsetting: Christianity decreed that people deserve punishment for offending God, Newman said. He concluded, therefore, that in Christian belief, "the fretfulness of a child is an infinite evil!" Newman wrote, "I was aghast that I could have believed it." As Charles read, how could he not think of his sick daughter? Annie, pleasant and brave during the day, cried herself to sleep at night. How could that be offensive to the Infinite Being? How could his little girl, or her fretfulness, be evil? How could he ascribe to a religion with that belief?

When Annie was recovered enough from the flu to travel, Charles and Emma decided it was time to take her for the water cure. Emma was pregnant again; she was seven months along, and they decided she should not make the trip. So Emma and Annie would be parted for a month at least. None of them was happy about that. But Charles would take Annie and Etty (for company), along with their nurse, Brodie, to Malvern. He would stay a few days, get them settled, and then come home. Miss Thorley, the governess, would join them there, too.

Annie and Emma sat on the sofa together as the bags were being loaded into the carriage. Annie cried and cried; she did not want to leave her mother.

Chapter 21

God Only Knows the Issue

*Without you when sick I feel most desolate. . . . I do
long to be with you and under your protection
for then I feel safe. God bless you.*
—CHARLES TO EMMA, MAY 27, 1848

If Annie hadn't been so sick, the trip would have been excit-
ing. The girls loved Brodie, and going to Malvern was an
adventure. They went by train to London, and the four of
them—Charles, Annie, Etty, and Brodie—stayed overnight
with Erasmus, which was always a treat. Erasmus was a kind,
funny, charming man, and an indulgent uncle. From his house
they took a Growler—a horse-drawn carriage with two seats
facing each other, big enough to fit all of them and their
luggage—to Euston Station for the train. They had to take a
train north to Birmingham, which they reached by lunch-
time, and then go south to Worcester, where they arrived in
late afternoon. From Worcester, they took a stagecoach to
Montreal House, one of the main hotels in Malvern.

Charles got them settled in Malvern and then he left to go back home to Emma. Annie would be in good hands—Miss Thorley would be arriving soon to help Brodie—but still it was hard for Charles to leave. He'd come back in a month to collect them—including, he hoped, a cured Annie.

Charles stopped again in London for a longer visit with Erasmus and other family before heading home. The relatives in London thought he looked "uncommonly well and stout," though that was often misleading. Even when he was feeling his worst physically, Charles's ruddy complexion made him look well. Inside he was sick with worry about Annie.

At first, all went according to plan at Malvern, and the letters home to Emma were happy. Etty reported that she and Annie bought oranges, that "yesterday I fell down twice," and that they were going to buy combs. They were doing art and looking forward to playing with the children of one of the doctors. Miss Thorley arrived, and they went on a donkey ride. Annie started getting the water treatment, and soon she was doing well. Charles, once home again, went back to work, and even started to return some of the barnacles he had borrowed from other collectors. One phase of his barnacles work was done.

But then things at Malvern took a terrible turn. Annie started vomiting. At first the doctor did not seem concerned. But then Annie got a fever that wouldn't go away. Within a week, she was very frail. Not willing to admit defeat, Dr. Gully assured Miss Thorley that Annie was progressing slowly and that there was no need to call Charles back.

Soon, though, Gully changed his mind. When he examined her on Tuesday evening, April 15, the doctor felt certain that Annie was dying. He wrote to Charles immediately, asking him to come to Malvern. The postman brought the terrible news to Down House at midday on Wednesday. Reading the doctor's letter, Charles and Emma decided he should leave right away. Emma achingly wanted to be with Annie, but since she couldn't take care of her daughter, she took care of everyone else. She arranged for Etty to come home as soon as possible and for their sister-in-law Fanny to go to Malvern and help Charles. She also prepared for her upcoming confinement. She asked one of her aunts to come stay with her. And she asked Elizabeth to get her some chloroform.

When Charles arrived at the hotel in Malvern the next afternoon, Miss Thorley took him aside. Quietly, in an outer room, she told him how bad it was. Charles flung himself facedown upon the sofa. Poor Etty watched in horror; she had had no idea how sick Annie really was.

Dr. Gully had diagnosed Annie with a bilious fever, which meant that along with a fever and stomach upset, she was vomiting bile. What this also meant, as Charles knew, was that Annie was in mortal danger. Unless there was a miracle, she was likely to die.

Miss Thorley took Etty out of the room so she didn't have to see Charles so upset. Now Charles could cry alone.

After he gathered himself, Charles went in to see Annie. "She looks very ill: her face lighted up and she certainly knew me," he wrote to Emma. He told her the doctor said that Annie was doing a little better. They were giving her camphor and ammonia to stimulate her and to stop her vomiting. Medicine had not advanced much in the twenty years since Emma's sister Fanny had died; all that could be done was to treat Annie's symptoms. There was nothing to directly attack a bacterial infection. (Antibiotics, such as penicillin, would not be discovered for almost eighty years.) Dr. Gully came in the evening and felt Annie's pulse. It was irregular, and he was afraid she would die that night. Gully stayed there to help however he could, and Charles wrote the next day to Emma that he had been "most kind."

On April 18, Good Friday, Annie had another bad vomiting attack, which this time they chose to interpret as a somewhat hopeful sign. At least she had the strength to vomit. And her pulse was regular again.

Charles reported all to Emma and responded to a letter of hers. "Your note made me cry much," he wrote, "but I must not give way, and can avoid doing so by not thinking about her. It is now from hour to hour a struggle between life and death."

And he added, "God only knows the issue."

When she vomited more green fluid, bile from her liver, they all knew it was very, very bad. But Charles kept up hope. "She appears dreadfully exhausted," he wrote to Emma again, "and I thought for some time she was sinking, but she has now rallied a little. The two symptoms Dr. G. dreads most have not come on—restlessness and coldness." While Charles was writing this letter, Dr. Gully came in and examined Annie. He felt sure she was dying, but he gave Charles something to hold on to. Charles continued his letter. "Dr Gully has been and thank God he says though the appearances are so bad, positively no one important symptom is worse, and that he yet has hopes—positively he has Hopes. Oh my dear be thankful." But he knew the situation was dire.

Charles wrote to Emma every day, even twice a day, and she wrote back to him. He told her what they were feeding Annie when she could eat (gruel with some brandy), what fluids they gave her ("Fanny gave her a spoonful of tea"), and what the doctor said at each visit. If Charles put a letter in the post by six thirty in the evening, it would get to Down around noon the next day. And if Emma gave the postman a letter in Down, it would get to Malvern by the next morning. On some days, Charles wrote every hour. It was the best release for him (he could cry while he wrote to her) and also for Emma. She wanted to know every single thing that transpired with her darling girl. As a result, Emma experienced the illness as much as Charles did—almost. He was bereft without her. She was in agony not to be there. She thought of Annie constantly.

Charles, Fanny, and Miss Thorley took turns sitting by Annie's bed with Brodie. Charles found the company a great comfort, especially Fanny, but when it was his turn to be with Annie, he just couldn't sit still.

When Annie had a peaceful night's sleep and Dr. Gully told Charles that she was turning the corner, Charles was so happy he sent an electronic telegram to Erasmus and asked him to send a servant to Down House so Emma would get the good news before she became distraught over the last letters. Emma was in the yard "looking at my poor darling's little garden to find a flower of hers" when the messenger drove up. Emma read the telegraph: "Annie has rallied—has passed good night—danger much less imminent."

Yet Charles wrote that Emma "would not in the least recognize her with her poor hard sharp pinched features." She looked nothing like "our former dear Annie." No wonder he couldn't sit still by her bed and just stare at her.

Annie drifted in and out of consciousness, often delirious. Even in her discomfort and illness, she was polite. When Charles moved her and it hurt, she said, "Don't do that please." When he stopped, she thanked him. "I never saw anything so pathetic as her patience and her thankfulness," Charles wrote to Emma. "When I gave her some water, she said, 'I quite thank you.' Poor dear darling child."

On Monday morning, the day after Easter Sunday, Emma received the letters from the weekend, which told a very different story from the telegram. She wrote back to Charles while the postman waited. "I am confused now and hardly know what my impression is, but I have considerable hopes. . . . Every word about her is precious. . . . Except at post-time my sufferings are nothing to yours," she told her husband.

Although she didn't know what to think, Emma kept hope alive. And she so appreciated Charles's letters: "Your minute accounts are such a comfort and I enjoyed sponging our dear one with vinegar as much as you did." Planning for Annie's recovery, she thought of what food they should give her first when she was up to eating more. She told them to try rice gruel flavored with cinnamon or currant jelly.

Late Tuesday afternoon, Dr. Gully came to see Annie. He told Charles and Fanny that she had not gained ground. They had to prepare for the worst. Fanny wrote to Emma that "he thinks her in imminent danger. . . . Oh that I have to send you such sad, sad news."

As the day wore on, Annie's pulse weakened. Her breaths became more and more shallow. She dropped into unconsciousness. At noon on Wednesday, April 23, with Charles beside her, Annie took her last breath.

Charles threw himself on his bed in physical and emotional agony.

At Down, with a gap in the letters, Emma feared the worst.

On Thursday, the postman brought the news.

"My dear dearest Emma," Charles had written when finally he could get up from his bed, "I pray God Fanny's note may have prepared you."

Emma read on. "She went to her final sleep most tranquilly, most sweetly at twelve o'clock today."

Dr. Gully had written up the cause of death as a "Bilious Fever with typhoid character."

"Our poor dear child has had a very short life, but I trust happy, and God only knows what miseries might have been in store for her," Emma read. "She expired without a sigh. How desolate it makes one to think of her frank cordial manners." A year earlier, Charles had had a picture of Annie made. He told Emma, "I am so thankful for the daguerreotype. I cannot remember ever seeing the dear child naughty. God bless her."

Charles ended his letter with another hope, a most heart-felt prayer: "We must be more and more to each other, my dear wife." Losing a child ruins many a marriage; he could not bear to live without Emma. "Do what you can to bear up, and think how invariably kind and tender you have been to her. I am in bed, not very well."

Emma wrote Charles that he should come home. "You must remember that you are my prime treasure (and always have been)." She needed to be with him as much as he needed to be with her. She feared for his health and his life, so she told him not to hurry. She could not bear it if he died, too. But she knew "we shall be much less miserable together."

In her diary, on the day for April 23, she noted simply, "12 o'clock."

Chapter 22

A Dear and Good Child

She must have known how we loved her. Oh, that she could now know how deeply, how tenderly, we do still and shall ever love her dear joyous face! Blessings on her!
—CHARLES, THE END OF HIS MEMORIAL TO ANNIE, APRIL 30, 1851

When he was on the *Beagle* voyage, Charles had witnessed the funeral of another beloved daughter, the daughter of a native chief in New Zealand. Charles recounted the scene in his *Journal*.

> The hovel in which she had expired had been burnt to the ground: her body being enclosed between two small canoes was placed upright on the ground, and protected by an enclosure bearing wooden images of their gods, and the whole was painted bright red, so as to be conspicuous from afar. Her gown was fastened to the coffin, and her hair being cut off was cast at its foot. The relatives of the family had torn the flesh of their arms, bodies, and faces, so that they were covered with clotted blood; . . . On the following

day some of the officers visited this place, and found the women still howling and cutting themselves.

There would be no howling, no tearing of flesh at Annie's funeral in Malvern. It would be a quiet ceremony in the grave-yard in the town where she died, but Charles did not want to stay. He would get no relief or release from his daughter's funeral. What comfort could he get from a Christian service? How could he believe that his dear Annie suffered for sins she committed? She had been an innocent; nothing could convince him otherwise. Even while she was dying, she was sweet and polite. Even while she was dying, she worried about her little sister. "Where is poor Etty?" she had asked Brodie. Annie was Annie until the end—sweet, considerate, sensitive.

Although Charles felt torn about leaving, because he was not one to shirk his duties, he just could not remain in Malvern. Fanny would stay, and Hensleigh would come, too. They, with Brodie and Miss Thorley, would be there to see Annie buried. He knew the only thing that would give him any consolation would be holding Emma and being held by her. Although Fanny had been a comfort, and although he wrote to Emma constantly, it was he alone who had watched their cherished daughter leave the earth. His letter to Emma telling her that Annie had died seemed calm and composed. He had been anything but. As the end came near, he had sat beside her crying, knowing there was nothing he could do; knowing deep in his soul that no matter what Emma believed about heaven, he would never see Annie again. Death was the true end, and his little girl was gone forever.

At home Emma waited for Charles and tried to comfort the other children. She had written that "my feeling of long-ing after our lost treasure makes me feel painfully indifferent to the other children, but I shall get right in my feelings to them before long." Yet according to her sister Elizabeth, Emma was being wonderful, crying at times, but also coming to the meals with the little children and helping them with their food, attending to their needs. Willy had arrived from school and, though he was grief-stricken, his presence was a gift to his mother. And she had the new life growing inside her. That was a gift, too. But she was bereft.

When Charles got home, Emma met him at the door. They clung to each other and wept. They went over the details of the last days again. It was necessary to go through it all together, side by side.

Charles said he took some consolation in the thought that had Annie lived she might have suffered a life of ill health, as he was now suffering. He also took solace in the knowledge that he had never said a mean word to his daughter. But these were small comforts compared to his grief.

Everyone at Down was devastated. Brodie, Annie's beloved nurse, took her death especially hard. She came back for a while, but at sixty she found it was just too painful to be at Down without her Annie. She was close to retirement anyway, so she left the family and Charles provided her with an annual pension for the rest of her life. She came back to Down House many times afterward for long visits.

Charles asked Erasmus to put a notice in the *Times* of London in the "Deaths" column: "On the 23rd inst; of April, at Malvern, of fever, Anne Elizabeth Darwin, aged 10 years, eldest daughter of Charles Darwin, Esq., of Down, Kent."

A week after Annie died, Charles took out pen and paper and wrote a memorial portrait of Annie. It was just for him and Emma to capture the essence of their child on paper.

"We have lost the joy of our household," he wrote, "and the solace of our old age."

Emma experienced premature labor pains the day Charles wrote the memorial, but then the pains stopped. Twenty days after they lost Annie, on May 13, a new child, a son, Horace, was born. Emma's sister Elizabeth was still there, and she and their aunts had hoped that Emma would be healed by the birth. When Elizabeth reported that Emma was still very much in grief, an aunt wrote, "We are disappointed at your account of dear Emma. . . . However, we must have patience and wait."

In July, with Emma recovered enough from the pregnancy and birth to travel, she and Charles took the family to London for a week. Emma held baby Horace close. The baby and the normal activities of everyday life were starting to help a little. In London the Darwins stayed with Erasmus, who hired three horse-drawn cabs for Charles, Emma, and all the children and their nurses and governesses to go to the Great Exhibition in Hyde Park. It had opened a week after Annie died. Held in the architecturally magnificent Crystal Palace, the "Great Exhibition of Works of Industry of all Nations" was a celebration of technology and progress. Charles enjoyed the exhibits. There were displays of power looms, rope-making lathes, marine engines, hydraulic presses, steam machines, and other tools, machines, and crafts from around the world. The children enjoyed the sweets Uncle Erasmus gave them. But the exhibit itself was boring for the young Darwins, and given a chance to go a second time, Etty stayed at her uncle's house to scrub the back stairs, which she thought would be much more fun.

After trips to the zoo and other excursions around town, Charles and Emma took their family home to Down. It was a relief to be back in the country. The city always made them both feel worse physically. And life had to go on. Charles had two books on barnacles coming out: *A Monograph on the sub-class Cirripedia* and *A Monograph on the fossil Lepadidae.* He planned to write at least two more. He had more work to do when he was ready. He would not have Annie to make his hair beautiful or whirl around the Sandwalk with him. But he had Emma and the other children.

Over the summer, Emma realized that Etty, who was not quite eight, was suffering terribly from her sister's death. She had lost her playmate just as Emma had lost Fanny all those years ago. But Etty was just a small child. She did not have a real understanding of death. Emma had told the children that Annie had gone to heaven. This did not comfort Etty at all.

One evening that summer, as the family listened to Miss Thorley sing, Emma noticed that Etty looked upset. She took her out of the room and asked her what was the matter.

"But Mamma," Etty said, "where do the women go, for all the angels are men."

Emma asked her if she was thinking of Annie. Etty said she had not been thinking of Annie, but then she burst into tears.

Etty agonized over heaven and hell because she felt she was not as good a girl as Annie had been. On a few occasions Emma tried to reassure her, but Etty focused on the fact that she was deficient somehow. She kept trying to be "better." The maids did not help—they told her that Annie had been much sweeter and nicer than she was.

"I used to be a very naughty girl when Annie was alive, do you think God will forgive me?" she asked her mother another evening. And she pleaded, "Will you help me to be good?"

"Annie was a good child," Emma told her. "I do not think you will find it difficult to be as good as she was." But something was bothering Etty. Emma asked her what made her so unhappy.

"I am afraid of going to hell," Etty replied.

Emma told her, "Annie is safe in heaven." The implication was that Etty, if she was a good girl, would go to heaven, too.

But Etty knew that she was not Annie.

"Come to me," Emma said, "and I will try to help you as much as I can."

"But you are always with somebody," Etty challenged her.

Emma *was* always busy, with other children, with servants, with visitors. But she was concerned enough about Etty to write down these conversations. She told Etty to pray, and she prayed with her, but Etty was not consoled. She worried that she was too proud, too selfish to go to heaven. Unlike Emma, who had been old enough at twenty-four to commit herself to faith and to being a good and religious person like Fanny, Etty was just eight. Emma had written that note to God: "help me to become more like her, and grant that I may join with Thee. . . ." But what could Etty, a small child, do to come to terms with her sister's death and to make herself feel better?

Emma took it as a good sign when Etty asked for some of Annie's hair to put in a locket, and that she was able to talk about her sister's death. The following February, Etty told Emma, "I think about Annie when I am in bed." And, "Mamma when I see anything belonging to Annie it makes me think of her. Sometimes I make believe (but I know it's not true) that she is not quite dead, but will come back again sometime."

Emma knew it was good for Etty to talk about Annie. But she found it too difficult and painful to talk about her lost daughter. So did Charles. He did not speak of Annie more than once or twice for the rest of his life.

Etty said later that her mother never got over Annie's

death. When Emma died, an old woman of eighty-eight, Etty found a "little packet of memorials" that Emma had kept: a half-finished piece of wool work, a child's desk, paper of texts in a child's hand, and two ornamental pocket books. Emma had also copied out part of a poem, "Early Death," by Hartley Coleridge:

> She pass'd away, like morning dew
> Before the sun was high;
> So brief her time, she scarcely knew
> The meaning of a sigh.

Charles had also kept something in addition to his memorial of Annie. He kept the notes he had taken of Annie's symptoms during her illness and while she lay dying.

Emma and Charles coped with Annie's death the best they could—both together and separately. What united them was their love for each other and their love for Annie and their other children. Would their religious differences divide them? Aunt Jessie had written a year and a half earlier, "We have none of us to choose our religion. It comes to us by the atmosphere in which we live, we modify it afterwards according to our different minds, and many by our hearts only." Would Emma and Charles modify their religious feelings together or separately?

Emma held on to the hope of heaven. Charles could not.

Soon after Annie died, Charles wrote to his cousin Fox, "I do not suppose you will have heard of our bitter & cruel loss. . . . Thank God, she suffered hardly at all, and expired as tranquilly as a little angel. . . . She was my favourite child; her cordiality, openness, buoyant joyousness and strong affections made her most lovable. Poor dear little soul. Well it is all over."

For Charles it was all over. Although he knew he would continue to think, to read, and to talk with Emma about his religious beliefs, he was certain he would never see Annie again.

When he had arranged for Annie's tombstone at Malvern, he put no quotes from scripture on it, as was usually done. The marker read only:

ANNE ELIZABETH
DARWIN
BORN MARCH 2. 1841
DIED APRIL 23. 1851
A DEAR AND GOOD CHILD

Chapter 23

Against the Rules

"Well, you have come quite wrong; you should have turned to the right, but I am going to Bromley myself and I will shew you the way." They then walked on with the kind old woman.
—FROM "THE POUND OF SUGAR,"
A STORY BY EMMA DARWIN

As time went on, life at Down House settled back into a routine. Everyone missed Annie, but there were still seven children and Charles had his work to continue. His health had deteriorated again, but with Emma to nurse him as she always did, he turned back to his barnacles by October 1851, six months after Annie's death. His spirit was not in it, but the work routine helped his grief.

Emma kept her grief private, but she would struggle with depression off and on for the rest of her life. Losing her beloved treasure, as she thought of Annie, Emma worried about what else could and would happen to those she loved; nobody, nothing was safe. And Charles's religious doubts continued to sadden her. She did find solace in prayer and in her faith. Her belief in an afterlife was not diminished by Annie's death; it had been strengthened, just as it had, years earlier, by Fanny's death. In her old age, Aunt Jessie had come to the same conclusion. She wrote to Emma, "Now that I stand at the end of my life, as it were, and commonly called a long one, too, the whole appears to me so short, so fleeting, as if nothing was worth thinking of but the Eternity in which we recover all our earthly loves."

Emma and Aunt Jessie had always kept in close touch through letters. Their fondness for each other went back many years, to the time that Emma and Fanny had lived with Aunt Jessie and Sismondi as young women. Emma and Aunt Jessie didn't see each other as often as either would have liked, even after Aunt Jessie moved back to England when Sismondi died. But Emma regaled her aunt with stories about the children, which Aunt Jessie loved to read. She wrote, "My dear Emma, how I do love you when you talk of your children! . . . You are poetic without knowing it, which is the prettiest poetry of all. . . . Blessed mother of happy children you are, my Emma."

Of course Aunt Jessie knew that Emma wasn't always happy, but the children kept her busy. Very busy. Down House was overflowing with rambunctious children, mostly boys. Etty and Lizzy (as Elizabeth was now called) were the only girls left. Lizzy felt the imbalance. One day she came out of the drawing room and saw her papa.

"I'm so dull," she told Charles. "There is only horrid beastly boys in the drawing room."

Charles had to agree. He wrote to his cousin Fox to congratulate him on his tenth child and said, "When I have a tenth, send only condolences to me. We have now seven

children all well, thank God, as well as their mother; of these
seven, five are boys; and my father used to say that it was
certain that a boy gave as much trouble as three girls; so that
bona fide we have seventeen children."

The boys *were* energetic, and each different from the next.
Of the older boys, George stood out for his enterprise. Charles
wrote to Willy at school that "Georgy draws every day many
Horse-guards, and Lenny is as fat as ever." George drew his pictures of horse-guards, knights, and castles on the backs of
Charles's manuscript drafts and notes, which Charles threw
into the cupboard under the stairs by the garden door, along
with the children's toys, tennis rackets, parasols, and croquet
mallets. As George got older, he needed more paper, for he
wrote stories to go with his pictures. So he foraged in the cupboard and wrote *The Fairies of the Mountain* on the back of his
father's notes about barnacles and observations about pigeons
and chickens. Emma and Charles kept the papers, not for
Charles's drafts, but for George's childhood creations. (The
barnacle notes on the back of George's story are the only ones
left; the rest got thrown away.) Aunt Jessie loved hearing about
George; she could tell he was brilliant and told Emma that if
he could find work he loved when he grew up, he would find
happiness.

Just as Etty had complained that there was always someone else who needed Emma, Charles seemed to sometimes
feel he needed more from Emma than he could get, too, and
he wanted a certain kind of attention from her. In October
1852, just half a year after saying they had enough children, he
joked to Fox, "Emma has been very neglectful of late & we
have not had a child for more than one whole year."

In early 1853, Aunt Jessie got ill; her heart started to fail.
Emma could not go to her, but she heard from Jessie's sisters

what happened next. On March 3, as she lay in bed, Jessie gave directions about her last wishes to her sisters. When she finished she was still for a few minutes and then said quietly, "I think that is all." After a pause, she cried, "Sismondi, I'm coming," and looked up as if she saw him standing before her. Then she died.

Emma would miss Jessie very much. Hearing that story had to be hard for her for another reason. Would Emma see Charles on her deathbed, beckoning her to the beyond? Who or what would he see on his deathbed? What would he be thinking—believing—at that moment?

Charles still struggled with religious questions, and with how Emma and other religious people would react to his going against the biblical story of creation. But he felt certain that his theory was right, that new species were created all the time by the process of natural selection. And he was finally working toward letting his theory out into the world. He started to tell more people about it, testing the waters. But he did not want to cause upheaval or controversy. He was an English gentleman to the outside world, and he did not want to ruin his reputation by breaking the rules of society.

At home it was a very different story. There were still few rules at Down House, and Charles was not very good at enforcing the ones he and Emma did make. This was well known among his children. In 1855, when Lenny was about five, Charles walked in to find his son jumping up and down and tumbling all over a new sofa.

"Oh Lenny, Lenny," Charles said. "You know it is against all rules."

"Then," Lenny said to his papa, "I think you'd better go out of the room."

And so Charles did.

* * *

Charles was a creature of habit, and the whole family's routine revolved around his. Yet the household really was focused on the children as much as it was on Charles. Not only was the furniture bought for sturdiness, chairs were made into trains; the children ran in and out of the house, taxing Parslow's patience at times. But Parslow doted on them as well. He had made a sliding board that went down the stairs so the children could play inside when the weather was bad.

There was no "children should be seen and not heard" rule, as was common in Victorian households. One visitor described luncheons at Down as violent. Much to the chagrin of some of the servants and to the consternation of Emma's sister Elizabeth, the children even used bad language such as "the devil take" or "I wish to God." Charles thought it was funny. He loved to tell about how one day Lenny, age six, was lying on his papa's lap. The boy looked up at his father and said coolly to him, "Well, you old ass."

Shocked by his own words he quickly said, "Really, I did not mean to spurt that out."

There was a morality to the house, and Emma was the moral center, the bribery notwithstanding. But she also struggled with rules—and sometimes disobeyed them, such as turning around during the Trinity prayer. She could not decide on rules for the family about what should and should not be done on Sunday.

Etty wrote later, "In the years when we were growing up I believe my mother was often puzzled as to what rules to make about keeping Sunday. I remember she persuaded me to refuse any invitation from the neighbours that involved using the carriage on that day, and it was a question in her own mind whether she might rightly embroider, knit or play patience." After Emma died, Etty found a list among Emma's papers. Just as her husband would have done, she wrote down the pros and cons "on the side of abstaining from what other people think wrong, tho' you do not" and "on the side of doing as you think right, without considering the opinion of others." She could barely think of anything to write on the first side— just that other people would think they were sinners if they did not behave on Sundays. But on the side of doing what you think is right she wrote, "The sincerity of showing yourself as you really are. The real good it would do, the world not to have artificial sins." Emma was, and had always been, sincere and without pretense. Besides, she thought that England "would be morally the better for some amusements on Sunday," as she continued on her list.

She did care what the servants thought: "Whether the servants know you as you are and do not take your opinions as any guide for theirs—whether they learn toleration in short."

But above all she was thinking of the children. How could they be happy being restrained even on one day of the week? "All this only applies to my own doings, as I do not feel at all sure enough in any way to interfere with the pleasures of sons of the age of mine."

Although Charles was the funny one, the one who told jokes and stories, the children adored Emma, too. She was much more reserved, but, according to Etty, "there was always about her a bright aliveness" and "a happy enjoyment of fun and humor." But she didn't laugh much. Etty later wrote that strangers were sometimes put off by her seeming sternness, though she wasn't actually stern at all. She was calm and sometimes solemn, and together that could be mistaken for gravity. But she was always welcoming to all visitors, known or unknown. As Etty later wrote, "She would hurry to the front door at Down, eager for the first moment of greeting. In summer weather she would be on the little mound which overlooks the entrance road, waiting to wave a welcome as the carriage drove up. The contrast of this outspringing of warmth with her usual calm demeanour, made every arrival a kind of special festival."

All the children knew she was tenderhearted, and although Etty had complained earlier that her mother was always with someone, she wrote later that her mother stopped whatever she was doing to watch what a child wanted her to watch—two titmice playing leapfrog in the garden that Etty pointed out to her, for instance. Emma also played piano for the children—a special galloping tune that made them run around the parlor.

The open-mindedness of Maer Hall won out over the strictness of the Mount at Down House. The children never felt disapproval or judgment from their parents.

When Elizabeth did not want to be confirmed, she felt free to tell her mother that she did not have the heart to pretend she believed in the Trinity. Emma must have had mixed feelings about her daughter not being confirmed, but she abhorred hypocrisy. She did not want her daughter to do something she didn't believe in just for appearances' sake. So she allowed Elizabeth to skip confirmation.

Emma taught them about morality through stories she wrote. One of their favorites was called "A Pound of Sugar." It features a little boy called Bobby—Charles's nickname as a baby—and his little sister, named Lizzy. Bobby's grandfather asks him to get a pound of sugar in town. Grandfather tells him to make sure he turns right when he crosses the road. So Bobby and Lizzy set out for Bromley, and Bobby turns left. The children get lost, but they are not punished for it; instead an old woman helps them find their way back into town. In town, neither child remembers what it is they were supposed to buy and they come home with a pound of salt instead of sugar. The tea tastes terrible with the salt in it, but Grandfather does not punish Bobby. He just sends the children out again the next day to buy sugar. They come home empty-handed because a boy thief tricks them out of their money. Again they are not punished. The story ends happily with Bobby and Lizzy buying not only sugar, but a toy as well. What was the moral of the story? That deviating from the rules does not get you punished and grown-ups are always there to help you? Was Emma trying to tell Charles something?

The real Bobby was all grown up now, and as other people turned right, he felt he must turn left. Would it turn out happily in the end? What would happen when Charles went against the rules?

Chapter 24

Terrible Suffering

*Yearly more are bred than can survive; the smallest grain
in the balance, in the long run, must tell on which death
shall fall, and which shall survive.*

—CHARLES IN HIS SPECIES SKETCH OF 1844

In 1854, Charles finally finished with the barnacles. He had worked so long on them that once when one of the boys, probably Lenny, went over to Sir John Lubbock's house to play with his son, he asked the Lubbock boy, "Where does your father do *his* barnacles?" Because, of course, all fathers must study barnacles—his had been doing it ever since the Darwin children could remember! But in fact Charles was the first person to fully study and classify barnacles.

And now that Charles was finished studying and describing all known *Cirripedia* in minute detail (1,200 pages' worth), he felt it was time to go back to the big picture. Charles turned to his species book. It was time to take the chance. He would make a leap of faith that everything would be all right. He still wasn't going to rush to publish it, although his friends were urging him to. Even Lyell, who did not agree with everything Charles was thinking, urged him to publish something about his theory of natural selection. Anything. Evolution was in the air; what if someone else came up with the same mechanism as Charles had? Charles was looking at selection in pigeons now. Lyell told him if he couldn't publish the whole thing, then just a small part: "pigeons if you please."

But Charles wanted his argument to be airtight, indisputably right, and for that he needed time. He kept studying the pigeons just as he had the barnacles; he kept amassing notes; and he kept retching in the curtained-off privy in his study. Maybe he wasn't ready, after all.

"I rather hate the idea of writing for priority," Charles wrote back to Lyell the next day. "Yet I shd be vexed if any one were to publish my doctrines before me."

By 1856 Charles was breeding his own pigeons—Squire, the other pigeon fanciers nicknamed him, referring to the country gentleman that he was. It was a term of respect. Charles wasn't a dilettante; he was serious about the breeding and created his own new lines of pigeons. He was also continuing his own line; Emma was pregnant again. At forty-eight, she was quite old to be having a baby in the medically perilous nineteenth century. She had a tiring and uncomfortable pregnancy. Etty, who turned thirteen in September, read to her mother to help her pass the time.

The baby, Charles Waring Darwin, was born on December 6, 1856. Charles wrote to his cousin Fox telling him about the birth of their last child. He also told him, "I am working very hard at my Book, perhaps too hard. It will be very big & I am become most deeply interested in the way facts fall into groups. am like Croesus overwhelmed with my riches in facts. & I mean to make my Book as perfect as ever I can."

This new little Darwin had a happy and placid temperament. Charles and Emma showered love and attention on him, and he loved them back. He also had a special fondness for Parslow, which pleased Charles no end. Whenever Parslow came into the room, baby Charles would stretch out his arms to be picked up. But usually the baby just lay in Charles's lap, staring up at his father's face with pleasure and equanimity. It soon became clear to Emma and Charles that something was wrong. Etty later said that the baby was born "without its full share of intelligence." Still, Emma and Charles were more relaxed about him than they had been about their other children—he was certainly going to be their last, and they enjoyed their moments with him. Charles described the baby as "backward in walking and talking, but intelligent and observant."

In the summer of 1858, Charles Waring was a year and a half old. At an age when his sisters and brothers had been talking and toddling around, he still lay docilely in his parents' laps. In a world in which survival depended on the ability to fight, Charles Waring would have lost. But with loving parents to take care of him, his future, though maybe not as bright and promising as his brothers', seemed secure.

On June 3, 1858, Emma wrote in her diary that it had been blazing hot for a week. But by June 8, it was lovely weather. Visitors came and went, as usual mostly family—Charles's sister Catherine, Emma's sisters Elizabeth and Charlotte. George had the measles but they had him stay at school because scarlet fever was sweeping through the countryside. Charles was busy working on his species book—he had hundreds of pages written—though he still was in no rush to get it done. He agonized over the earthquake his theory would cause.

On June 18, Emma wrote in her diary, "Etty taken ill." She had a sore throat and felt very weak. While that was not in and of itself serious, it could progress into something dangerous. Etty had been sickly since she was thirteen, two years before. (At that time she was told not to get up for breakfast but to take it in bed. She had breakfast in bed for the rest of her life!) Charles and Emma were always worried when one of their children was ill, but it hit them especially hard when it was one who was already sickly. It was so much more likely that a sickly child would die from even a common illness.

Charles knew that he was seeing up close, in his family, what he was thinking about and writing about in his study. Right there in front of him was the "struggle for existence" that he was writing about in his book. But here he was seeing it in his beloved children. Again.

On that same day, June 18, the post brought a diversion. But it was not a welcome one. It was a letter from Alfred Russel Wallace, a young naturalist who was currently traveling around the world collecting specimens just as Charles had done. The two had corresponded before. But this letter was a shock. It included an essay Wallace had written called "On the Tendency of Varieties to Depart Indefinitely from the Original Type."

Charles read it immediately. He was shocked and upset. Lyell had been right in urging him to get on with publishing his views. This essay was so close to Charles's theory as to make him very uncomfortable. Wallace had many of the same ideas Charles had had for years, and Wallace also had gotten some of them from reading Malthus's *Essay on Population*.

Charles sat down at his desk and wrote to Lyell so that the letter would go out the same day: "Your words have come true with a vengeance that I shd. be forestalled. You said this when I explained to you here very briefly my views of 'Natural Selection' depending on the Struggle for existence.—I never saw a more striking coincidence, if Wallace had my M.S. sketch written out in 1842 he could not have made a better short abstract! Even his terms now stand as Heads of my Chapters."

Charles wasn't ready to publish, but he certainly did not want someone else to come first. What was he going to do?

Wallace had not asked Charles to publish his essay, but Charles thought perhaps he was duty bound to arrange for publication. Wallace had asked him to send the essay to Charles Lyell, which Charles did. He told Lyell that he would send it to a journal if Lyell thought he should. He worried that "all my originality, whatever it may amount to, will be smashed." But he also felt that it might not hurt his book. "Though my Book, if it will ever have any value, will not be deteriorated; as all the labour consists in the application of the theory." He told Hooker about Wallace's paper, too.

But his immediate concerns lay with Etty and the other children. Scarlet fever was hitting the area hard; some children in the village were already seriously ill. Later they would realize that they should have packed up the family and left, but they couldn't have moved Etty, anyway; she was too sick.

Five days after receiving the letter from Wallace, on June 23, baby Charles got sick with a fever. And it was now clear that Etty had diphtheria, a disease that was new to England. It had come from France in epidemic proportions just that year. There was no cure, and it could be fatal.

Charles stuck to his routine as much as possible, but when he walked on the Sandwalk he worried. He worried about Etty and the baby, about George sick at school with measles, and about Wallace's essay. Emma worried with him about the children; Lyell and Hooker worried with him about Wallace. He wrote to Lyell almost every day during this week. On June 25, he wrote that "there is nothing in Wallace's sketch which is

not written out much fuller in my sketch copied in 1844"—
the one he had given to Emma in case of his sudden death—
"and read by Hooker some dozen years ago." He had also sent
the sketch to Asa Gray, the American botanist, about a year
earlier "so that I could most truly say & prove that I take nothing from Wallace." He wrote Lyell that he would be "extremely
glad now to publish a sketch of my general views in about a
dozen pages or so. But I cannot persuade myself that I can do
so honourably."

Charles had not intended to publish his sketch—he was
waiting for the whole book to be done. Could he do so now,
honorably, when Wallace was closing in on him? "I would far
rather burn my whole book," he told Lyell, "than that he or any
man shd think that I had behaved in a paltry spirit."

Charles was tormented by this decision. Although their
views were not identical, they were virtually the same. "I
could send Wallace a copy of my letter to Asa Gray to show
him that I had not stolen his doctrine. But I cannot tell
whether to publish now would not be base & paltry."

The next day, June 26, Etty was very weak but seemed to be
getting better. The baby, though, had a high fever, and, as
Charles wrote to Lyell, "What has frightened us so much
is, that 3 children have died in village from Scarlet Fever, &
others have been at death's door, with terrible suffering."

This letter was a PS to the one the day before. He wrote it
to tell Lyell that he felt his first instinct had been right: He
should not publish anything now. But he needed Lyell's guidance, because distraught as he was about this as well as his children, he could not make a decision himself. "I have always
thought you would have made a first-rate Lord Chancellor," he
told his friend, and "I now appeal to you as Lord Chancellor."

How could he think clearly when their sweet baby
was suffering? Charles and Emma took turns rocking him,

comforting him as best they could. He was miserable; they were miserable. To watch their usually happy, placid baby cry in pain was horrible. To watch another child of theirs suffer was almost more than they could bear.

By the next day, they were certain the baby had scarlet fever; "Baby worse," Emma wrote in her diary. Their nurse Jane also seemed to have the disease. When the doctor came to visit, he declared that the baby was not dangerously ill. Charles reported the situation in a letter to William Fox. But before Charles could even seal that letter for the post, the baby took a turn for the worse. Charles wrote a PS: "Since this written our Baby has become suddenly most ill. . . . the doctor can only say there is yet some hope."

This was all too familiar. At least this time Charles and Emma were together.

And this time it was quick.

In her diary on June 28, next to where she had already written "G. holidays"—George was scheduled to come home from school—she wrote, "Death." Their youngest child had died.

Charles wrote to Hooker, "It was the most blessed relief to see his poor little innocent face resume its sweet expression in the sleep of death. Thank God he will never suffer more in this world. Poor Emma behaved nobly and how she stood it all I cannot conceive."

Charles himself was done in; he had no ability to focus on the Wallace crisis. Lyell and Hooker took matters into their own hands. They decided that Charles should send them a paper, and they would present it together with Wallace's essay to the Linnaean Society in London.

On June 29, the day after the baby died, Charles wrote to Hooker, "I am quite prostrated & can do nothing but I send

Wallace & my abstract of abstract of letter to Asa Gray." He sent Hooker the sketch of 1844, the exact copy that Hooker had read before. Charles hoped "that you may see by your own handwriting that you did read it." As if Hooker could have forgotten.

Charles could not bear to look at the draft right now. It was too much, on top of the baby's death, to think that his years of work could be upstaged. He still felt badly that he was so worried about establishing priority, of ensuring that all would know that he was the first of the two men to have the idea. But it must be done. A perfectionist, he added a note with the sketch: "This MS. work was never intended for publication, and therefore was not written with care.—C.D. 1858."

And then Charles turned his attentions away from his study, back into his home life. He and Emma had a baby to bury.

Chapter 25

The Origins of *The Origin*

I fear I shall never be able to make it good enough.
—CHARLES TO JOSEPH HOOKER ON WRITING
WHAT HE CALLED HIS ABSTRACT,
THE ORIGIN OF SPECIES

On July 1, 1858, Emma wrote nothing in her little diary. There was no need to; a mother never forgets the date of her child's funeral. Charles Waring Darwin was buried in the cemetery at the churchyard at Down where Mary Eleanor lay. Etty later said that after their original sorrow, Charles and Emma had a sense of relief. What would his future have been? But at the time they were heartbroken; they had adored him. And they knew there would be no more babies.

On the very same day as the funeral of Charles Waring Darwin, the Linnaean Society fit in an extra meeting. The joint paper of Charles Darwin and Alfred Russel Wallace was read in a stately room on Piccadilly Street in London. Wallace had no knowledge this was happening; he was too far away, in

Ternate, Indonesia, for them to let him know in time. He would find out three months later.

The title of the paper was "On the Tendency of Species to form Varieties; and on the Perpetuation of Varieties and Species by Natural Means of Selection. By CHARLES DARWIN, Esq., F.R.S., F.L.S., & F.G.S., and ALFRED WALLACE, Esq. Communicated by Sir CHARLES LYELL, F.R.S., F.L.S., and J. D. HOOKER, Esq., M.D., V.P.R.S., F.L.S, &c."

Lyell and Hooker wrote, as an introduction, "The gentlemen having, independently and unknown to one another, conceived the same very ingenious theory to account for the appearance and perpetuation of varieties and of specific forms on our planet, and both fairly claim the merit of being original thinkers in this important line of inquiry; but neither of them having published his views, though Mr. Darwin has for many years past been repeatedly urged by us to do so, and both authors having now unreservedly placed their papers in our hands, we think it would best promote the interests of science that a selection from them would be laid before the Linnaean Society."

The members of the society present, sitting in wooden churchlike pews, heard Charles's theory spelled out in a short but painstaking manner. His essay began with the notion that

> all nature is at war, one organism with another, or with external nature. Seeing the contented face of nature, this may at first be well doubted; but reflection will inevitably prove it to be true. The war, however, is not constant, but recurrent in a slight degree at short periods, and more severely at occasional more distant periods; and hence its effects are easily overlooked. It is the doctrine of Malthus applied in most cases with tenfold force.

Using birds as an example, Charles showed that in nature, if every egg hatched and every fledgling survived, populations would grow too big: "Suppose in a certain spot there are eight pairs of birds, and that only four pairs of them annually (including double hatches) rear only four young, and that these go on rearing their young at the same rate, then at the end of seven years (a short life, excluding violent deaths, for any bird) there will be 2048 birds, instead of the original sixteen." But bird populations do not explode. What happens, instead, is a struggle for existence, with slight variations in the birds giving some advantages over others.

On the same day that baby Charles was being put into the ground, the members of the Linnaean Society heard his father's words:

> Now, can it be doubted, from the struggle each individual has to obtain subsistence, that any minute variation in structure, habits, or instincts, adapting that individual better to the new conditions, would tell upon its vigour and health? In the struggle it would have a better chance of surviving; and those of its offspring which inherited the variation, be it ever so slight, would also have a better chance. Yearly more are bred than can survive; the smallest grain in the balance, in the long run, must tell on which death shall fall, and which shall survive.

Charles had figured out, looking at the finches and mocking birds from the Galapagos all those years ago, that certain variations helped the birds survive. The small variations that caused individual birds to survive would be passed down to their offspring, creating—eventually—new, separate species. The same thing happened with dogs and foxes, with ferns and flowers, with all living things.

The survival of a species also depended upon how successful males and females were in reproducing their lines. Three of Charles's children had not survived. But seven had; some of them, he hoped, would reproduce.

Since survival in nature depended on reproduction, courtship was crucial. Charles wrote about "the struggle of the males for the females. These struggles are generally decided by the law of battle, but in the case of birds, apparently, by the charms of their song, by their beauty or their power of courtship, as in the dancing rock-thrush of Guiana. The most vigorous and healthy males, implying perfect adaptation, must generally gain the victory in their contests." He had some vigorous and healthy males left in his five sons.

In this paper, he didn't come right out and say that God had nothing to do with the process, but he knew that the people listening would hear that between the lines: "An organic being, like the woodpecker or mistletoe, may thus come to be adapted to a score of contingences—natural selection accumulating those slight variations in all parts of its structure, which are in any way useful to it during any part of its life." In other words, species were constantly adapting. This was the moment he had been scared of for so many years—his theory made public. He wasn't there in the great meeting room to see the reaction of his peers. He was home with his family.

And in the Linnaean Society meeting room, Charles's and Wallace's papers were met with—no reaction. There were, if not literal, then theoretical yawns. No one seemed to understand the import of what the two men were saying.

At home the next day, Charles focused on getting all the children who were well enough—that is, all but Etty—out of Down and away from the scarlet fever. He had to protect his offspring. He and Emma arranged for her sister Elizabeth to take them into her house in Hartfield, Sussex, south of Down (Elizabeth lived in a house next to their other sister, Charlotte). Etty was too ill to move, so until she was stronger Charles and Emma stayed with her.

When Charles received word of the reaction at the meeting, he was relieved. He would edit and polish his paper, making it ready for publication. And then maybe he would write his book, finally.

Once Etty was well enough to be moved, Charles and Emma took the whole family for a holiday on the Isle of Wight. While there, Charles got his paper ready for the Linnaean Society's publication of the proceedings; both his and Wallace's papers would be published at the same time. Meanwhile, Hooker wrote to Wallace and told him what they had done. Charles was seriously worried about Wallace's reaction. He was worried about the reaction when the papers were printed, as well. But neither reaction was earth-shattering. Wallace was very generous and understanding; he gave Darwin priority. He even later wrote a book about the theory, which he called "Darwinism."

As to the reaction of the members of the Linnaean Society—only a few who read the papers had any idea what impact the theory would make. The firestorm Charles had long feared had not come to pass.

So by the time he got back home in August, Charles was well into the writing of his book. He would call it not *Natural Selection* as he once planned, but *On the Origin of Species*. He was committed, but he was still scared. And sick. He wrote to Hooker how ill writing the book was making him: "My God how I long for my stomach's sake to wash my hands of it—for at least one long spell." But he kept working on the book, veering away from it sometimes to help Frank with his beetles. Frank recently had started collecting them, and Charles's old interest was renewed. He wrote to Fox that his son had "caught the other day *Brachinus crepitans*. . . . My Blood boiled with old ardour when he caught a *Licinus*—a prize unknown to me."

The biggest and most difficult task he had with the book was to make it short enough to be readable. He called the book his "Abstract," for it was only a fraction of what he had written over the years. He knew that it is often harder to write short than to write long. (Across the ocean, the essayist Henry David Thoreau had written to a friend just the year before, "Not that the story need be long, but it will take a long while to make it short.")

Charles worked harder than he ever had. He sat not at a desk, but in his armchair, which had been raised high to accommodate his long legs, with a board across his knees to write on. He was surrounded by his years of notes and research. The children ran in and out, as usual, and he took breaks for reading the mail, striding around the Sandwalk, listening to Emma read, playing backgammon, and writing letters. But he made great progress quickly. After all the hesitation, all the delay, he finished the book he had been sitting on for more than fifteen years in just thirteen months and ten days.

Chapter 26

Dependent on Each Other in So Complex a Manner

*Then how should I manage all my business if I were
obliged to go every day walking with my wife?*
—CHARLES, 1838, CONTEMPLATING WHETHER TO MARRY

In 1859, when Charles finished the manuscript for his book, he gave it to Emma. He also sent it to some of his scientific friends, but he was in many ways most interested in Emma's reaction. She was a representative of the religious world he was up against—he was sleeping with the enemy! And she told things as she saw them.

He respected Emma's mind and trusted her implicitly. She was brilliant, had been an avid reader her whole life, and she was a terrific literary critic, editor, and proofreader. Emma helped him with all his papers and books, and this one was the most important. Charles wanted *The Origin of Species* to be simple enough for a nonscientist to read and understand, as well as accurate and cogently argued enough to convince a scientist. His scientific friends would speak to the latter question. But Emma was his first and most important nonscientific reader.

In fact, Emma was not all that interested in science. She was only interested in Charles's science because it was his. Once, as they sat together listening to a lecture at the British Association for the Advancement of Science, he turned to her and said, "I am afraid this is very wearisome to you."

"No more than all the rest," she answered him quietly.

Charles often told this story; he thought it was funny. He had never wanted a scientific partner. He wanted a constant companion, which he got. He also got a devoted nurse who would not leave him alone for a night because it made him anxious. He got a woman who was, according to an aunt of Emma's, "an exception to every wife" in her devotion.

But he also got a good—and tough—reader.

Now, sitting in the drawing room, Emma read page after page of *The Origin of Species*. In the book, Charles was trying to make a strong, coherent, cogent argument for creation by natural selection. It was, in many ways, a response to the argument put forth by William Paley in *Natural Theology*. Charles modeled his own book after Paley's, because he wanted *The Origin* to have the same effect on others that Paley's had had on him when he first read it at Cambridge. And Charles's book was, after all, an argument against the concept of God as creator that Paley had espoused.

Emma and most of Charles's religious friends and family did not ascribe to the miracle-creating, vengeance-meting, wrathful-king God of the Hebrew scriptures. They believed in the prevailing concept of God: God as benevolent Father who created every single species as it existed now, unchanged. This God created a world that ran like clockwork, with every plant, animal, and creature a cog in the great machine. This

God created a world with people at the top, near the angels, and all the other animals down below, unrelated to human beings. This God had revealed himself through his son, with a promise of everlasting life.

In *The Origin*, Charles wasn't trying to murder Emma's God; he was trying to show how he believed creation really occurred.

He knew he was right; he just had to make his argument clear enough so as to be, as much as was possible, irrefutable. And he wanted to be polite about it. Charles wrote the way he spoke, as an English gentleman. At Down, when he wanted a servant to do something, he did not order him in an imperious way. Instead he said, "Would you be so good" as to light the fire, empty the chamber pot, fix my dinner? There was no doubt that Charles was the master, but he was kind and respectful. Now in his book he was saying, Would you be so good as to listen to what I have to say—and agree with me?

In what was to become one of the most famous passages in the book, he wrote:

It may metaphorically be said, that natural selection is daily and hourly scrutinising, through the world, every variation, even the slightest; rejecting that which is bad, preserving and adding up all that is good; silently and insensibly working, *whenever and wherever opportunity offers*, at the improvement of each organic being in relation to its organic and inorganic conditions of life.

"It may metaphorically be said" was a bit of British reserve, but it was clear what Charles was arguing. It may be said that new species are forming all the time. It may be said that God did not create all the species at once, as you have been told to believe. Old species die out; new species are created. It may be said that this is actually beautiful. For Charles this process *was* beautiful. For Emma death was bearable because there was an afterlife. In Charles's view of the world, death looked very different, but he found meaning and grandeur in that view.

As Emma read the pages, there were parts that made her cringe; passages that she worried would move people farther away from God. But she only criticized the argument to help Charles spell it out more clearly. Emma rewrote awkward sentences, and if she didn't understand what he was trying to say, they talked it through so that he could write it in a more lucid fashion. She also helped him with his grammar and his atrocious spelling. She teased him about his misuse of commas—and fixed them for him.

In a brilliantly persuasive move, Charles included a chapter called "Difficulties of the Theory." He had thought long and hard about what people would object to, and he had worked hard to answer their objections as best he could. "Long before the reader has arrived at this part of my work," he said in chapter VI, "a crowd of difficulties will have occurred to him. Some of them are so serious that to this day I can hardly reflect on them without being in some degree staggered; but, to the best of my judgment, the greater number are only apparent, and those that are real are not, I think, fatal to the theory."

In this chapter, he addressed difficulties such as Emma's concern about the development of the eye. He wrote, "To suppose that the eye with all its inimitable contrivances for adjusting the focus to different distances, for admitting different amounts of light, and for the correction of spherical and chromatic aberration, could have been formed by natural selection, seems, I freely confess, absurd in the highest degree." But he went on to compare the reader's doubt to another long-held assumption that was known now to be wrong: "When it was first said that the sun stood still and the world turned round, the common sense of mankind declared the doctrine false; but the old saying of *Vox populi, vox Dei*, as every philosopher knows, cannot be trusted in science." *Vox populi, vox Dei:* "The voice of the people is the voice of God." Not true, Charles was saying. Just because everyone thinks so doesn't mean it is right.

He argued to Emma and to all his readers:

> Reason tells me, that if numerous gradations from a simple and imperfect eye to one complex and perfect can be shown to exist, each grade being useful to its possessor, as is certainly the case; if further, the eye ever varies and the variations be inherited, as is likewise certainly the case; and if such variations should be useful to any animal under changing conditions of life, then the difficulty of believing that a perfect and complex eye could be formed by natural selection, though insuperable by our imagination, should not be considered as subversive to the theory.

He went on to delineate and, he hoped, prove his point.

In that chapter he also included other difficult problems. He admitted that one could not see the intermediate stages of a species' development in the fossil record. He also said that he did not know how, exactly, traits were passed down through the generations. Charles never figured this out because to do so he needed to know about genes. Gregor Mendel, the Austrian monk and scientist, was working this out in his monastery at about the same time, but Charles was not aware of him. Very few people were. Even though Mendel's paper was published in 1866, it wouldn't be until after both Charles's and Mendel's deaths that Mendel's work would be rediscovered and the process of heredity through genes would become known and understood.

Charles did not address the origin of the human species in this book. He was not ready for that fight. He had already figured out that humans had a common ancestor with apes (not that people evolved from apes, as many people still misunderstand it). But he held that back—for now.

Even though the book was long, Charles always felt as though it was just an abstract. And it was. He had intended his book to be much longer; he had hundreds more pages written that he had culled from. He had worked hard to make it short. And he worked hard to make it irrefutable.

If the *Not Marry* side of his list had been longer—or stronger—than the *Marry* side, and he had stayed single in London with Erasmus and his crowd, perhaps he would have grown farther away from the church and the established, conservative, religious society. Had he spent more time with freethinking, liberal intellectuals and less time sitting on the sofa with Emma, who rubbed his stomach when he was ill and put a cool hand on his feverish head, perhaps then he would not have been quite so conciliatory and conservative in his writing of the book. He hoped that even if there was controversy, it wouldn't be personal. He hoped the public, though they might disagree with what he was saying, would still like the person who was saying it. Emma did.

His life at Down informed his work in many ways. Back when he was thinking about getting married, he worried that taking walks with his wife would infringe on his work time. But in the last paragraph of *The Origin*, Charles wrote about a spot near Down House where he and Emma often walked together. He wrote, "It is interesting to contemplate an entangled bank, clothed with many plants of many kinds, with birds singing on the bushes, with various insects flitting about, and with worms crawling through the damp earth, and to reflect that these elaborately constructed forms, so different from each other, and dependent on each other in so complex a manner, have all been produced by laws acting around us. . . ."

So different from each other, and dependent on each other in so complex a manner. He could have been writing about his marriage.

Chapter 27

What the Lord Hath Delivered

I hope you are not working too hard. For Heaven's Sake,
think that you may become such a beast as I am.
—CHARLES TO THOMAS HENRY HUXLEY, SEPTEMBER 10, 1860

The day *The Origin of Species* was published, November 24, 1859, Charles was in Ilkley, taking another water cure. Finishing the book had almost done him in. Now he and Emma had to wait for the reaction.

The publisher, John Murray, and Charles had put out advance word about the book, and the first printing sold out in one day. It was not a huge printing, only 1,500 copies, but Mudie's lending library had bought 500 copies, which meant that many more people would read *The Origin*. Mudie's lent books all over Britain and had 25,000 subscribers. Emma was proud of her husband. She wrote to their son William, "It is a wonderful thing the whole edition selling off at once & Mudie taking 500 copies. Your father says he shall never think small beer of himself again & that candidly he does think it very well written." The fact that the public wanted more was a satisfaction to Charles, though it didn't sell as quickly as that anonymous book, *Vestiges,* had done.

Charles did his best to help the book along, as any dedicated author will. He sent copies to friends, colleagues, family members—anyone whom he thought could and would be a good advocate. With each copy, he wrote a personal letter, geared to the recipient and to the fears Charles had about the recipient's reaction. He told his cousin Fox, for instance, knowing that he was religious, that he didn't think the book would convert him.

Darwin called the book one long argument, and that's what it was, but the style was accessible and readable. Many people gobbled it up, much as they were gobbling up the novels of Charles Dickens. Although some readers found it hard to get through—especially if they couldn't buy his argument.

The first published review confirmed all Charles's fears. An anonymous review (many reviews then were anonymous—which meant they could be written by close friends, known enemies, sometimes even family members) in the weekly literary magazine the *Athenaeum* declared that the book was too dangerous for most people to read and that it should be read only by theologians who could answer it best. "If a monkey has become a man—what may not a man become?" the reviewer asked. Charles had not written anything about human evolution, but there it was. And it was also incorrect. A monkey did not become a man; monkeys and men had a common ancestor. Charles was furious, and at the same time, he was surprised at how upset he was. He had been expecting a religious uproar, hadn't he? He had been worrying about this ever since those months in 1838 when he contemplated marriage. But the public reaction was very hard for him to take; it was that avalanche of negative opinion that had always terrified him.

Privately some of his friends also told him they had problems with taking God out of creation. If God could be put back into the equation, then many people would have no trouble reading Charles's book and accepting the scientific argument. It was fine if the exact account of creation in Genesis wasn't exactly true. As long as one could still *believe*. But most of his religious friends were not angry with Charles; they saw very clearly the soundness of his argument. And they knew his lack of enmity against them and their beliefs. These kinds of discussions were similar to talks he and Emma had been having for years; they were much easier for him to handle.

But one friend's reaction upset him terribly. It came in a letter. The post brought many letters in reaction to the book—two hundred in the first six months after publication. His old professor Adam Sedgwick wrote to him, "I have read your book with more pain than pleasure." He admired parts of it, he said, but he laughed at other parts. Laughed at! And he was angry about others. He felt that Charles had ignored morality, and that to accept the argument of creation by natural selection would "sink the human race into a lower grade of degradation than any into which it has fallen since its written records tell us of its history." He begged Charles to accept God's revelation so the two of them would meet, eventually, in heaven.

Charles showed Sedgwick's letter to Emma. She agreed with much of what Sedgwick said but was upset at his tone. She comforted her husband. Etty knew about this letter, for it caused much excitement and discussion at Down. But Emma refused to show it to her, even though she was sixteen. Perhaps Emma wanted to keep the pointed criticism away from her so as not to diminish the daughter's respect for the father. But Etty's doubts after Annie's death could not have been forgotten; perhaps Emma felt there was no need to fan the flames of religious doubt by showing her what some thought of her father's "heresy." Emma clearly was upset by the letter, too, and about the religious controversy around the book. No matter how open-minded she was, Emma was not comfortable at all with Charles's role as heretic.

There were many other reviews very soon after that first one, and a great number of them were positive, including a review by Julia "Snow" Wedgwood, Hensleigh and Fanny's daughter. She was a novelist and literary critic. Not surprisingly, she gave the book a positive review. Charles kept everything—all the reviews, mentions, and notices. Over the years there were close to two thousand reviews, notices, and articles about the book. He put the magazines and journals on his shelves; he put the newspaper articles in a drawer and Parslow or the children glued them into leather-bound albums when they had the time. But he didn't just save the reviews, he made notes of interesting criticisms and ideas for changes in further revisions. As usual he was organized, forward-thinking, and self-critical.

Charles said there were so many reviews and notices that he got sick of reading about himself. He didn't get sick of his theory, though. He never stopped thinking about his argument, honing it, and figuring out how to put it across better in future editions of the book.

He still puzzled over the question of God's role in nature and about his own faith. He listened to what people said, and he and Emma continued to think, read, and talk about the subject. But whether it was Sedgwick's letter or the negative reviews or whether he had always known he would handle it this way, Charles came to the conclusion fairly quickly that he wanted to stay out of the controversy as much as possible. He wanted to stay home with Emma. Fortunately, she wanted him to.

Also fortunately for him, he had friends who were able and eager to do battle for him out in the world. Although Charles guided the offense and defense from his sanctuary at Down, it was Charles Lyell, Joseph Hooker, Asa Gray, and especially a man named Thomas Henry Huxley who fought his battles in person. Huxley was the most vocal and pugnacious of them all, and earned the nickname of Darwin's bulldog. When he first read Charles's book, he cried, "How extremely stupid not to have thought of that!" And to Charles he wrote, "I trust you will not allow yourself to be in any way disgusted or annoyed by the considerable abuse & misrepresentation which unless I greatly mistake is in store for you" and declared, "I am sharpening up my claws & beak in readiness." Darwin was fortunate that the regular reviewer for the London *Times* passed off the book to Huxley to review, which meant *The Origin* got a rave review in that most important of papers.

Joseph Hooker took the botany side of natural selection and showed how Charles's theory seemed to work among plants. Asa Gray, in America, also argued for him, although he believed that God created the good variations in species. Charles liked Gray and thought that in many ways he understood the theory best; Charles called Gray's reviews good natural theological commentary. Charles Lyell took the geological side, and he wrote a book a few years later called *The Antiquity of Man*, which argued against the biblical story of the creation and the flood. But he was never able to believe that human beings had no divine genesis, and he always believed that humans possessed a soul. He once joked to Huxley that he could not "go the whole orang." Like Emma, Lyell and Gray were willing to support Charles, even with their differences. But it was Thomas Henry Huxley who was Charles's biggest proponent. Huxley's role was established during the summer of 1860.

In June 1860 there was a weeklong conference of the British Association for the Advancement of Science at Oxford University. The meeting was an annual gathering place for most of the preeminent scientists of the day. Charles and Emma had thought about going; they had enjoyed the meeting a previous year. But not long before the meeting began, Charles became too ill to attend. He went for yet another water cure instead. So although it became one of the most famous scientific meetings in history, one in which evolution and religion fought on center stage, Charles Darwin was not there. Afterward he heard all about it, first in a letter from Huxley and later from all his friends who attended.

This year many of the scientists had gone to Oxford specifically to discuss Charles's book. Richard Owen, formerly a friend and colleague of Charles's, one who had analyzed many of his specimens from the voyage, was there not as a supporter but as an enemy. He came armed. He was furious about *The Origin of Species* and hated Charles's theory of natural selection. He argued with Huxley and others about anatomy, claiming that the brains of apes and of people were vastly different. Part of Owen's reaction was due to professional jealousy and jockeying for position in the scientific world. He had been upstaged by the younger man. But he also truly disagreed with Charles's theory on both scientific and religious grounds.

The religious world also was represented at the conference,

most notably by the Bishop of Oxford, Samuel Wilberforce. He had written a critical review of *The Origin* in the *Quarterly Review*, using some arguments supplied to him by Owen. He claimed that Charles said that human beings had developed from oysters. It was with Wilberforce that Huxley had the biggest battle and the most fun.

Wilberforce addressed the crowd first. He was happy to have an audience so he could argue for the divine creation of human beings. At one point during his speech he turned to Huxley and asked him if he was related to an ape on his grandfather's side or on his grandmother's. Even though Charles had not written about human beings in his book, it was front and center, as he had feared. But Huxley was not scared. He believed Charles was right, and he loved a fight. He is reported to have whispered to the man next to him after Wilberforce's speech, "The Lord hath delivered him into mine hand."

The people in the audience waited; the atmosphere was tense and charged. What would Huxley say? The audience was made up not only of Charles's critics, but also of his friends—in addition to Huxley there were Hooker, Henslow, and Sir John Lubbock, the famous astronomer (and the Darwins' neighbor, who did not do barnacles). Huxley began with a well-reasoned argument about anatomical structure and how Charles had compiled his theory using such data as had never been used before. What everyone later remembered was not so much Huxley's long scientific argument but how he ended his speech. He concluded by saying he would rather have an ape for a grandfather than be descended from a man who introduced ridicule into a serious scientific discussion.

The audience cheered. And word went out that Darwin's champion, Huxley, would rather have an ape for a grandfather than a bishop. Also at the meeting was Robert FitzRoy, Charles's captain from the *Beagle*. He had brought his Bible with him and waved it around furiously, trying to get attention. He shouted that Charles was wrong; he shouted that he was sorry that he had given him the opportunity to collect the specimens that led to his theory. He begged all assembled to believe the Bible as God's holy word, as the truth about creation, not Charles Darwin. Not that many people heard FitzRoy over the crowd, but those who did found him pathetic and desperate. He was; he had financial problems, and mental ones as well. He killed himself five years later.

The meeting in Oxford did not do much to further serious discussion about science and religion. That subject stayed heated and contentious. Huxley was ready to continue the fight. But as Huxley and the others battled on, Charles stayed home at Down, working on a new edition of the book, with some revisions, and arranging for foreign publication as well. For the second edition, Charles made one significant change in reaction to some of the criticism. He put God back in—in the last sentence of the book.

In the first edition, Charles had ended the book: "There is grandeur in this view of life, with its several powers, having been originally breathed into a few forms or into one." In the second edition, he added three new words, "by the Creator." The last sentence now read, "There is grandeur in this view of life, with its several powers, having been originally breathed by the Creator into a few forms or into one."

He later said he regretted it. But he never took God back out.

Chapter 28

Feeling, Not Reasoning

I wish you knew how I value you; and what an inexpressible blessing it is to have one whom one can always trust, one always the same, always ready to give comfort, sympathy and the best advice. God bless you, my dear, you are too good for me.
—CHARLES TO EMMA, 1859

Every day the postman brought bundles of letters to Down House—letters in reaction to the book. There were five hundred a year, every year, after *The Origin of Species* was published. Charles answered all of them—even the ones from quacks. He had lifelong correspondents, he had fans, he had critics, he had people who wrote asking to meet him, to give him gifts, to take his photograph. He took each letter seriously and gave it the time he felt it needed. During his lifetime he had two thousand correspondents. He wrote at least seven thousand letters and received as many.

But whenever he could, he did experiments, just as he had when he was in high school. Only now they weren't chemical explosions; they were studies of plants, mostly orchids and a

flower called *Drosera*. *Drosera*, also called sundew, fascinated
Charles for its carnivorous eating habits. He was so
enthralled, he wanted to write a poem about it. Sadly for history, he didn't. Charles was always one to anthropomorphize
creatures, seeds, rocks even, and could be overheard talking
to them as if they understood.

Emma wrote to Charles Lyell's wife (the former Mary
Horner, now Lady Lyell) that Charles was given to anxiety but
that "his various experiments this summer have been a great
blessing to him . . . at present he is treating *Drosera* just like a
living creature, and I suppose he hopes to end in proving it to
be an animal."

He was also obsessed with orchids and was working on a
book about them. He studied orchids because they were so
beautiful and people used them as an argument for God's
hand in nature. Why would something be so beautiful for no
apparent reason? they argued. But Charles felt if he could see
the evidence for the evolution of orchids by his process of
natural selection, then that would be a good argument against
God as the designer of every single species. Most importantly,
it would be another example to illustrate his theory. The book
was eventually published in 1862 with the title *On the Various
Contrivances by which British and Foreign Orchids Are Fertilized by
Insects, and on the Good Effects of Intercrossing*.

Charles's American friend Asa Gray was one of those people
who wanted to see God's hand in the design of flowers, but he
also thought that Charles's argument for natural selection was
right. Gray wanted both to be true—a God-directed evolution.
Because Charles valued Gray's friendship and needed his help
in promoting natural selection, he did not rule out the possibility. He also could not seem to rule out the possibility for
himself. Over the course of many letters back and forth across

the ocean, the two friends discussed God and design. Charles argued that "there seems too much misery in the world." He could not persuade himself that a "beneficent & omnipotent God" would have created parasites and would have cats play with and torture mice. He listened to Gray, and also to Lyell, and was, as always, aware of Emma's feelings. In the end, he could not believe that the world was all God's design. And yet he did not think everything happened by chance. He wrote to Gray, "I am conscious that I am in an utterly hopeless muddle. I cannot think that the world, as we see it, is the result of chance; & yet I cannot look at each separate thing as the result of Design."

Although Charles discussed religion and science with Gray and other close friends, he demurred when strangers wrote to him asking what he believed about God. He said that theologians should answer questions about religion, scientists about science.

In 1861, illness was still a big part of life at Down. Etty kept getting sick; she was, at seventeen, an invalid, very weak and at times close to death. An infection—probably typhoid fever—had left her so debilitated the year before that she had needed twenty-four-hour nursing care for months. The youngest Darwin, Horace, was ten, Annie's age when she died, bringing back bad memories, along with fear and anxiety for Charles. Horace was a sickly child, and around this time he started having shaking and crying fits. It seemed to be his stomach—another Darwin with Charles's bad digestion. Or perhaps it was love; every time he had a fit, he was comforted and held by the children's new, pretty governess. When she was sent away for a time, Horace got much better.

But scarlet fever epidemics still raged, and with seven children, there was always something to worry about. Charles was especially concerned about Etty, but he also worried about Lenny, who, funny as he was, seemed backward in his lessons. And when George, the scholar, came home for some dental work on his horribly rotting teeth, Charles watched him lose consciousness from the chloroform. It looked so much like death that Charles got sick to his stomach.

Yet Emma, even with most of her time spent taking care of Charles and nursing whatever child was sick, even with the bouts of sadness and anxiety that she had since Annie's death, maintained an equanimity and serenity in the midst of it all. As one of her great-aunts had written about her when she was a little girl, she possessed "so much affection in her nature as will secure her from selfishness." In March 1861, with her house and hands already full of needy people, in the busy aftermath of the publication of *The Origin*, Emma had a heart big enough to take on even more duties, and more sorrow. At Charles's suggestion, she encouraged Thomas Henry Huxley's wife, Henrietta, and their three small children to come to Down for two weeks to rest. The Huxleys had just lost their oldest child, a little boy, Noel, at age four. Mrs. Huxley was devastated, and as she told it later, even though they barely knew each other, Emma "begged me to come to her and bring the three children and nurse, and I should have the old nurseries at Down."

Henrietta Huxley wrote back that she was too weak. She was so ill and depressed she could not even get downstairs until one o'clock. Emma replied that "that was the usual state of the family at Down," and they should come because they would fit in perfectly well.

Mrs. Huxley and the children arrived on March 9, which Emma noted in her diary along with "good day," for Etty. They did stay for two weeks, in the old nursery, where they had a view of the beautiful mulberry tree growing outside the window. Mr. Huxley stopped in a few times while they were there, to take breaks from his bulldogging and to get more direction and advice from Charles.

The visit did Mrs. Huxley good. Emma, of course, knew just how the bereaved mother was feeling. She made her feel at home and at ease. Emma always made sure Down House was a tranquil place; she was said to keep the peace among the servants with a sledgehammer if necessary. Years later Mrs. Huxley wrote to Etty, "Towards your mother I always had a sort of nestling feeling. More than any woman I ever knew, she comforted."

But Charles was not doing well. He spent many days in a row vomiting hour after hour. His nights were sleepless and filled with anxiety, giddiness, heart palpitations, and agony, even with Emma by his side. His old friend and Cambridge professor John Stevens Henslow was dying and he could not bring himself to go to Henslow's deathbed. They had remained close, even though they had not always seen eye to eye. Henslow did not accept natural selection. He just could not see creation without God. Charles was disappointed and upset that his mentor could not see the merits of his theory. He often said that Henslow was the man who made him what he was. He would miss him.

Emma knew that it took work to keep things calm and tranquil, both outside and inside. Although she was serene by nature, life had dealt her enough blows and she had suffered enough tragedy that sometimes she had to work to stave off the anxiety she felt. She worried about Charles's and the children's illnesses. She never knew when another one of her loved ones would die. And she was still concerned about Charles's lack of faith. She was able to relieve her anxiety—or at least bear it—through prayer.

Knowing how much her husband was suffering both physically and emotionally, she recommended to Charles— with hesitation, but also strong feeling—what worked for her. In the spring of 1861 she sat down and wrote him another letter about faith. She told him that, even if she didn't always say so, she knew how sick he felt and that she was grateful for "the cheerful and affectionate looks you have given me when I know you have been miserably uncomfortable." She confessed, "My heart has often been too full to speak."

She assured him that she minded his sufferings almost as much as her own and that the only way she could get through either was "to take it as from God's hand, and to try to believe that all suffering and illness is meant to help us to exalt our minds and look forward with hope to a future state." Ten years after losing her Annie, Emma still held on to the promise of an afterlife. There were so many people she had lost: Annie and the two babies, her dear sister Fanny, her parents. She hoped to see them all in heaven. But what about Charles? She could not bear to think that they would not be together always.

Once again, she reassured Charles—and herself—that he was a good man, a moral man, and should get into heaven. But she still felt that it would only happen, that they would only be able to love each other into eternity, if he were to offer his prayers to God. Quoting from Isaiah, she continued, "I often think of the words, 'Thou shalt keep him in perfect peace whose mind is stayed on thee.'"

And to the scientist she knew so well, she once again implored him to stop thinking of faith the same way he thought about science: "It is feeling and not reasoning that drives one to prayer."

After more than twenty years she still felt sad about the

differences in their religious belief, and yet she also felt as though she should not, really, be telling him what to do. She felt "presumptuous in writing this to you." But she could not help it—their eternal life together, as well as his current happiness—depended on it.

Emma held on to this letter until she felt less upset and resolved to give it to him when "I feel cheerful and comfortable again about you." She knew she wrote it partly to help him and partly "to relieve my own mind."

When she did give him the letter, Charles read it. There was so much to say, but also nothing to say. He would not pray, he would not accept the Revelation. Although Charles knew what pain it gave Emma to believe he would burn in hell, he couldn't lie to her. He knew later, after he was gone—for certainly he would go first—she would see this letter. Like the others she had written him, he kept it always.

He wrote on it, simply:

God bless you. C.D.
June, 1861.

Chapter 29

Such a Noise

I remember when in Good Success Bay, in Tierra del Fuego,
thinking . . . that I could not employ my life better than in adding
a little to natural science. This I have done to the best
of my abilities, and critics may say what they like,
but they cannot destroy this conviction.
—CHARLES, IN HIS *AUTOBIOGRAPHY*

One day Charles walked into the drawing room and found
Lenny sitting on the sofa—not jumping on it—and reading a
copy of *The Origin of Species*. It was the first time Lenny was
home from boarding school. He was about thirteen. Being
out in the world by himself, he had discovered that everyone
was talking about his father's book—even boys his own age.
When Charles saw Lenny reading it, he said, "I bet you half a
crown that you do not get to the end of that book." Charles
was right; but Lenny never paid up.

George, about five years older and a better student, was
reading his father's book on orchids and had convinced the

headmaster at school to read part of it with him and do some of the experiments at school.

Soon Horace, the youngest boy, would go to school, too, and then it would be just the two girls at home. The girls did not go to school, but learned at home and, according to Etty, had a spotty education. But that was how it was done in many upper-class Victorian families: the boys went to school, and the girls stayed home. Charles and Emma remained involved and loving parents—to the boys in person on school holidays and through the mail the rest of the year. "Your last letter was not interesting, but very well spelt, which I care more about," Emma wrote to Lenny. She tried gallantly to produce a generation of Darwins who could spell, unlike their famous father.

With more time on her hands now that the children needed her less, Emma found a passion that brought her into touch with the world outside of Down. She waged a campaign to invent a more humane trap for game-hunting. She wrote a letter titled "An Appeal," in which she said:

> An English gentleman would not himself give a moment's unnecessary pain to any living creature, and would instinctively exert himself to put an end to any suffering before his eyes; yet it is a fact that every game preserver in this country sanctions a system which consigns thousands of animals to acute agony, probably of eight or ten hours duration, before it is ended by death. I allude to the setting of steel traps for catching vermin.

Emma got the Society for the Prevention of Cruelty to Animals involved, and they had a contest to see who could invent the most humane but effective trap. Although no trap was good enough to win, the cause became known.

Emma also took up gardening more than she had before; it

was something she and Charles shared, a love for flowers. Although Charles continued to direct the battle for evolution behind the scenes and work on new books for his publisher, what gave him the most pleasure was doing experiments with his orchids and other plants. He wanted to see how they grew, how they moved toward the light, and how they crossed to produce new plants. He put nets on Emma's azaleas to see if it would change the way they grew. Emma didn't mind his experiments with her flowers or his forages into her sewing box for threads to use in his experiments. She didn't mind that he had seedlings in little pots all over the place, but Charles decided it was silly for him to keep going to his neighbor's greenhouse—where he had his bigger plants—so he built his own in the backyard. It was finished in 1863.

Only once did gardening come between them. Both Charles and Emma loved the Sandwalk; they walked on it together day after day, year after year. When they had first moved in, Emma had planted bluebells and anemones, primroses, cowslips, and wild ivy, which she especially loved. But as will happen in gardens, other plants grew there—dog's mercury and Jack-in-the-hedge—and they tended to overtake the plants Emma loved. A good example of survival of the fittest! So occasionally she hired someone to pull up the dog's mercury and the Jack-in-the-hedge so that her favorites could flourish. Once she hired a young boy to pull up those plants and he pulled up the ivy by mistake. Emma was distraught; she loved that ivy. Much to her chagrin, Charles laughed at how upset she was, which made Emma furious. He claimed it was the only time she was ever cross with him.

While his theory was being challenged and extolled, Charles's health continued to plague him. Once it got so bad that he vomited for twelve days in a row. Emma insisted that Charles have another water cure and that they should also give Horace some treatment, for he was still sickly. In September 1863, they headed for Malvern, staying with Erasmus in London on the way. Erasmus thought Charles seemed sicker than he had in a long time; they all hoped the water cure would help both him and Horace. But going back to the place where Annie had died was too much for Charles in his weakened physical and emotional state. Once there, he became so feeble and frail that he could barely leave the villa they had rented. Etty later wrote that during this time Charles seemed to have lost his memory and may even have had an epileptic seizure.

One day during their stay in Malvern, Emma went to the churchyard to find Annie's grave. She had never seen it; neither had Charles. Emma walked and walked through the cemetery, searching for her daughter's tombstone, but she could not find it. When she went back and told Charles of her failure, he sent a letter to his cousin Fox, who had visited Malvern before and had written to Charles describing the grave. Charles wrote, "Will you tell us what you can remember about the kind of stone & where it stood; I think you said there was a little tree planted . . ."

Before they got his answer, Emma went out again, and this time she did find the stone. Annie would have been twenty-two had she lived, but to them she was still ten years old, still the dear and good child she had always been.

While they were at Malvern, they got word that the Hookers' six-year-old daughter had died. Like Charles, Hooker had no hope that he would see his "flower of my flock" again in heaven. But Charles wrote to him and reassured him that in time he would remember her with much less pain, as he did Annie. "My dear old Friend," Charles wrote, "your note is most pathetic I understand well your words: 'wherever I go, she is there'.—I am so deeply glad that she did not suffer so much, as I feared was inevitable. This was to us with poor Annie the one great comfort.—Trust to me that time will do wonders, & without causing forgetfulness of your darling."

Two years later, in 1865, still suffering, Charles tried an ice cure, which also did not help. But although he felt sick most days for much of the day and often slept terribly at night, he kept writing and publishing books and articles, on orchids and climbing plants. He was also revising *The Origin* for more editions, adding details from new research and correcting errors. He was very productive, even with his illness. "I am surprised at my industry," he said. And he continued to love his work.

In 1867, he sent out questionnaires about facial expression and body motions to people in different parts of the world. He had been interested in emotions and expressions in people and in animals since his first notebook jottings, through the observations of animals and his own children. He wanted to widen his research to people outside his family and to people of different races and nationalities so that he could make a more definite study and eventually publish a book about his findings. He asked seventeen questions, including: "Is astonishment expressed by the eyes and mouth being opened wide, and by the eyebrows being raised?" and "Does shame excite a blush when the colour of the skin allows it to be visible? and especially how low down the body does the blush extend?" and "Is contempt expressed by a slight protrusion of the lips and by turning up the nose, with a slight expiration?" and "Do the children when sulky, pout or greatly protrude the lips?" and "Can guilty, or sly, or jealous expressions be recognized? though I know not how these can be defined."

Charles's long-range goal was to write the huge book he had intended from the beginning, including all the material and evidence he had amassed and would continue to amass about evolution by natural selection. But his publisher did not think one huge book would sell well and encouraged him to publish smaller books about more specific topics, which is what he did. All his later books can be said to be continuations of *The Origin of Species*.

Because of Charles's fame, the biggest change at Down was that there were more and more visitors who made pilgrimages to meet him. Fans came from all over, including foreign countries. Sometimes they stayed to lunch. Emma wrote to one of her sons in later years, "We have been rather overdone with Germans this week." But both Charles and Emma liked having visitors; Emma still ran to the front door when she heard someone coming up the drive. Charles attached a mirror to the outside of the house so that when he was in his study he could see who was coming up the walk—visitors and the all-important postman.

Even with the hubbub, Charles's routine stayed the same: He would rise early in the morning and go for a walk before breakfast. From about eight o'clock, he would work in his study for an hour and a half, when he would take a break to listen to Emma read letters or a novel. Sometimes, though, Charles would just wear himself out with work. He would say, in the middle of writing a sentence, "I am afraid I must leave off now." And it would be time for a rest.

Lunch was the main meal of the day and was served at about one. After that, Charles read the newspaper, wrote letters, or read until three. Then he'd rest, and sometimes Emma would read to him. He'd work again from about four thirty to five thirty, when he would take another rest. Then he and Emma would have a simple tea at seven thirty, followed by a couple of games of backgammon, or Emma would play the piano or read to him, as they had begun to do their first week of married life on Gower Street.

Charles took two or three walks around the Sandwalk every day with Emma and one of the dogs. They had a Newfoundland called Bob, who loved to go on walks with Charles. The routine changed slightly after Charles built the greenhouse. Now before his walks he often stopped into the hothouse to take a look at his plants. This dismayed Bob, who would put on his "hot-house face of despair" as Charles called it. Bob hated for their walk to be delayed.

Charles loved dogs—and when his grown children started calling him and Emma Father and Mother instead of Papa and Mama, he declared, "I would as soon be called Dog." Dog was better than Father, anyhow, but Papa was best of all.

Charles's motto was "It's dogged as does it," and while it may not have been a reflection of his love of dogs, it was a reflection of his work ethic. He never stopped working, even when he was ill. In 1871, when Horace was twenty, Charles finally finished his book on the origin of the human species, *The Descent of Man*. It was not until he wrote this book that he used the word *evolution* to describe how species change. The book met with mixed reviews—some people were, of course, angry at the argument that humans and animals have a common ancestor. Religious people were upset that Charles rejected the idea of God as creator. But the response was not loud; most people criticized the ideas, not the author. And the book sold very well.

That same year, Etty got married. She was the first Darwin child to do so. Both Charles and Emma had become very close to Etty over the years—Charles even depended on her to read his drafts. Though she would continue to do so, Charles would miss her presence very much. In later years he would rest on the sofa in the drawing room and look at some old china and pictures that Etty had arranged. He called it Henrietta's shrine. Charles and Emma took her marriage hard and felt they did not know the man, Richard Litchfield, well enough. But other people vouched for him, including Erasmus, whose opinion they always valued. And apparently Litchfield was happy to have Etty as his wife, even though, like Charles, she did not conceal her religious doubts. She told him that she did not believe in a personal God. She did have more faith than Charles, however; she was, after all, a child of Emma's, too.

When Etty was away on her honeymoon, Charles wrote to her, "From your earliest years you have given me so much pleasure and happiness that you well deserve all the happiness that is possible in return; and I do believe that you are in the right way for obtaining it." He told her he would miss her sadly, but "I have had my day and a happy life, notwithstanding my stomach; and this I owe almost entirely to our dear old mother, who, as you know well, is as good as twice refined gold." He advised her to use Emma as an example, and then her husband would not only love her but would worship her "as I worship our dear old mother."

Emma missed Etty terribly and wrote to her constantly. She gave her all kinds of news and gossip, and reported on the goings-on at Down, including those that involved Etty's dog, Polly, a rough-haired fox terrier, whom she left there. Polly adopted Charles.

"I think she has taken it into her head that F. [Father] is a very big puppy," Emma told Etty. "She is perfectly devoted to him . . . will only stay with him and leaves the room whenever he does. She lies upon him whenever she can, and licks his hands so constantly as to be quite troublesome. I have to drag her away at night, and she yelps and squeaks some time."

Polly was known to be a cunning dog and could get Charles to give her what she wanted. When it was nearing dinnertime, if Charles passed by, she would tremble with misery. Even though he knew her character, he would declare her to be "famishing" and in need of food, quickly. He used to make her catch biscuits off her nose, and told her to "be a very good girl."

In 1872, Charles published his book *The Expression of the Emotions in Man and Animals*, in which he was able to use all those notes he made about the children growing up. He wrote about his babies, his experiments on them, and on his screaming sons. He also wrote about his dogs, and made Bob famous for his hothouse face of despair. By now, he was not afraid to admit that he thought Jenny the orangutan was cousin to us all.

The outside world loved and reviled Charles Darwin. He received honors and lavish reviews; he received angry reviews and nasty letters. People made portraits and statues of him; they drew disrespectful, mocking cartoons about him. "My views have often been grossly misrepresented," he wrote later, "bitterly opposed and ridiculed, but this has been generally done, as I believe, in good faith." He also said, "On the whole I do not doubt that my works have been over and over again greatly over praised."

He withstood it all, with his friends out in the world fighting for him and with Emma by his side at home, as she had been since they made their leap.

Emma was bemused and also proud. In 1873, she wrote to an aunt, "I sometimes feel it very odd that anyone belonging to me should be making such a noise in the world."

Chapter 30

Mere Trickery

I have been speculating last night what makes a man
a discoverer of undiscovered things. . . . As far as I can conjecture
the art consists in habitually searching for the causes and
meaning of everything which occurs.
—CHARLES TO HIS SON HORACE, 1871

Over the years of their marriage, Emma and Charles each became more like the other in their beliefs—or at least their differences seemed less important. While Emma never stopped believing in God and Jesus, her faith seems to have become less intense. Always an open-minded person, she became more tolerant of Charles's views, and she seemed to be less concerned about his lack of faith. Etty later wrote that she thought Emma was sad to have lost the convictions she had had. Etty said, "She kept a sorrowful wish to believe more, and I know it was an abiding sadness to her that her faith was less vivid than it had been in her youth." But it could also have been that she was just content to be quiet about her beliefs and not impose them on others, including Charles.

For his part, Charles admitted that Emma had been right when she said that his looking at the world in a scientific way probably precluded him from looking at it in a religious way. Perhaps to do the great science he did, he had to focus entirely that way—to let religion in would have diluted his effort. That did not mean he would deny Emma—or anyone—their beliefs. But for him, science was the way to get answers.

Perhaps in reaction to doubts about traditional religion, various kinds of spirituality had become popular in England, even among some of Charles and Emma's intellectual friends and family, including Hensleigh Wedgwood. Emma's smart and widely read brother attended séances, communed with spirit guides, and collected photographs that seemed to show ghosts and spirits. Both Emma and Charles were upset by Hensleigh's obsession. He wanted to talk about little else, and he urged Charles and Emma, and even Thomas Henry Huxley, to get involved. Hensleigh sent Huxley a photograph he thought showed a ghost. When Huxley told him that the photographer had superimposed an image on the plate, and it could not be real, Hensleigh did not believe him. Hensleigh was not the only one in their circle captivated by spirits and ghosts. All over London, séances were being held in parlors and living rooms and at dining tables. Even Alfred Russel Wallace, the naturalist who had also come up with the theory of natural selection, was a spiritualist, now working on a book that would be published soon—*Miracles and Modern Spiritualism*.

It was only a matter of time before the Darwins would find themselves in one of those darkened rooms. It was intriguing even for the skeptical.

In January 1874, Emma and Charles headed to London. Emma was sixty-five, Charles was about to turn sixty-five. Charles now had a long white beard, which he had started growing in 1863 because eczema made it uncomfortable for him to shave. He was thinner than ever, and frail. He looked like the wise old sage he was now considered to be. For even with the controversy—and there was still some—evolution had become more or less accepted as fact.

It was, in all ways but one, a typical trip to London. They were going to visit Erasmus. They would see their grown children who lived in London. Charles would see his publisher and also some doctors. But Charles and Emma also were going to attend a séance—in Erasmus's house. Eras, like many people who held séances, was a skeptic, but intrigued. If they held the séance in his house, he could try to make sure there was nothing done beforehand to fake the results.

One cold winter afternoon, Erasmus gathered some friends and family around his dining room table. It was a close and cozy crowd. Etty was there with her husband, Richard, as was Hensleigh, of course, with his wife, Fanny, and their daughter Snow. Emma was thrilled by the presence of one of the guests—the novelist known as George Eliot, author of one of Emma's favorite books, *Middlemarch*. Her real name was Mary Ann Evans, and she had come with her longtime companion, George Lewes, who wrote about natural history and was an advocate of Darwinism. Emma and Charles's son George came; he had hired the medium, a Mr. Williams. Charles wanted Huxley to come, and he may have been there—but anonymously. Huxley was evolution's public champion, still fighting for Darwinism. He coined the term *agnostic* to mean one who believes you cannot know whether God exists because you cannot prove God's existence. He did not want to be recognized by a medium who could claim later that Huxley believed in conjuring up the dead. Huxley, if he *was* there, showed up for the fun of it, as did most of the attendants.

They darkened the room, closing the curtains and shutting the doors. The group sat down around the table. George and Hensleigh sat next to Mr. Williams on either side, holding down his hands and feet so he couldn't make anything happen. No one wanted this to be an ordinary séance, meaning one that was contrived by the medium. It was more of a test. The rest of the group joined hands and they all sat quietly—or tried to. Lewes could not help making jokes. Etty found him troublesome; they were supposed to "play the game fairly."

Etty later wrote that "The usual manifestations occurred, sparks, wind-blowing, and some rappings and movings of furniture."

Charles Darwin was not in the room to see what happened. He had gone upstairs to lie down, as he reported later, "before all these astounding miracles, or jugglery, took place." He said he was too hot and tired to stay. Lewes later wrote that he and Mary Ann Evans left, too, in disgust, when the medium demanded that the room be totally dark.

When it was over, Charles came downstairs. Upon seeing all the chairs disarranged, he was mystified. He knew that what had happened—Emma reported that the chairs had been lifted up high over their heads—was a result of trickery, not spirits from the other world. But "how the man could possibly do what was done passes my understanding," Charles said. He did not doubt that it was all a hoax. He declared, "The Lord have mercy on us all, if we have to believe in such rubbish." He thought it was too bad that people spent so much time and energy investigating the supernatural when there was so much to figure out about reality.

Yet, after this séance, Thomas Henry Huxley definitely did go to another séance, and reported about it to Charles. Huxley used diagrams to explain how Williams must have produced various effects. Charles wrote back, "To my mind an enourmous weight of evidence would be requisite to make one believe in anything beyond mere trickery. . . ."

Not long afterward, Williams was proved to be a fraud. But that didn't mean to everyone that *all* spiritualism was false. Many people still believed.

Emma was not convinced one way or the other, though she remained cynical and thought it was almost certainly trickery. Still, according to Etty, Emma, as always, kept an open mind.

Chapter 31

Warmth to the End

*I cannot bear her notion that God took him away because
she was so deeply attached to him. Not that I think a person
cannot be selfish in their love; but it is not the strength
of the love that is the sin, but the selfishness.*
—EMMA, WRITING TO AN AUNT ABOUT A MEMOIR THEY BOTH READ

Charles and Emma played backgammon every night, and
they kept track of who won and who lost. They took it all
very seriously. When Charles wasn't winning, he would yell,
"Bang your bones!" He was quoting Jonathan Swift's *Journal
to Stella*.

In a letter to Professor Asa Gray on January 28, 1876, he wrote:

Pray give our very kind remembrances to Mrs. Gray. I know
that she likes to hear men boasting, it refreshes them so
much. Now the tally with my wife in backgammon stands
thus: she, poor creature, has won only 2490 games, whilst I
have won, hurrah, hurrah,

2795 games!

Charles could brag about winning more games, but Emma won more gammons, which meant that when she won, Charles still had all his pieces on the board. That doubled the number of points he lost. They played doggedly on, battling on the backgammon board.

In 1876, Emma and Charles looked forward to the birth of their first grandchild. Frank was married to a woman named Amy, whom they loved; they could not wait for the baby. In September, Bernard Darwin was born. But Emma and Charles's happiness was short-lived. Amy became ill, and with Frank and Charles by her side, died a few days later. Another life cut too short. Frank, of course, was devastated. Charles told a friend that his son walked around bewildered and dazed. Looking at Frank's suffering, Charles knew for sure that he did not want to outlive Emma. He couldn't take it.

Emma was distraught as well, and, unusual for her, had become so undone that it was Charles who took over and gave all of them the emotional support they needed. But she soon rallied, and it was decided that Frank, who was working as Charles's secretary, would live at Down with Bernard.

Emma took charge of the nursery, and Bernard became, in a very real way, Emma's last baby. She devoted herself to him and his care as if she were a young woman. Although Amy's death had filled Emma with anxiety, Bernard was a happy, easy, and healthy baby, which eased Emma's anxiety quite a bit. Both of his grandparents doted on him. "Your father is taking a good deal to the Baby," Emma wrote to Etty. "We think he (the Baby) is a sort of Grand Lama, he is so solemn."

Frank helped his father with a collection of letters that he wanted to publish, and with an autobiography that Charles was preparing for his children and grandchildren. Frank had also become fascinated by plants. At Down, he and Charles worked together studying the movement of plants in relation to light and gravity. They also looked at the evolution of plants.

And Charles had a new obsession. He had had so many in his life—beetles, barnacles, orchids, and now worms. Years ago, Uncle Josiah had suggested to Charles that worms moved the dirt around; it looked as though that movement made rocks sink into the ground. Charles now had time to test out the theory. He put chalk and small pieces of wood on the ground and noted how deeply rocks sank over time. In his twenties now, Horace made a mechanical instrument that helped his father study how far a stone moved vertically. He carried out many of the experiments and observations.

Charles decided to study worms more closely—their behavior and how their movements affected the ground. Once again, he thought that tiny actions brought about cumulative effects and great change. Most of his studies he conducted at home, but he looked at worms wherever he went. In June 1877, he and Emma, along with Frank, Bernard, and the baby's nursemaid, made a pilgrimage to the great prehistoric monument Stonehenge. Emma wrote to Etty before they left that she was afraid it would "half kill" Charles. She wrote to Etty almost every day now.

It would be a two-hour train ride and a twenty-four-mile drive in a coach. Emma was eager to see the stone monuments and the Cathedral Church at nearby Salisbury. But Charles was "bent on going, chiefly for the worms." He liked to look at the action of worms in different types of soil. When they arrived at Stonehenge, the guard allowed him to dig as much as he wanted. Charles is probably the only tourist (adult, anyway) ever to pay more attention to the ground at Stonehenge than to the huge stone monoliths.

Back at Down, Charles involved the whole family in his worm obsession. One day, he decided to see if he could figure out what worms hear. They gathered in the drawing room around the piano. Emma played the piano, Frank the bassoon, and Elizabeth, who was unmarried and also lived at home, shouted. Even little Bernard joined in on the metal whistle. The worms did not react to the noise at all. But when he placed the worms on Emma's piano—in flower pots—then the worms responded to the vibrations they felt. If Emma struck a single note, high or low, the worms retreated into the soil.

Charles kept to his routine as much as possible, with Frank by his side. The routine was the same as when Frank had been a child, though now his father walked stooped over when he took his turns around the Sandwalk.

Frank and Charles worked hard together on the collection of letters, which would focus mostly on the scientific ones, especially his correspondence with his closest associates: Hooker, Henslow, Huxley, Gray, and his dear friend Charles Lyell, who had died in 1875 and been buried in Westminster Abbey.

Frank relished the time with his father. He later said, "How often, when a man, I have wished my father was behind my chair, that he would pass his hand over my hair, as he used to do when I was a boy. He allowed his grown-up children to laugh with and at him, and was, generally speaking, on terms of perfect equality with us."

As the children grew up, they all remained close to Emma and Charles and with each other. It is often the case that with a great father the sons feel they cannot fill his shoes; the Darwin boys did not try. There were no hard feelings in the Darwin family. Charles and Emma had always loved their children for who they were. And they were proud parents. In a letter to George, Charles wrote, "Oh Lord, what a set of sons I have, all doing wonders."

Charles and Emma rarely parted from each other. He hated to be away from her for even one night. She was his "constant companion (& friend in old age)" as he had hoped his wife would be. In 1877 when he was awarded an honorary degree at his old university, Cambridge, Emma went with him and wrote to William how proud she was. "I felt very grand walking about with my LL.D. in his silk gown."

And together they had gone on the journey of faith. In a letter in 1879, Charles wrote what he now believed about science and faith and how he had gotten there. He said that it was absurd to doubt that a man could be a theist and an evolutionist, as someone had said. Charles pointed to his friend Asa Gray, who was both. As for his own views, he said they were of "no consequence to any one except myself." Knowing, certainly, that his views were indeed important to other people, he answered the question—in part. He said, "My judgment often fluctuates. Moreover whether a man deserves to be called a theist depends on the definition of the term: which is much too large a subject for a note."

In his autobiography, which he intended just for his family, he wrote that although he was "very unwilling to give up my belief . . . disbelief crept over me at a very slow rate, but was at last complete." But in the 1879 letter, which was to a member of the public, he wrote that even at his most "extreme fluctuations," he was never an atheist "in the sense of denying the existence of a God.—I think that generally (& more and more so as I grow older) but not always, that an agnostic would be the most correct description of my state of mind." Whether he wrote that because he knew the letter would likely become public and that is how he wanted to be known, or whether that was an accurate appraisal of his beliefs, we'll never be certain. But it does seem as though with age came acceptance of his own ignorance. As Emma had told him, he could not prove or disprove the existence of God. Religion was not a science.

Happily for Charles—and perhaps not coincidentally— with age also came better health. His symptoms were much less severe, and he spent much less time in pain. Since he was old and had lived such a sickly life, he didn't do more than he used to. Yet he had always been extremely busy and productive, even when he was ill. To his gardener it looked like he wasn't doing much at all when he walked about the grounds observing the flowers. Asked about his master's health, the gardener said, "He moons about in the garden, and I have seen him standing doing nothing before a flower for ten minutes at a time. If he only had something to do, I really believe he would be better." In fact he was, as usual, making scientific observations.

In the cold January of 1880, Charles's children, concerned that he never dressed warmly enough, gave him a fur coat. He was delighted at the thought but told Emma privately that he doubted he would ever need to wear such a thing. He wrote to the children, "The coat . . . will never warm my body so much as your dear affection has warmed my heart." Though he did add, "I should not be myself if I did not protest that you have all been shamefully extravagant to spend so much money over your old father." But he put on the coat almost immediately and wore it so constantly, as Emma told Lenny, that he was "afraid it will soon be worn out."

That summer Emma became obsessed with the worms, too. Charles had taken to attempting to train them, but Emma told Lenny he "does not make much progress, as they can neither see nor hear." So they could not respond to cues they were given. Still she spent hours with Charles in the garden, watching the worms. She wrote, "They are, however, amusing and spend hours in seizing hold of the edge of a cabbage leaf and trying in vain to pull it into their holes."

In 1881, Erasmus Darwin died and was buried at Down. When Horace's first child was born in December, he named him Erasmus. They had all loved their uncle. As William said, "To me there was a charm in his manner that I never saw in anybody else."

That year Charles also published *The Formation of Vegetable Mould Through the Action of Worms, with Observations on Their Habits*. In the conclusion, he wrote, "Worms have played a more important part in the history of the world than most persons would at first suppose." And more people were interested in worms than Charles would have thought. This book sold better than any of his others!

In early 1882, Charles suffered several heart attacks. Though not fatal, they left him weak and unable to walk without pain in his chest.

In March he was so sick that it was an occasion on the days he got up to look out the window. But then, when spring came and it got warmer—"exquisite weather," Emma wrote—Charles was able to get outside. He had lost his lifelong pleasure of walking, but he spent many happy hours sitting in the orchard with Emma. They both knew that the end was probably near as they sat and listened to the birds sing in the spring sunshine and admired the crocuses opening up.

In many ways, both Charles and Emma had been preparing for his death since they were first married. He had been so sickly, and it was really only in his last years of life that his health was fairly normal. Emma nursed him one last time and recorded his symptoms in her diary. And as she sat by his bed, he told her what he needed her and the family to know. "Tell all my children to remember how good they have been to me," he whispered to her.

Like Annie, Charles was always polite and grateful when he was sick. "I was so sorry for you, but I could not help you, " he told Emma, thanking her for all her years of taking care of him. And, as he often had told her over the course of their lives together, "It's almost worthwhile to be sick to be nursed by you."

On Monday, April 17, Emma wrote in her little diary that Charles did some work and went into the orchard with her twice. On Tuesday, she wrote "ditto"—another day of work and sitting in the orchard. But then, at midnight, he had a "fatal attack."

The next morning, Charles reassured Emma, "I am not the least afraid of death."

As he slipped slowly away into unconsciousness, he told her what he had said many times before, what she already knew, but what he had to say again: "Remember what a good wife you have been to me."

Emma held Charles to her one last time.

Chapter 32

Happy Is the Man

His body is buried in peace, but his name liveth evermore.
—FROM GEORGE FRIDERIC HANDEL'S FUNERAL ANTHEM,
SUNG AS THE COFFIN OF CHARLES DARWIN
WAS LOWERED INTO THE GRAVE

On Wednesday, April 19, 1882, Emma wrote in her diary, "3½." Charles had died at three thirty, with Emma holding him. Etty, Elizabeth, and Frank were also by his side. Charles was seventy-three.

That afternoon, Emma went down to the drawing room for tea as usual. Etty and the others watched in wonder as she let herself be amused. She smiled a little, and once almost even laughed. It was so like Emma to bear her grief alone, to hold it inside and be strong for the others, who were crying inconsolably. Charles's absence would hit Emma again and again over the years, painfully, but for now she had a family to take care of and a funeral to consider.

Emma wanted Charles buried at the church graveyard

at Down. He had wanted to be buried at Down, too, in the village where he had spent most of his life. That was where the two babies lay; that was where Charles had buried his brother Erasmus the year before. Down was near Emma; it was home.

The next day, as the rest of the family began to arrive, Polly, the dog who had been so attached to Charles, suddenly grew deathly ill. Frank had to put her down. In her diary, Emma wrote "Polly died" and "all the sons arrived."

They buried Polly under a Kentish Beauty apple tree.

The undertaker came to Down House and laid Charles out in the coffin on his wheeled cart. The plan was still to bury him in the church graveyard near his babies and his brother. But when Frank informed Huxley, Hooker, Lubbock, and other friends of his father's death, they felt strongly that Charles should be given a hero's burial. A quick campaign began, and within a day or two, twenty members of Parliament signed an edict that Charles should be buried in Westminster Abbey. He would be laid to rest in the nave, next to Sir John Herschel, the astronomer, whose quote calling the origin of species the "mystery of mysteries" Charles had used in the introduction to his *Origin of Species*. He would also be near the great Sir Isaac Newton. Emma, who finally agreed that Charles would have graciously accepted the offer, only wished he could be closer to his friend Charles Lyell, who was buried in the nave of the abbey, too.

The funeral was held on April 26. Emma and Charles had been married just over forty-three years. Emma did not go to London. She stayed at Down, at home, where she felt closer to Charles. She wanted to mourn alone. She told Etty she wanted now, and later, to live through her desolation by herself and be left to rebuild her life as well as she could without Charles. She wanted time, too, to think about her precious past with him.

The rest of the family went up to London, as did Parslow and a few other servants.

It was a stately affair, large and ceremonious. Charles's body had been moved from the country coffin to an elegant city casket draped in black velvet and sprinkled with white blossoms. Most of the important people of the day came to show their respects to the great man of science. And as he was buried in a church, a gulf—there, at least—was bridged. A special hymn was written for the occasion. It began with words from the Book of Proverbs: "Happy is the man that findeth wisdom, and getteth understanding."

William, as the eldest son, the one upon whom "the nation's eyes" rested, as the family always said afterward, lent the affair a casual, no-nonsense Darwin atmosphere. After he removed his hat, as one had to do in church in polite society, his bald head got cold. Not wanting to offend by putting his hat back on, but worried, of course, as any Darwin child would be, about getting sick, he balanced his black gloves on the top of his skull to keep it warm. He sat that way through the whole service.

Chapter 33

Unasked Questions

*I feel a sort of wonder that I can in a measure
enjoy the beauty of spring.*
—EMMA TO LEONARD, 1882

Emma spent that summer at Down, but she felt it would be too lonely to stay there without Charles in the winter. The house was large, and it would be too empty without the person on whom Emma fixed all her routines, as she said. In summer the children and grandchildren would come and help her fill up the empty space, the empty hours. But for the rest of the year, she needed a different place to live. So she bought a house in Cambridge, where two of her sons, George and Horace, already lived. Her new house, the Grove, gave her a place to rebuild her life without Charles, though she never went anywhere without her "precious packet"—the few letters she had saved that he had written to her over the years. She wished she had saved every scrap, every note he had written to her.

Frank and Bernard moved to Cambridge with her. And when Frank got engaged the following year, he built a house on Emma's property so that Bernard could see his grandmother every day, as ever.

George married an American, and they had a baby whom they named Gwen. Emma took much pleasure in this baby, as she did in all her grandchildren. She wrote to Etty when Gwen was three months old, "I am so pleased to find how comfortable I can make this baby. She is so placid and spends her time devoted to the gas; but answering any attention by a smile and gathering herself in a lump with both fists in her mouth."

But she missed Charles. Reading over his books and letters made her feel closer to him. Three years after he died, she sat down and read his *Voyage of the* Beagle again. There was Charles's voice, his hand reaching out to her, Come with me. She told Etty, "It gives me a sort of companionship with him which makes me feel happy—only there are so many questions I want to ask."

That year there was an unveiling of a statue of Charles in the Natural History Museum in London. Emma would have liked to be there, but she did not want to have to see people. "I should prefer avoiding all greetings and acquaintances." She went later to see the statue, and she liked the pose, though she did not think it looked enough like Charles. How could a stone image look to her like the man she had loved for so long?

Frank was working to publish his father's letters, as well as reminiscences he culled from the autobiography Charles had written. Emma read the letters, too, and found that "in almost every one there is some characteristic bit which charms one. A little mention of me in a letter . . . sent me to bed with a glow about my heart coming on it unexpectedly."

But Emma was worried about the publication of the autobiography. Charles had written it for his family, not for
strangers. And there were things Charles had written that she
felt would offend others, because they offended her. Not surprisingly, they were about religion. She asked Frank to take
out certain passages, writing to him, "There is one sentence in
the *Autobiography* which I very much wish to omit, no doubt
partly because your father's opinion that all morality has
grown up by evolution is painful to me; but also because
where this sentence comes in, it gives one a sort of shock. . . ."
The sentence Charles had written was "Nor must we over-
look the probability of the constant inculcation in a belief in
God on the minds of children producing so strong and perhaps inherited effect on their brains not yet fully developed,
that it would be as difficult for them to throw off their belief
in God, as for a monkey to throw off its instinctive fear and
hatred of a snake." Emma felt this sentence would give people
"an opening to say, however unjustly, that he considered all
spiritual beliefs no higher than hereditary aversions or lik-
ings, such as the fear of monkeys towards snakes."

Emma told Frank she thought it was fine to leave in the
first part of the sentence, but asked that he take out the last—
it was not good to equate religious feeling with the fear of
snakes. She added, "I should wish if possible to avoid giving
pain to your father's religious friends who are deeply attached
to him, and I picture to myself the way that sentence would
strike them." She named some friends, Charles's sister Caroline, and "even the old servants."

Emma asked Frank to omit other sentences as well, and he
complied. She did not exactly censor Charles's autobiography,
but she did clean it up as much as she could so that nothing
would be misunderstood, and nothing, she hoped, would give

offense. She was, as always, Charles's editor. But he wasn't there to argue his points.

She left in "I gradually came to disbelieve in Christianity as a divine revelation" but took out "Beautiful as is the morality of the New Testament, it can hardly be denied that its perfection depends in part on the interpretation which we now put on metaphors and allegories."

Most significantly, Emma expurgated this passage: "I can indeed hardly see how anyone ought to wish Christianity to be true; for if so the plain language of the text seems to show that the men who do not believe, and this would include my Father, Brother and almost all my best friends will be everlastingly punished. And this is a damnable doctrine."

Was this true? Were Erasmus and Dr. Darwin, and Charles himself, in hell? Would she see Charles again? These were questions that could not be answered.

Other than helping Frank, Emma spent the years of her life after Charles's death much as she had the years before she married him. She read constantly and offered, in letters to Etty mostly, her literary criticism. She read some of her favorite old books again. She spent much of her time reading, and in 1894 she wrote, "I am rather ashamed to find I use up rather more than a volume a day of novels." She read the Brontës and Robert Louis Stevenson. She read the novels of Jane Austen and Elizabeth Gaskell. One of Mrs. Gaskell's books, her last one, was left unfinished. In this book, *Wives and Daughters*, Roger Hamley, a wonderful, likeable hero, was modeled after Gaskell's friend Charles Darwin. Because Gaskell died in 1866 before finishing the book, Roger and his sweetheart, Molly, were not yet together. But the book points to a happy ending.

Emma continued to read books on religion as well, and on politics; she read the Psalms, but was not much impressed by

them, and as usual she called it as she saw it. She wrote in a letter to Etty, "I am reading the Psalms and I cannot conceive
how they have satisfied the devotional feelings of the world
for such centuries." She also did needlework, played patience
and whist, played the piano, and wrote many letters.

Emma enjoyed her grandchildren immensely, playing
with them and bribing them just as she had done with her
own children. They climbed into her bed as she ate breakfast;
Emma pulled licorice out of her sewing basket and gave them
treats. Her daughters-in-law loved her, too, and she returned
the feeling. "My dear daughter in heart," she called William's
wife.

One day in Cambridge she was playing with her grandchildren, watching them fly a kite. Afterward she had them
over for tea and a game of hide-and-seek. Little Erasmus, then
about three, said, "Grandmama, did your little children have
kites?" Emma wondered whether he realized who her little
children were.

She entertained visitors in Cambridge and in Down, often
old servants and the children of old servants. Etty said she
seemed very happy and less anxious in her later years. "Her
buoyant spirit and the essential reserve of her nature pre-
vented our knowing how much she dwelt on the past."

In his autobiography, Charles told his children that their
mother was his greatest blessing. "I marvel at my good fortune, that she, so infinitely my superior in every single moral
quality consented to be my wife. . . . She has been my wise
adviser and cheerful comforter. . . . She has earned the love
and admiration of every soul near her."

On September 27, 1896, Emma fell ill. She was eighty-eight
years old. Charles had been gone for fourteen years. She wrote

to Etty and said she was feeling fine; there was no need to come. But Etty hurried to take care of her mother just as her mother had taken care of her when she was sick.

Getting ready for bed on October 2, Emma wound up her watch as she always did before she went to sleep. Then she put her head back on her pillow and she died.

So Much to Worship

There is a grandeur in this view of life....
—CHARLES, IN *THE ORIGIN OF SPECIES*

I suppose one does admire one's own view absurdly.
—EMMA, 1889, LOOKING AT THE VALLEY FROM THE FIELD AT DOWN

Charles Darwin left an unparalleled legacy to science. He gave future generations of scientists "a theory by which to work." His theory will continue to evolve. The debate between evolution and religion continues, too. He and Emma would certainly say that people from both worlds should keep talking to each other.

Together Emma and Charles left a legacy in generations of Darwins. Frank, George, and Horace had children, and these three sons also continued in their father's footsteps: Frank was a botanist and edited his father's letters and published the *Autobiography*. He was knighted in 1913. George did grow up to find work he loved, as Aunt Jessie had hoped. He was an astronomer and mathematician and studied the evolution of the solar system. Horace made scientific instruments and was for a short time mayor of Cambridge.

As Charles had said, all the sons were doing wonders, though not all in science. William was a banker. Lenny became a soldier in the Royal Engineers, taught at the School of Military Engineering, and served in the Ministry of the War (in the Intelligence Division) and in Parliament. Henrietta Darwin Litchfield edited her mother's personal letters and published them in 1904 with many biographical notes. Etty had no children but was a devoted wife and aunt. Elizabeth Darwin did not marry or have children; she was a loving and attentive aunt to her nieces and nephews and took care of elderly people at the workhouse in Cambridge.

Emma and Charles's first grandchild, Bernard, grew up to be a lawyer and a famous golf writer. And George's daughter, Gwen (the baby who put both fists in her mouth), grew up to be an artist and writer named Gwen Raverat. She wrote a memoir about her childhood called *Period Piece*, in which she described her grandmother Emma, her Darwin aunts and uncles, and Down House.

Gwen spent many summers at Down before Emma died. And as a little girl, she adored everything about Down House. She wrote,

> The path in front of the veranda was made of large round water-worn pebbles, from some beach. They were not loose, but stuck down tight in moss and sand, and were black and shiny, as if they had been polished. I adored those pebbles. I mean literally, adored; worshipped. . . . And it was adoration that I felt for the foxgloves at Down, and for the stiff red clay out of the Sandwalk clay-pit; and for the beautiful white paint on the nursery floor.

When the Darwins had first moved to Down House, Charles had planted flowers so that Emma would be as happy there as she had been at Maer. The offspring of those flowers still bloomed, alongside new ones that Emma had planted. Just as Emma had felt about the flowers at Maer—that they were the prettiest anywhere—so Gwen felt about the ones at Down. "All the flowers that grew at Down were beautiful," she said, "and different from all other flowers."

Even though she never met her grandfather, his presence filled the house. "The faint flavour of the ghost of my grandfather hung in a friendly way about the place, house, garden and all." Charles Darwin was a person to be revered. "Of course, we always felt embarrassed if our grandfather were mentioned, just as we did if God were spoken of."

Gwen looked at Charles's study with awe. It had been left just as it was when he died, for the pilgrims who came to Down to see where the great man worked and lived. On the tables and shelves were remnants of his experiments, including something weird in a bottle. Gwen and her cousins ran through Charles's study to get outside, but it felt "faintly holy and sinister, like a church."

"At Down," Charles and Emma's granddaughter wrote, "there were more things to worship than anywhere else in the world."

In 1838, when Charles had decided to ask Emma to marry him, he had made a leap of faith. When she agreed, they made that leap together.

"Marry—Marry—Marry Q.E.D."

It had been demonstrated; it had been proved.

Acknowledgments

Writing this book was a labor of love. Sometimes it was a little heavy on the labor part, but it was never too light on the love part. That's because I fell in love with Charles and Emma and their whole family. And speaking of love, this book is a love letter to my husband, Jonathan Weiner, and it is he whom I have to thank first. He is the one who got me into this, after all. Jon's been writing about science and evolution since we met. I had just graduated from college with a major in religious studies. We started talking immediately—about science and religion and writing and pretty much everything else—and we haven't stopped since.

One day, about seven years ago, Jon said to me, "You know, Charles Darwin's wife was religious." I looked at him. He continued, "And they loved each other very much. She was afraid he would go to hell and they wouldn't be together for eternity."

If bells had chimed right then or fireworks had exploded in the sky above us at that moment (as they did once in Italy for no apparent reason other than it was our anniversary), I would not have been surprised. I knew right then I had a book to write. So thank you, Jon, for that moment, and for all the other zillions of moments since. You put up with a lot as I wrote this book. You owed me, sure, but you have paid me back in spades. I'm ready for your next one. Jon read the book front to back in many drafts, and if there are any mistakes, blame him. (That's not what you're supposed to say, I know, but . . . hey, he's my husband, so why not?)

Other people helped me enormously, and none of the mistakes (if there are any; God, I hope not) are theirs. I would like to thank those who read the whole book in different drafts: John Tyler Bonner, great scientist, writer, and dear friend; Martha Hewson, who saved my life and my sanity by being a terrific editor; Tali Woodward, who made terrific suggestions, and helped me check facts and track down loose ends at a moment's notice; and a special thanks to Janet Browne, who knows more about Darwin than anyone ever, including Darwin himself. I would also like to thank Reverend Nathan Humphrey for consultations. The following writer friends read chapters and gave me great advice and much encouragement. Thank you to Kay Winters, Sally Keehn, Pat Brisson, Wendy Pfeffer, Elvira Woodruff, Joyce McDonald, Pamela Curtis Swallow, Susan Korman, Gail Carson Levine, Elizabeth Winthrop, and the other three Four Vines—Patricia Lakin, Marguerite Holloway, and Laurent Linn. Barbara Kerley, Marfé Ferguson Delano, and Laurie Halse Anderson held my hand from afar.

My sons, Aaron and Benjamin, consulted, consoled, cajoled, and jumped to when I needed a quick fact or piece of advice. Benjamin helped out by going to college just as I had to finish the book. Those two sons of ours are doing wonders, and they inspire me every day. I also have to thank the friends and family I neglected while working on this book. They knew not to call before noon most days (if they remembered) and not to call at all sometimes. For their support and patience I thank especially Julie Stockler, Nancy Sandberg, Laurie Brotman (and Henry), Essie Goldsmith, Linda Miller, Cherie Vogelstein, Doris and Morton Fleischer, Bonnie Long, Jerome Weiner, and my whole Pennsylvania family. I'm sorry if I'm missing anyone. Thanks also to Gail and Steve Rubin.

Now to my book team. First to Ken Wright, who has the best homophonic name for an agent (yes, you Can Write!). Thank you, Ken, for looking at me at our first meeting, and saying, "So what do ya got?" and lighting up when I told you about Charles and Emma. Thank you, too, for your (almost) limitless capacity for patience, and for your humor, your great e-mails, and, you know, everything. (I don't want to sing your praises too high because I don't want to share you more than I already have to.) Noa Wheeler is probably the most brilliant associate editor in the universe and also perhaps the funniest. She not only kept us all in line and held it all together, miraculously, but she also came up with the second-best title for this book (*Charles, Emma, and God: The Darwins at Home*). A very special thanks to my editor, Laura Godwin, who dispensed pearls of wisdom just when I needed them and somehow managed to make me laugh at the same time. I don't know how she does it.

And, finally, thank you to Charles and Emma. You two are just the best. I am going to miss you.

The Darwin Family

Erasmus Darwin m. Mary Howard
(1731–1802)　　(1739–1770)

4 other
children

Robert Waring m. Susannah
Darwin　　　　Wedgwood
(1766–1848)　　(1765–1817)

5 children 〔 Marianne
(1798–1858)

m. Henry Parker
(1788–1856)

4 children 〔 Caroline Sarah
(1800–1888)

m. Josiah Wedgwood
(1795–1880)

Susan Elizabeth
(1803–1866)

Erasmus Alvey
(1804–1881)

Emily Catherine
(1810–1866)
as second wife

m. Charles Langton
(1801–1886)

Charles Robert
(1809–1882)

m. Emma Wedgwood
(1808–1896)

William m. Sara
Erasmus　Sedgwick
(1839–1914)（1839–1902)

Anne
Elizabeth
(1841–1851)

Mary
Eleanor
(1842–1842)

Henrietta m. Richard
Emma　　Buckley
(Etty)　　Litchfield
(1843–1930)（1831–1903)

George m. Maud
Howard　Du Puy
(1845–1912)（1861–1947)

Gwendolen Mary
(1885–1957)

3 other children

The Wedgwood Family

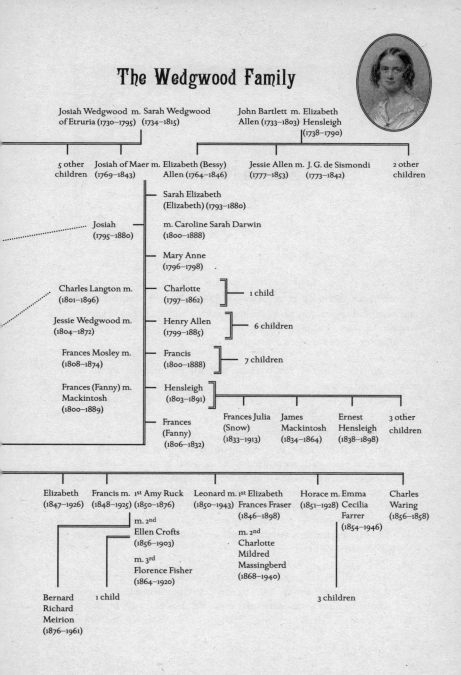

Josiah Wedgwood m. Sarah Wedgwood
of Etruria (1730–1795)   (1734–1815)

John Bartlett m. Elizabeth
Allen (1733–1803) Hensleigh
(1738–1790)

5 other | Josiah of Maer m. Elizabeth (Bessy) | Jessie Allen m. J. G. de Sismondi | 2 other
children | (1769–1843) Allen (1764–1846) | (1777–1853) (1773–1842) | children

Sarah Elizabeth
(Elizabeth) (1793–1880)

Josiah
(1795–1880)

m. Caroline Sarah Darwin
(1800–1888)

Mary Anne
(1796–1798)

Charles Langton m.   Charlotte   1 child
(1801–1896)   (1797–1862)

Jessie Wedgwood m.   Henry Allen   6 children
(1804–1872)   (1799–1885)

Frances Mosley m.   Francis   7 children
(1808–1874)   (1800–1888)

Frances (Fanny) m.   Hensleigh
Mackintosh   (1803–1891)
(1800–1889)

Frances   Frances Julia   James   Ernest   3 other
(Fanny)   (Snow)   Mackintosh   Hensleigh   children
(1806–1832)   (1833–1913)   (1834–1864)   (1838–1898)

Elizabeth | Francis m. 1st Amy Ruck | Leonard m. 1st Elizabeth | Horace m. Emma | Charles
(1847–1926) | (1848–1925) (1850–1876) | (1850–1943) Frances Fraser | (1851–1928) Cecilia | Waring
| | (1846–1898) | Farrer | (1856–1858)
m. 2nd		(1854–1946)
Ellen Crofts	m. 2nd
(1856–1903)	Charlotte
	Mildred
m. 3rd	Massingberd
Florence Fisher	(1868–1940)
(1864–1920)

Bernard   1 child   3 children
Richard
Meirion
(1876–1961)

Source Notes

A note about citations: In most cases, quotes from letters, notebook entries, and diary entries have not been altered and appear as originally written. In a few instances, punctuation or spelling was changed very slightly to enhance a reader's appreciation of the content.

Please see the Selected Bibliography for full information about the sources listed below.

Chapter 1: Better Than a Dog

5   ". . . shape of his head . . .": Barlow, p. 79

5   The *Marry, Not Marry* list, which runs throughout this chapter, has been reproduced many times. The original is in the Cambridge Library. You can see the image here: http://darwin-online.org.uk/content/frameset?viewtype=side&itemID=CUL-DAR210.8.2&page-seq=1 You can also look at it in *Autobiography*, p. 232

7   ". . . greater store of accurate knowledge": Darwin Correspondence Project footnote www.darwinproject.ac.uk/darwinletters/calendar/ entry-372.html

8   "in horizontal position . . .": Porter, p. 997

10   "above all praise" and "a great name . . .": Susan Darwin to Charles Darwin, November 22, 1835, Darwin Correspondence Project www.darwinproject.ac.uk/darwinletters/calendar/entry-288.html

10   "A man who dares to waste . . .": Charles Darwin to Susan Darwin,

August 4, 1838, Darwin Correspondence Project www.darwinproject
.ac.uk/darwinletters/calendar/entry-306.html

12   "Owls. transport mice alive?": *Notebooks*, p. 191

12   "How easily does Wolf & Dog cross?": *Notebooks*, p. 204

13   "Children have an uncommon pleasure . . .": *Notebooks*, p. 582

13   "sprang up, and waving . . .": *Voyage*, Penguin, p. 171

15   "Where true Love burns . . .": Coleridge, Samuel Taylor, "Desire," published 1834

15   "In Man it has been said, there is instinct . . .": *Notebooks*, p. 172

Chapter 2: Rat Catching

17   "I do not believe that anyone . . .": *Autobiography*, p. 44

19   "featherbed to catch . . .": *Life and Letters*, Volume 1, p. 513

19   "the number of thoughts . . .": *Autobiography*, p. 25. The quote continues, ". . . and seem hardly compatible with what physiologists have, I believe, proved about each thought requiring quite an appreciable amount of time"

20   "to the prayers and not to my . . .": *Autobiography*, p. 25

21   "You care for nothing but shooting . . .": *Life and Letters*, Volume 1, p. 30

Chapter 3: Conceal Your Doubts

22   "Man in his arrogance . . .": *Notebooks*, p. 300

24   ". . . acrid fluid, which burnt my tongue": *Life and Letters*, Volume 1, p. 43

24   "the man who walks with Henslow": *Autobiography*, p. 64

24   "a wild scheme": *Autobiography*, p. 228

25   "I have given Uncle Jos . . . the subject again": *Autobiography*, p. 227

25   Uncle Josiah's answers, "I should not think it would be in any disagreeable . . . as happens to few": *Autobiography*, pp. 229–30

27   "extreme misery thus caused . . .": *Autobiography*, p. 95

28   "Conceal your doubts!": *Autobiography*, p. 95

Chapter 4: Where Doors and Windows Stand Open

29   "Emma's handwriting . . .": Litchfield, Volume I, p. 62

29   "excuse this scrawl . . .": Fanny Owen to Charles Darwin, late January 1828, Darwin Correspondence Project www.darwinproject.ac.uk/darwinletters/calendar/entry-38.html

29   "was very pleasant for walking or riding" and the rest of Charles's description of Maer: *Life and Letters*, Volume 1, p. 38

30 "I never saw anything pleasanter...all this sounds and is delightful": journal entries of Emma Caldwell cited in Litchfield, Volume 1, pp. 59–60

32 "I was not the least sure of his feelings...": Litchfield, Volume II, p. 5

32 "Fanny Owen has quite the preference...": Caroline and Catherine to Charles, April 11, 1826, Darwin Correspondence Project, www.darwinproject.ac.uk/darwinletters/calendar/entry-31.html

33 "write me one last adieu...": Fanny Owen to Charles Darwin, December 2, 1831, Darwin Correspondence Project, www.darwinproject.ac.uk/darwinletters/calendar/entry-151.html

33 "It may be all very delightful..." and "I am at a loss...": Charles to Caroline, April 5 & 6, 1832, Darwin Correspondence Project, www.darwinproject.ac.uk/darwinletters/calendar/entry-164.html

34 "my love of natural science...": *Autobiography*, p. 141

35 "quite weary of it": Litchfield, Volume I, p. 255

Chapter 5: Little Miss Slip–Slop

36 "I love Maer much too well...": Litchfield, Volume I, p. 190

36 "My dear Emma..." to "...we will have another goose": Charles to Emma, August 7, 1838, Darwin Correspondence Project, www.darwinproject.ac.uk/darwinletters/calendar/entry-423.html

37 "most radiant in her person...": Litchfield, Volume I, p. 193

38 "I like the Coloes...": Litchfield, Volume I, p. 117

39 "I marvel at the strength of the girls' spirits...secure her from self-ishness": Litchfield, Volume I, pp. 134–35

40 "in such a whirl of noise...": Litchfield, Volume I, p. 161

40 "The whole Theatre was quite full...": Litchfield, Volume I, pp. 187–88

41 "My dear Fanny and Emma...": Litchfield, Volume I, p. 201

41 "Emma Woodhouse, handsome, clever, and rich...": Austen, *Emma*, p. 1

Chapter 6: The Next World

42 "The sorrows and distresses of life...": Malthus, p. 150

42 "On Monday 13th August..." and Emma's other notes from Fanny's illness: Healey, pp. 129–30

44 "seemed very ill for two days with vomitings...": Caroline to Charles, September 12, 1832, Darwin Correspondence Project, www.darwinproject.ac.uk/darwinletters/calendar/entry-185.html

44 "At 9 came the fatal attack...": Litchfield, Volume I, p. 250

44 "Uncle Jos was terribly over come..." to "so intimately connected

with her": Caroline to Charles, September 12 1832, Darwin Correspondence Project, www.darwinproject.ac.uk/darwinletters/calendar/entry-185.html

45 "Oh Lord . . ." and "I feel a sad blank . . . Worthy of being with her": Litchfield, Volume I, pp. 250–51

46 "education and environment produce only a small effect . . .": *Life and Letters*, Volume 1, p. 21

Chapter 7: The Sensation of Fear

47 "My experience of English lovers . . .": Raverat, p. 108

47 "There was no difficulty in standing upright, but . . .": *Voyage*, Penguin, p. 228

48 "threw herself on her back, kicked & cried . . .": Charles to Susan Darwin, April 1, 1838, Darwin Correspondence Project, www.darwinproject.ac.uk/darwinletters/calendar/entry-407.html

48 "Children understand before they can talk . . . put them in—like child": *Notebooks*, p. 567

51 "theory by which to work": *Autobiography*, p. 120

52 "Oh you materialist!": *Notebooks*, p. 291

52 "Fear must be . . ." and Charles's other notes on this topic through ". . . I believe, in Materialism": *Notebooks*, p. 532

53 "If one does not marry soon . . . trust to chance": Complete Work of Charles Darwin Online, http://darwin-online.org.uk/content/frameset?viewtype=side&itemID=CUL-DAR210.8.2&pageseq=2

Chapter 8: A Leap

55 "E. says she can perceive sigh . . .": *Notebooks*, p. 584

56 "I went straight into . . .": Litchfield, Volume II, p. 7

56 "too much bewildered . . ." and "Indeed I was so glad to find . . ." and Emma's other descriptions of the event: Litchfield, Volume II, pp. 5–6

58 "The day of days": http://darwin-online.org.uk/content/frameset?viewtype=side&itemID=CUL-DAR158.1-76&pageseq=30

58 "drawn a prize": Litchfield, Volume II, p. 4

58 "It is very like . . .": Litchfield, Volume II, p. 12

Chapter 9: A Busy Man

60 "I hardly expected such good fortune . . .": Litchfield, Volume II, pp. 2–3

60 "You will be forming theories about me . . .": Darwin Correspondence

Project www.darwinproject.ac.uk/darwinletters/calendar/entry492
.html

61   "I have the very good . . .": Litchfield, Volume II, p. 1
61   "How truly & warmly . . .": Charlotte Langton to Charles Darwin,
      November 14, 1838, Darwin Correspondence Project, www
      .darwinproject.ac.uk/darwinletters/calendar/entry-436.html
62   "It is a marriage which . . .": Erasmus Darwin to Charles, Darwin
      Correspondence Project, www.darwinproject.ac.uk/darwinletters/
      calendar/entry-435.html
62   "Everything I have ever heard . . . from your hands": Litchfield, Vol-
      ume II, pp. 9–11
63   "He is the most open . . .": Litchfield, Volume II, p. 6
63   "there was never anyone so lucky . . ." and Charles's other words
      to Emma through "Dearest Emma, good-bye": Litchfield, Volume II,
      pp. 3–5
65   "I positively can do nothing . . .": Litchfield, Volume II, p. 13
65   "Jealousy probably originally . . .": Notebooks, p. 557
65   "Sexual desire makes saliva . . ." and Charles's other notes on this
      topic: Notebooks, p. 574
66   "Shyness is certainly very much . . ." and notes on blushing through
      ". . . a most modest person": Notebooks, pp. 577–78
67   "I am so glad he is a busy man": Litchfield, Volume II, p. 6

Chapter 10: Melancholy Thoughts

68   "My reason tells me that honest . . .": Emma to Charles, Novem-
      ber 21–22, 1838, Darwin Correspondence Project, www.darwin
      project.ac.uk/ darwinletters/calendar/entry-441.html
68   "dressed in good taste . . .": Litchfield, Volume II, p. 9
68   "I bless the railroad . . .": Litchfield, Volume II, p. 7
69   "When I am with you . . ." and other excerpts from Emma's letter
      through ". . . not at all too dashing": Emma to Charles, November
      21–22, 1838, Darwin Correspondence Project, www.darwinproject
      .ac.uk/darwinletters/calendar/entry-441.html
72   "These deeds are done . . .": Voyage, Harvard Classics, p. 503
73   "I am sitting with Mamma . . .": Emma to Charles November 25,
      1838, Darwin Correspondence Project, www.darwinproject.ac.uk/
      darwinletters/calendar/entry-444.html
73   "it is not possible to give . . .": Voyage, Harvard Classics, p. 34

Chapter 11: A Whirl of Noise and Motion

75   "I quite agree with you ∴": Litchfield, Volume II, p. 16
75   "I have seen no one for these two days...": Litchfield, Volume II, p. 15
76   "whirl of noise and motion...": Dickens, p. 29
77   "Houses are very scarce...": Litchfield, Volume II, p. 13
77   "I suspect conscience, an hereditary...": *Notebooks*, p. 600
77   "It does not hurt the conscience...": *Notebooks*, p. 572
78   "breathless haste" and "spread the news": *Life and Letters*, Volume 1, p. 27
78   "destitute of faith, yet terrified of skepticism": Carlyle, p. 39
78   "Belief allied to instinct": *Notebooks*, p. 602
79   "The emotions of terror & wonder...": *Notebooks*, p. 605
79   "When two races of men meet...": *Notebooks*, p. 414
79   "It is a beautiful part of my theory...": *Notebooks*, p. 416
80   "makes me feel how much...": *Notebooks*, p. 540
80   "I quite approve of your plan...": Emma to Charles, November 30, 1838, Darwin Correspondence Project, www.darwinproject.ac.uk/darwinletters/calendar/entry-447.html
80   "Some London houses...": Dickens, p. 8
81   "a front drawing-room with three windows..." and "Gower Street is ours...": Litchfield, Volume II, p. 18
81   "But why does joy, & OTHER EMOTION ... joy & sublimity": *Notebooks*, pp. 578–79
82   "I long for the day...": Litchfield, Volume II, p. 18

Chapter 12: Heavy Baggage, Blazing Fires

83   "I take so much pleasure...": Litchfield, Volume II, p. 24
83   "I am very sorry to spoil..." and other descriptions of the event through "The little garden is worth its weight in gold" reported in a letter to Emma, Litchfield, Volume II, p. 19
85   "My good old friend Herbert...": Litchfield, Volume II, pp. 23–24
85   "What passes in a man's mind...": *Notebooks*, p. 579
85   "You will have a few days more time...", through "... corrupting your mind": Emma to Charles, January 7, 1839, Darwin Correspondence Project, www.darwinproject.ac.uk/darwinletters/calendar/entry-485.html
86   "By the way now we seem to be clearing old scores...": Emma to Charles, January 9, 1839, Darwin Correspondence Project, www.darwinproject.ac.uk/darwinletters/calendar/entry-486.html

87   "soon teach me there is greater happiness . . ." and "I made a very stu-
      pid mistake yesterday . . ." through "my own dear future wife . . .":
      Charles to Emma, January 20, 1839, Darwin Correspondence Project,
      www.darwinproject.ac.uk/darwinletters/calendar/entry-489.html

87   "I am rather ashamed of writing . . .": Emma to Charles, December
      30, 1838, Darwin Correspondence Project, www.darwinproject
      .ac.uk/darwinletters/calendar/entry-465.html

87   "Today the Miss Northens are coming very early . . .": Emma to
      Charles, January 20–21, 1839, Darwin Correspondence Project,
      www.darwinproject.ac.uk/darwinletters/calendar/entry-490.html

88   "You need not fear my own dear Charles . . .": Emma to Charles, Jan-
      uary 23, 1839, Darwin Correspondence Project, www.darwinproject.
      ac.uk/darwinletters/calendar/entry-492.html

88   "quite cured me" to ". . . news I have to tell": Litchfield, Volume II, p. 24

89   "We ate our sandwiches . . .": ibid, p. 26

Chapter 13: Definition of Happiness

90   "A thousand thanks to you . . .": Litchfield, Volume II, p. 30

90   "Happiness in marriage is entirely a matter of chance . . ." and "It is
      better to know as little as possible . . .": Austen, *Pride and Prejudice*, p. 20

91   "made up his mind to give up . . .": Litchfield, Volume II, p. 61

91   "a sort of clarety-brown satin": Litchfield, Volume II, p. 29

91   "I often bless all novelists . . .": *Autobiography*, pp. 138–39

92   "went slopping . . .": Litchfield, Volume II, p. 29

92   "a large dose of music every evening": Litchfield, Volume I, p. 32

93   "when the plum-pudding appeared . . .": Litchfield, Volume II, p. 33

93   "the thoughts of this precious child . . .": Litchfield, Volume II, p. 28

93   "honours yet": Litchfield, Volume II, p. 33

93   "Charles said his face . . ." and "My Charles has been very unwell
      since Sunday . . .": Browne, *Voyaging*, p. 405

94   "Emma is looking very pretty . . .": Litchfield, Volume II, p. 34

94   "Erasmus drank tea . . ." and other excerpts from Emma's diaries:
      Complete Work of Charles Darwin Online, http://darwin-online
      .org.uk/EmmaDiaries.html

Chapter 14: Pregnant Thoughts

96   "I should be most unhappy if I thought . . .": this letter, which is
      quoted throughout this chapter, can be found in Darwin's *Auto-
      biography*, p. 237, as well as on the Complete Work of Charles

Darwin Online, http://darwin-online.org.uk/content/frameset?
viewtype=side&itemID=CUL-DAR210.8.14&pageseq=1

97   "write about coral formations..." to "... undeniably growing": Charles
      to Caroline, October 27, 1839, Darwin Correspondence Project, www
      .darwinproject.ac.uk/darwinletters/calendar/entry-542.html

Chapter 15: Little Animalcules

101   "The baby performed his first smile to-day...": Litchfield, Volume
      II, p. 52

101   "Charles got some of his father's good doctoring" through "... time
      to read it yet": Litchfield, Volume II, p. 42

102   "it beat all other nonsense he has ever read on the subject":
      Charles to Caroline, October 27, 1839, Darwin Correspon-
      dence Project, www.darwinproject.ac.uk/darwinletters/calendar/
      entry-542.html

102   "so entirely happy in her lot...": Litchfield, Volume II, p. 42

103   "first-rate landscape-painter with a pen": Browne, *Voyaging*, p. 417

103   "The scene, as beheld through the hazy atmosphere..." and "The
      island would generally be considered...": *Voyage*, Penguin, pp. 41–42

104   "In the thirteen species of ground-finches...": *Voyage*, Penguin, p. 287

104   "The success of this my first literary child...": *Autobiography*, p. 116

105   "What an awful affair a confinement is...": Charles to Fox, June 7,
      1840, Darwin Correspondence Project, www.darwinproject.ac.uk/
      darwinletters/calendar/entry-572.html

105   "It cost me a good cry...": Litchfield, Volume II, p. 44

105   "little prince": Charles to T. C. Eyton, January 6, 1840, Darwin
      Correspondence Project, www.darwinproject.ac.uk/darwinletters/
      calendar/entry-549.html

105   "prodigy of beauty and intellect": Charles to William Fox, June 7,
      1840, Darwin Correspondence Project, www.darwinproject.ac.uk/
      darwinletters/calendar/entry-572.html

105   "my baby, and a very nice looking one it is...": Litchfield, Volume II,
      p. 50

106   "I find as you always prophesied...": Charles to FitzRoy, February 20,
      1840, Darwin Correspondence Project, www.darwinproject.ac.uk/
      darwinletters/calendar/entry-555.html

106   "During first week...": Complete Work of Charles Darwin
      Online, http://darwin-online.org.uk/content/frameset?itemID=
      CUL-DAR210.11.37&viewtype=side&pageseq=1

106   "I made in his presence many odd noises and strange grimaces ..."
       and other descriptions of Charles's experiments: *Expression*, p. 358
107   "His sympathy with the grief ...": *Life and Letters*, Volume 1, p. 109
107   "A child crying. Frowning ...": *Notebooks*, p. 595
108   "extremely difficult to prove that our children ...": *Expression*, p. 358
108   "It is a great advantage to have the power of ...": Litchfield, Volume
       II, p. 52

Chapter 16: Down in the Country

109   "A frog jumped near him ...": Litchfield, Volume II, p. 60
109   "My little Annie ...": Litchfield, Volume II, p. 69
110   "The London air ...": Litchfield, Volume II, p. 67
110   "I presume you did not know any more than I" and "anything about
       our children ...": Litchfield, Volume II, p. 59
111   "Charles is very busy finishing ...": Litchfield, Volume II, pp. 69–70
111   "An individual organism placed under ..." and other excerpts
       from this species sketch: Complete Work of Charles Darwin
       Online,   http://darwin-online.org.uk/EditorialIntroductions/
       Freeman_Sketchesof1842and1844.html text views
114   "Down-in-the-mouth": Charles to Leonard Horner, October 4, 1842,
       Darwin Correspondence Project, www.darwinproject.ac.uk/dar-
       winletters/calendar/entry-648.html
115   "In a country neighborhood you move ...": Austen, *Pride and Prejudice*,
       p. 40
115   "He so filled every instant of my life ...": Litchfield, Volume II, p. 72

Chapter 17: Sudden Deaths

116   "I think I have found ...": *Voyage*, p. 111
116   "very feverish, violent headaches" and other notes from Emma's diary:
       Complete Work of Charles Darwin Online, http://darwin-online
       .org.uk/content/frameset?itemID=CUL-DAR242%5B.8%5D&view-
       type=image&pageseq=1 (diary entries are listed by date)
117   "Our sorrow is nothing to ...": Litchfield, Volume II, p. 78
117   "I can still see the horse with the man's ...": *Autobiography*, p. 24
117   "Charles is well to-day and the funeral over ..." and "I keep very well
       and strong and am come ...": Litchfield, Volume II, p. 78
117   "I feel sure I shall become deeply attached to Down ...": Charles to
       Catherine, September 16, 1842, Darwin Correspondence Project,
       www.darwinproject.ac.uk/darwinletters/calendar/entry-633.html

119 "I don't want to have that shilling . . .": Litchfield, Volume II, p. 81

120 "I got into a transport over . . .": Litchfield, Volume II, pp. 86–87

120 "At last gleams of light have come . . .": Charles to J. D. Hooker, January 11, 1844, Darwin Correspondence Project, www.darwin project.ac.uk/darwinletters/calendar/entry-729.html

121 "My hairdresser (Willis) says that . . .": *Notebooks*, p. 338

122 "My. Dear. Emma. I have just finished my sketch . . .": Charles to Emma, July 5, 1844, Darwin Correspondence Project, www.darwinproject .ac.uk/darwinletters/calendar/entry-761.html

123 "A great assumption/E.D. . . ." and Emma's other editorial comments: Desmond and Moore, p. 319

123 "it will be necessary to show how the first eye is formed": *Notebooks*, p. 337

124 "I have also read the 'Vestiges,' but . . .": Charles to J. D. Hooker, *Life and Letters*, Volume 1, pp. 301–2

Chapter 18: Barnacles and Babies

126 "My chief enjoyment and sole employment . . .": *Life and Letters*, Volume 1, p. 65

126 "In the morning I was baddish . . .": Litchfield, Volume II, p. 93

127 "patient look," "Don't you think you could not come in again . . ." and "I well remember lurking about . . .": *Life and Letters*, Volume 1, p. 113

128 "hard at work dissecting a little animal . . .": *Life and Letters*, Volume 1, p. 317

129 "at present I am suffering from . . .": *Life and Letters*, Volume 1, p. 320

129 "I asked one of my boys to shout as loudly . . .": *Expression*, p. 158

129 "I suppose now and be-hanged to you . . ." and "This. lovely day makes me pine . . .": Litchfield, Volume II, pp. 117–18

131 "You will be surprised to hear that we all . . ." and Charles's other description of the water cure: Darwin Correspondence Project, www.darwinproject.ac.uk/darwinletters/calendar/entry-1241.html

132 "At Down ill health was considered normal": Raverat, p. 122

Chapter 19: Doing Custards

133 "A good, cheerful, and affectionate daughter . . .": Litchfield, Volume II, p. 2

133 "doing custards": My description of Annie in this chapter is taken, unless otherwise noted, from Charles's memorial to her, which can be found in a complete version at the Complete Work of

Charles Darwin Online, http://darwin-online.org.uk/content/frameset?itemID=CUL-DAR210.13.40&viewtypeside&pageseq=1

133 "always so candid and kind-hearted" and "always found her a child whose heart it was easy to reach": Keynes, p. 163

134 "how neatly Annie takes hold...": Notebook of Observations of the Darwin Children, Complete Work of Charles Darwin Online, http://darwin-online.org.uk/content/frameset?viewtype=text&itemID=CUL-DAR210.11.37&pageseq=1

135 "Annie first failed about this time": Emma's Diary, Complete Work of Charles Darwin Online, http://darwin-online.org.uk/Emma-Diaries.html

136 "I was so bold during my wifes confinement...": Charles to J. S. Henslow, January 17, 1850, Darwin Correspondence Project, www.darwinproject.ac.uk/darwinletters/calendar/entry-1293.html

Chapter 20: A Fretful Child

137 "Her sensitiveness appeared extremely early in life...": Charles's memorial to Annie, Complete Work of Charles Darwin Online, http://darwin-online.org.uk/content/frameset?itemID=CUL-DAR210.13.40&viewtype=side&pageseq=1

140 "Annie began bark": Emma's Diary, Complete Work of Charles Darwin Online, http://darwin-online.org.uk/EmmaDiaries.html

140 "well not quite" and other notes about Annie's state: Keynes, p. 174

142 "the fretfulness of a child is an infinite evil!" and "I was aghast...": Newman, Phases of Faith, p. 78

Chapter 21: God Only Knows the Issue

143 "Without you when sick I feel most desolate...": Litchfield, Volume II, p. 119

144 "uncommonly well and stout": Litchfield, Volume II, p. 131

144 "yesterday I fell down twice": Keynes, pp. 182–83

145 "She looks very ill: her...": Darwin Correspondence Project, www.darwinproject.ac.uk/darwinletters/calendar/entry-1399.html

146 "most kind" and "Your note made me cry much...": Darwin Correspondence Project, www.darwinproject.ac.uk/darwinletters/calendar/entry-1400.html

146 "She appears dreadfully exhausted...": Darwin Correspondence Project, www.darwinproject.ac.uk/darwinletters/calendar/entry 1401.html

146 "Fanny gave her a spoonful of tea": Litchfield, Volume II, p. 135
147 "looking at my poor darling's little garden...": Litchfield, Volume II, p. 134
147 "would not in the least recognize her...": Darwin Correspondence Project, www.darwinproject.ac.uk/darwinletters/calendar/entry-1402.html
147 "Don't do that please" to "Poor darling child": Charles to Emma, April 20, 1851, Darwin Correspondence Project, www.darwinproject.ac.uk/darwinletters/calendar/entry-1406.html
148 "I am confused now...": Darwin Correspondence Project, www.darwinproject.ac.uk/darwinletters/calendar/entry-1409.html
148 "Your minute accounts..." and "imminent danger...": Darwin Correspondence Project, www.darwinproject.ac.uk/darwinletters/calendar/entry-1411.html
148 "My dear dearest Emma..." and other excerpts from Charles's letter about Annie's death: Litchfield, Volume II, pp. 136–37

Chapter 22: A Dear and Good Child

150 "She must have known how we loved her..." and other excerpts from Charles's memorial to Annie throughout the chapter: Complete Work of Charles Darwin Online, http://darwin-online.org.uk/content/frameset?itemID=CUL-DAR210.13.40&viewtype=side&pageseq=1
150 "The hovel in which she had expired...": *Voyage*, Penguin, pp. 314–15
151 "Where is poor Etty?": Litchfield, Volume II, p. 135
151 "my feeling of longing after...": Litchfield, Volume II, p. 137
152 "On the 23rd inst; of April, at Malvern...": Darwin Correspondence Project, www.darwinproject.ac.uk/darwinletters/calendar/entry-1416.html
153 "We are disappointed at your account...": Litchfield, Volume II, p. 40
154 "Where do the women go, for all the angels are men" and other details about Etty's worries and Emma's responses: *Correspondence*, Volume 5, p. 542
156 "little packet of memorials": Litchfield, Volume II, p. 139
156 "We have none of us to choose our religion...": Litchfield, Volume II, p. 125
156 "I do not suppose you will have heard...": Darwin Correspondence Project, www.darwinproject.ac.uk/darwinletters/calendar/entry-1425.html

Chapter 23: Against the Rules

158   "Well, you have come quite wrong; you should...": E. Darwin, "Pound of Sugar," p. 4

159   "Now that I stand at the end of my life..." and "My dear Emma, how I do love...": Litchfield, Volume II, p. 144

159   "I'm so dull...": *Correspondence*, Volume 4, p. 146

159   "When I have a tenth...": Charles to William Fox, March 7, 1852, Darwin Correspondence Project, www.darwinproject.ac.uk/darwinletters/calendar/entry-1476.html

160   "Georgy draws...": Litchfield, Volume II, p. 145

160   "Emma has been very neglectful...": Darwin Correspondence Project, www.darwinproject.ac.uk/darwinletters/calendar/entry-1489.html

161   "I think that is all" and other details of Jessie's deathbed scene and death: Litchfield, Volume II, p. 152

161   "Oh Lenny, Lenny...": *Life and Letters*, Volume 1, pp. 111–12

162   "Well, you old ass... spurt that out": *Correspondence*, Volume 4, p. 430

162   "In the years when we were growing up..." and information about Emma's list: Litchfield, Volume II, p. 201

163   "there was always about her a bright aliveness...": Litchfield, Volume II, pp. 45–49

Chapter 24: Terrible Suffering

166   "Yearly more are bred than can survive...": Complete Work of Charles Darwin Online, http://darwin-online.org.uk/content/frameset?itemID=CUL-DAR210.13.40&viewtype=side&pageseq=1

166   "Where does your father do *his* barnacles?": Browne, *Darwin's Origin*, p. 55

167   "pigeons if you please": Lyell to Darwin, May 1–2, 1856, Darwin Correspondence Project, www.darwinproject.ac.uk/darwinletters/calendar/entry-1862.html

167   "I rather hate the idea of writing for priority...": Darwin to Lyell, May 3, 1856, Darwin Correspondence Project, www.darwinproject.ac.uk/darwinletters/calendar/entry-1866.html

167   "I am working very hard at my Book...": Darwin to Fox, February 8, 1857, Darwin Correspondence Project, www.darwinproject.ac.uk/darwinletters/calendar/entry-2049.html

168   "without its full share of intelligence": Litchfield, Volume II, p. 162

168   "backward in walking and talking, but intelligent and observant":
        Correspondence, Volume 7, Appendix V

168   "Etty taken ill" and other notes from Emma's diaries throughout
        this chapter: Complete Work of Charles Darwin Online, http://
        darwin-online.org.uk/EmmaDiaries.html

169   "Your words have come true with a vengeance . . ." and other excerpts
        from Charles's letters to Lyell: *Letters: A Selection*, pp. 188–89

171   "What has frightened us . . ." and "I have always thought you would
        have made . . .": Darwin Correspondence Project, www.darwinproject
        .ac.uk/darwinletters/calendar/entry-2295.html

172   "It was the most blessed relief . . .": Darwin Correspondence Project,
        www.darwinproject.ac.uk/darwinletters/calendar/entry-2297.html

172   "I am quite prostrated . . .": *Letters: A Selection*, p. 190

173   "This MS. work was never intended for publication . . .": Complete
        Work of Charles Darwin Online, http://darwin-online.org.uk/
        content/frameset?viewtype=side&itemID=F350&pageseq=1

Chapter 25: The Origins of *The Origin*

174   "I fear I shall never be able to make it good enough": *Life and Letters*,
        Volume I, p. 489

175   "On the Tendency of Species to form Varieties . . ." and "The gentlemen
        having, independently and unknown to one another . . ." and other
        excerpts from his paper: Complete Work of Charles Darwin Online,
        http://darwin-online.org.uk/content/frameset?viewtype=side&item
        ID=F350&pageseq=1

178   "My God how I long for my stomach's sake . . .": Darwin Correspon-
        dence Project, www.darwinproject.ac.uk/darwinletters/calendar/
        entry-2450.html

179   "caught the other day *Brachinus crepitans* . . .": *Life and Letters*, Volume I,
        p. 496

179   "Not that the story need be long, but it will take a long while to
        make it short": Thoreau, p. 311

Chapter 26: Dependent on Each Other

180   "Then how should I manage all my business . . .": Complete Work of
        Charles Darwin Online, http://darwin-online.org.uk/content/
        frameset?itemID=CUL-DAR210.8.2&viewtype=side&pageseq=1

181   "I am afraid this is very wearisome to you": Litchfield, Volume II, p. 48

181 "an exception to every wife": Litchfield, Volume II, p. 183

182 "Would you be so good": *Life and Letters*, Volume I, p. 115

182 "It may metaphorically be said . . .": *Origin*, p. 90

183 "Long before the reader has arrived . . .": *Origin*, p. 158

183 "To suppose that the eye . . ." "When it was first said that the sun . . ." and "Reason tells me, that if numerous gradations . . .": *Origin*, pp. 168–69

185 "It is interesting to contemplate . . .": *Origin*, p. 450

Chapter 27: What the Lord Hath Delivered

187 "I hope you are not working too hard . . .": Charles to Huxley, September 10, 1860, Darwin Correspondence Project, www.darwinproject .ac.uk/darwinletters/calendar/entry-2909.html

187 "It is a wonderful thing . . . Mudie taking 500 copies": Darwin Correspondence Project footnote, www.darwinproject.ac.uk/darwinlet ters/calendar/entry-2549.html

188 "If a monkey has become a man . . .": Browne, *Power of Place*, p. 87

189 "I have read your book with more pain than pleasure": Sedgwick to Charles, November 24, 1859, Darwin Correspondence Project, www.darwinproject.ac.uk/darwinletters/calendar/entry-2548.html

191 "How extremely stupid not to have thought of that!": Browne, *Darwin's Origin*, p. 94

191 "I trust you will not allow yourself . . ." and "I am sharpening up my claws & beak in readiness": Huxley to Darwin, November 23, 1859, Darwin Correspondence Project, www.darwinproject.ac.uk/ darwinletters/calendar/entry-2544.html

192 "go the whole orang": Browne, *Power of Place*, p. 79

194 "There is grandeur in this view of life . . .": *Origin*, p. 450

Chapter 28: Feeling, Not Reasoning

195 "I wish you knew how I value you . . .": Litchfield, Volume II, pp. 171–72

196 "his various experiments this summer . . .": Litchfield, Volume II, p. 177

197 "there seems too much misery in the world": Charles to Gray, May 22, 1860, Darwin Correspondence Project, www.darwinproject .ac.uk/darwinletters/calendar/entry-2814.html

197 "I am conscious that I am in an utterly hopeless muddle . . .": Charles to Gray, November 26, 1860, Darwin Correspondence Project, www .darwinproject.ac.uk/darwinletters/calendar/entry-2998.html

198 "so much affection in her nature as will secure her from selfishness": Litchfield, Volume I, p. 135

198 "begged me to come to her and bring the three children . . ." and other details of Emma's invitation to Mrs. Huxley: Litchfield, Volume II, p. 186

200 "the cheerful and affectionate looks . . ." and other excerpts from this letter: Litchfield, Volume II, pp. 174–75

Chapter 29: Such a Noise

202 "I remember when in Good Success Bay . . .": *Life and Letters*, Volume 1, p. 73

202 "I bet you half a crown . . .": Browne, *Power of Place*, p. 207

203 "Your last letter was not interesting . . .": Litchfield, Volume II, p. 181

203 "An Appeal . . .": Litchfield, Volume II, pp. 178–80

205 "Will you tell us what you can remember . . .": Charles to Fox, September 4, 1863, Darwin Correspondence Project, www.darwinproject.ac.uk/darwinletters/calendar/entry-4292.html

205 "flower of my flock": Hooker to Charles, October 1, 1863, Darwin Correspondence Project, www.darwinproject.ac.uk/darwinletters/calendar/entry-4317.html

206 "Your note is most pathetic . . .": Charles to Hooker, October 4, 1863, Darwin Correspondence Project, www.darwinproject.ac.uk/darwinletters/calendar/entry-4318.html

206 "I am surprised at my industry": *Autobiography*, p. 119

206 "Is astonishment expressed by the eyes . . .": Complete Work of Charles Darwin Online, http://darwin-online.org.uk/content/frameset?viewtype=side&itemID=F873&pageseq=1

207 "We have been rather overdone with Germans . . .": Litchfield, Volume II, p. 223

207 "I am afraid I must leave off now": Litchfield, Volume II, p. 170

208 "hot-house face of despair": Litchfield, Volume II, p. 197

208 "I would as soon be called Dog": Litchfield, Volume II, p. 192

208 "It's dogged as does it": *Life and Letters*, Volume I, p. 125

209 "From your earliest years you have given me . . ." to ". . . dear old mother": Litchfield, Volume II, pp. 204–5

210 "I think she has taken it into her head . . .": Litchfield, Volume II, p. 198

210 "famishing" and ". . . good girl": *Life and Letters*, Volume I, p. 92

210 "My views have often been grossly misrepresented" through "On the whole I do not doubt that my works . . .": *Autobiography*, pp. 125–26

211 "I sometimes feel it very odd . . .": Litchfield, Volume II, p. 211

Chapter 30: Mere Trickery

212   "I have been speculating last night . . .": Charles to Horace, December 15, 1871, Litchfield, Volume II, p. 207

212   "She kept a sorrowful wish . . .": Litchfield, Volume II, p. 175

215   "play the game fairly" and "The usual manifestations occurred . . .": Litchfield, Volume II, pp. 216–17

215   "before all these astounding miracles . . ." and Charles's other thoughts about the dance: *Life and Letters*, Volume III, p. 187

Chapter 31: Warmth to the End

217   "I cannot bear her notion . . .": Litchfield, Volume II, p. 213

217   "Pray give our . . .": Litchfield, Volume II, p. 221

218   "Your father is taking a good deal . . .": Litchfield, Volume II, p. 225

219   "half kill" and "bent on going, chiefly for the worms": Litchfield, Volume II, p. 226

220   "How often, when a man, I . . .": *Life and Letters*, Volume I, p. 112

221   "Oh Lord, what a set of sons I have . . .": Litchfield, Volume II, p. 224

221   "I felt very grand . . .": Litchfield, Volume II, p. 231

221   "no consequence to any one except myself" and other excerpts from his 1879 letter: Charles to John Fordyce, May 7, 1879, Darwin Correspondence Project, www.darwinproject.ac.uk/darwinletters/calendar/entry-12041.html

221   "very unwilling to give up my belief . . .": *Autobiography*, p. 86

222   "He moons about in the garden . . .": Morris and Wilson, p. 46

222   "The coat . . . will never warm . . ." and "afraid it will soon be worn out": Litchfield, Volume II, pp. 239–40

223   "does not make much progress . . .": Litchfield, Volume II, p. 241

223   "To me there was a charm in his manner . . .": Litchfield, Volume II, p. 247

223   "Worms have played a more important part . . .": *Worms*, p. 288

224   "Tell all my children . . ." through ". . . to be nursed by you": Litchfield, Volume II, p. 253

224   "ditto" and other notes from Emma's Diaries: Complete Work of Charles Darwin Online, http://darwin-online.org.uk/EmmaDiaries.html

Chapter 32: Happy Is the Man

225   "His body is buried in peace, but his name liveth evermore" and "Happy is the man that findeth wisdom . . ." from Charles's funeral program: Complete Work of Charles Darwin Online, http://darwin-online.org.uk/content/frameset?itemID=A204&viewtype=side&pageseq=1

Chapter 33: Unasked Questions

228   "I feel a sort of wonder . . .": Litchfield, Volume II, p. 254

228   "precious packet": Litchfield, Volume I, p. 261

229   "I am so pleased to find how comfortable I can . . ." and "It gives me a sort of companionship . . .": Litchfield, Volume II, p. 272

229   "I should prefer . . ." and "in almost every one . . .": Litchfield, Volume II, p. 280

230   "There is one sentence in the *Autobiography* . . ." and "I should wish if possible to avoid giving pain . . .": *Autobiography*, pp. 93–94

231   "I gradually came to disbelieve in Christianity as a divine revelation," through "I can indeed hardly see how . . .": *Autobiography*, pp. 86–87

231   "I am rather ashamed to find I use up rather more . . .": Litchfield, Volume II, p. 275

232   "I am reading the Psalms . . .": Litchfield, Volume II, p. 305

232   "My dear daughter in heart": Litchfield, Volume II, p. 304

232   "Grandmama, did your little children have kites?": Litchfield, Volume II, p. 273

232   "Her buoyant spirit and the essential reserve . . .": Litchfield, Volume II, p. 283

232   "I marvel at my good fortune . . .": *Autobiography*, p. 97

Epilogue: So Much to Worship

234   "There is a grandeur in this view of life . . .": *Origin*, p. 450

234   "I suppose one does admire one's own view absurdly": Litchfield, Volume II, p. 286

235   "The path in front of the veranda . . ." and "All the flowers that grew at Down . . .": Raverat, p. 141

236   "The faint flavour of the ghost . . ." through "faintly holy and sinister, like a church": Raverat, p. 153

236   "At Down there were more things to worship . . ." Raverat, p. 142

Selected Bibliography

In researching this book, I relied as much as possible on primary sources (letters, diary entries, Charles Darwin's notebooks and manuscripts, as well as his autobiography and other published books). I was not always able to do so, however, and fortunately was able to rely on the scholarship of others. Below is a list, albeit incomplete, of the books that helped me. The resources on the Internet are almost infinite. But the two sites I used most and would recommend are The Darwin Correspondence Project (www.darwinproject.ac.uk) and The Complete Work of Charles Darwin Online (http://darwin-online.org.uk). These sites are continually updated.

Austen, Jane. *Emma*. New York: Pantheon, The Novel Library. First published 1816 in London.

———. *Pride and Prejudice*. New York: Pantheon, The Novel Library. First published 1813 in London.

Browne, Janet. *Charles Darwin. The Power of Place: The* Origin *and After—The Years of Fame*. New York: Alfred A. Knopf, 2002.

———. *Charles Darwin. Voyaging*. New York: Alfred A. Knopf, 1995.

———. *Darwin's* Origin of Species: *A Biography*. New York: Atlantic Monthly Press, 2006.

Darwin, Charles. *The Autobiography of Charles Darwin, 1809–1882: With original omissions restored.* Ed. Nora Barlow. New York: W.W. Norton & Company, 1958 (1969 edition).

———. *Charles Darwin's Letters: A Selection, 1825–1859.* Ed. Frederick Burkhardt. Cambridge: Cambridge University Press, 1996.

———. *Charles Darwin's Notebooks, 1836–1844.* Eds. Paul H. Barrett, Peter J. Gautrey, Sandra Herbert, David Kohn, and Sydney Smith. British Museum (Natural History). Ithaca: Cornell University Press, 1987.

———. *Correspondence of Charles Darwin. Volumes 2, 4, 5, 7.* Ed. Frederick Burkhardt. Cambridge: Cambridge University Press.

———. *The Descent of Man.* London: Penguin Books, 2004.

———. *The Expression of the Emotions in Man and Animals.* Chicago: University of Chicago Press, 1965.

———. *The Formation of Vegetable Mould Through the Action of Worms, with Observations on Their Habits.* London: John Murray, 1904.

———. *The Life and Letters of Charles Darwin Including an Autobiographical Chapter,* Volume I. Ed. Francis Darwin. New York: D. Appleton and Company, 1893.

———. *The Life and Letters of Charles Darwin Including an Autobiographical Chapter,* Volume II. Ed. Francis Darwin. New York: D. Appleton and Company, 1911.

———. *The Origin of Species.* New York: New American Library, 1958.

———. *Voyage of the Beagle.* Harvard Classics. New York: P. F. Collier & Son, 1909.

———. *Voyage of the Beagle.* London: Penguin, 1989.

Darwin, Emma. "The Pound of Sugar." Cambridge Library, 2002.

———. *Emma Darwin: A Century of Family Letters, 1792–1896.* Volumes I and II. Ed. Henrietta Litchfield. New York: D. Appleton and Company, 1915.

Desmond, Adrian, and James Moore. *Darwin: The Life of a Tormented Evolutionist.* New York: Warner Books, 1991.

Dickens, Charles. *Nicholas Nickleby*. Oxford: Oxford University Press, 1994. (First published in book form October 1839.)

Flanders, Judith. *Inside the Victorian Home*. New York: W.W. Norton, 2003.

Gaskell, Elizabeth. *Wives and Daughters*. Oxford: Oxford University Press, 1987.

Healey, Edna. *Emma Darwin: The Inspirational Wife of a Genius*. London: Headline, 2001.

Keynes, Randal. *Darwin, His Daughter, and Human Evolution*. New York: Riverhead Books, 2002.

Malthus, T. R. *An Essay on the Principle of Population*. Oxford: Oxford University Press, 1993.

Morris, Solene, and Louise Wilson. *Down House: The Home of Charles Darwin*. English Heritage, 1998.

Newman, Francis William. *Phases of Faith or Passages from the History of My Creed*. London: J. Chapman, 1850.

Pool, Daniel. *What Jane Austen Ate and Charles Dickens Knew: From Fox Hunting to Whist: The Facts of Daily Life in 19th-Century England*. New York: Simon and Schuster, 1993.

Porter, Duncan M. "The *Beagle* Collector and His Collections." Chapter 31 in *The Darwinian Heritage*, edited by David Kohn. Princeton: Princeton University Press, 1986.

Raverat, Gwen. *Period Piece*. Ann Arbor: The University of Michigan Press, 1992.

Thoreau, Henry David. *I to Myself: An Annotated Selection from the Journal of Henry D. Thoreau*. Ed. Jeffrey Cramer. New Haven: Yale University Press, 2007.

Wedgwood, Barbara, and Hensleigh Wedgwood. *The Wedgwood Circle, 1730–1897: Four Generations of a Family and Their Friends*. Westfield, New Jersey: Eastview Editions, 1980.

Weiner, Jonathan. *The Beak of the Finch: A Story of Evolution in Our Time*. New York: Vintage, 1995.

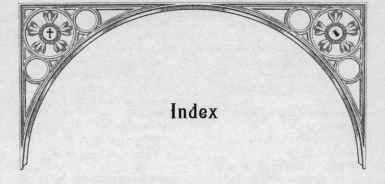

Index

Austen, Jane, 35, 41, 45, 58, 90–91, 115, 231

Beagle (ship), 1, 2, 5, 6, 13, 22, 24, 33, 51, 83, 95, 139, 150, 194
Bevan, Edward, 84
Bible, 11, 27, 51, 70, 72–73, 78, 94, 140, 141, 189, 191, 227, 231–32
British Association for the Advancement of Science, 8, 181, 192–94
Buffon, George-Louis Leclerc, 84

Cambridge University, 8, 23–24, 32, 33, 76, 124, 181, 199, 221
Carlyle, Jane, 6, 31, 75
Carlyle, Thomas, 6, 31, 75, 78
Chopin, Frédéric, 39
Christianity, 18–19, 26–27, 42, 46, 141–42, 151, 231
Coleridge, Hartley, 156
Coleridge, Samuel Taylor, 15
Covington, Syms, 6, 83–84, 92, 110

Darwin, Amy (Frank's wife), 218
Darwin, Anne Elizabeth (daughter), 109, 115, 119, 120, 122, 133–35
   birth of, 108
   death of, 148–49, 151–59, 190, 197, 198, 200, 205–206
   funeral of, 151
   illness of, 135–48, 156, 224
   musical talent of, 129–30, 134
Darwin, Bernard (grandson), 218–20, 229, 235
Darwin, Caroline (sister), *see* Wedgwood, Caroline Darwin
Darwin, Catherine (sister), 8, 18, 19, 30–33, 58, 63, 85, 117, 130, 133, 168
Darwin, Charles
   appearance of, 7–8
   autobiography of, 202, 218, 221, 229–31, 234
   birth of, 18
   births of children of, 105–106, 108, 116, 120, 126, 129, 136, 153, 167–68
   childhood of, 14, 17–20, 77–78

Darwin, Charles (*cont.*)
  child-rearing philosophy of,
    119–20, 127, 161–65
  children's relationship with, 107,
    108, 126–28, 132–35, 154, 159–60,
    202–203, 209, 220–21
  country house purchased by,
    111–20
  courtship of Emma, 30–32,
    34–37, 47
  daily routine of, 162, 207–208
  death of, 223–26
  deaths of children of, 116–17, 119,
    120, 135–49, 148–49, 151–59,
    171–74, 190, 197, 198, 200,
    205–206, 224
  development of species theory
    by, 10–12, 48–53, 79–80, 97, 108,
    111–12, 120–25, 128–30, 137–38, 161
    (*see also Origin of Species, The*)
  education of, 20–21, 23–24, 33
  engagement of Emma and, 54–69
  facial expression research of,
    206–207
  fame of, 210–11
  funeral of, 226–27
  grandchildren of, 218, 223, 235–36
  illnesses of, 95, 96, 101, 105, 111,
    129–32, 144, 158, 192, 199,
    204–206, 223
  legacy of, 234–36
  London house of Emma and,
    75–77, 80–96, 109–10
  in London intellectual circle,
    6–7
  marriage considered by, 5, 6, 8–17,
    22, 27–28, 98
  married life of, 90–95, 102–103
  observational studies by, 47–48,
    66, 80, 106–108, 129, 210, 219–20,
    222–23
  old age of, 217–23

personality of, 63, 163
plant studies of, 195–96, 204, 206,
    218–19
religious views of, 23, 26–28, 34,
    47, 52, 59, 69–74, 77–79, 97–100,
    140–42, 158, 161, 196–97, 200–201,
    212–13, 221–22, 230, 231
romance of Fanny Owen and,
    32–34
at séance, 213–16
on voyage, 5–10, 13, 24–26,
    33–34, 44, 47, 50–51, 58, 86,
    101, 102, 150
and Wallace paper, 169–75, 177, 178
wedding of, 88–89
Darwin, Charles Waring (son),
    167–68, 170–74, 176, 200, 226
Darwin, Elizabeth (daughter), 129,
    135, 136, 159, 160, 164, 203, 225, 235
Darwin, Emma Wedgwood
  appearance of, 31
  birth of, 37
  births of children of, 105–106, 108,
    116, 120, 126, 129, 136, 153, 167–68
  and Charles's daily routine,
    207–208
  and Charles's death, 223–26
  childhood and adolescence of,
    37–40
  child-rearing philosophy of,
    119–20, 127, 161–63
  children's relationship with, 132,
    134–36, 152, 155, 159–60, 202–203,
    209, 220–21
  country house purchased by,
    111–20
  courtship of, 30–32, 34–37, 47
  death of, 156, 232–33
  deaths of children of, 116–17, 119,
    120, 135–49, 148–49, 151–59,
    171–74, 190, 197, 198, 200,
    205–206, 224

drafts of Charles's works read by, 122–23, 180–81, 183

engagement of Charles and, 54–69

Erasmus as potential husband for, 15

gardening and, 203–204

grandchildren of, 218, 223, 229, 232, 235–36

illnesses of, 95, 110

legacy of, 234–36

London house of Charles and, 75–77, 80–82, 84–86, 109–10

married life of, 90–95, 102–103

musical talent of, 38, 92, 130, 134

old age of, 217–23, 228–32

personality of, 29, 31, 38, 163, 198–99

pregnancies of, 96, 97, 101, 108, 112, 115, 120, 142, 167

and publication of *The Origin of Species*, 185, 187, 189–92

religious views of, 45–47, 52, 53, 69–74, 78, 87–88, 97–100, 140–41, 154–55, 158–59, 161, 181–83, 189, 197, 199–201, 212–13, 221–22, 231–32

at séance, 213–16

and sister's illness and death, 42–46

travels of, 40–41

visitors and, 163–64, 207, 232

wedding of, 88–89

Darwin, Erasmus (brother), 8, 12, 31, 77, 84, 85, 88–89, 92–93, 102, 112–15, 122, 153, 205, 209, 231

and Annie's illness and death, 143, 144, 147, 152

and Charles and Emma's engagement, 62

childhood of, 18, 19, 46

death of, 223, 226

education of, 20, 21

and father's death, 130

female friends of, 14–15, 94

intellectual circle of, 6–7, 49, 185

poor health of, 138

religious views of, 78, 98, 141

séance at home of, 214–16

Darwin, Erasmus (grandfather), 18–19

Darwin, Erasmus (grandson), 223, 232

Darwin, Francis (Frank; son), 4, 129, 136, 160, 179, 218–21, 225, 226, 229–31, 234

Darwin, George (son), 47, 130, 136, 160, 172, 198, 221, 226, 228

birth of, 126

education of, 202–203

illness of, 168, 170

marriage and family of, 229, 234

scientific career of, 234–35

at séance, 214, 215

Darwin, Gwen (granddaughter), 229, 235–36

Darwin, Henrietta (Etty; daughter), *see* Litchfield, Henrietta Darwin

Darwin, Horace (son), 153, 160, 197, 203, 205, 208, 212, 221, 223, 226, 228, 234, 235

Darwin, Leonard (Lenny; son), 136, 160–62, 166, 198, 202, 203, 221, 222–23, 226, 235

Darwin, Marianne (sister), 8, 19, 63, 85, 130

Darwin, Mary Eleanor (daughter), 116–17, 119, 120, 137, 174, 200, 226

Darwin, Maud du Puy (George's wife), 47

Darwin, Robert (father), 5, 16–20, 33, 63, 78, 110–11, 114, 160, 231

and Charles's education, 20–21

Darwin, Robert (father) (cont.)
  and Charles and Emma's
    engagement, 58, 133
  child-rearing philosophy of, 18
  death of, 130–31, 139
  declining health of, 115, 129
  marital advice to Charles from,
    22, 27–28, 59, 66–67, 99
  medical practice of, 17, 20,
    44, 101
  religious views of, 18–20, 23, 27
  and voyage of the Beagle, 24–26
  and wife's death, 14
Darwin, Susan (sister), 8, 19, 63, 85, 130
Darwin, Susanna Wedgwood
    (mother), 14, 18–20, 77, 79, 117
Darwin, William Erasmus (son),
    109, 110, 114, 115, 119, 120, 122, 130,
    134, 187, 226, 221
  and Annie's illness and death,
    139, 141, 152
  birth of, 105
  at boarding school, 135, 160
  career of, 235
  at Charles's funeral, 227
  marriage of, 232
  observations as infant of, 105–108
Descent of Man, The (Darwin), 208
Dickens, Charles, 6, 49, 76, 80–81
Down House, 115–19

Edmonstone, John, 20
Evans, Mary Ann, 214, 215
Expression of Emotions in Man and
    Animals, The (Darwin), 107, 210

FitzRoy, Robert, 24, 51, 71, 78, 95, 102,
    104, 106, 128, 194
Fleming, John, 84
Fox, William Darwin, 105, 156,
    159–60, 167, 172, 188, 205
Franklin, Benjamin, 71

Galapagos Islands, 9, 11, 50, 51, 80,
    137–38, 176
Gaskell, Elizabeth, 231
Geological Society, 76
Gould, John, 51
Grant, Robert, 76
Gray, Asa, 123, 171, 173, 191, 192, 196–97,
    217, 220, 221
Gully, James, 131, 139, 140, 144–49

Henslow, John Stevens, 24, 85, 102,
    122, 131, 136, 193, 220
  death of, 199
  marital advice to Charles
    from, 86
  religious views of, 73, 78,
    112, 199
  specimens sent to, 8, 10
Herschel, John, 226
Holland, Henry, 139, 140
Hooker, Joseph, 116, 120, 123, 124, 129,
    174, 191, 193, 205–206, 220, 226
  and Wallace paper, 170–73,
    175, 178
Horner family, 7, 8, 31, 61, 80, 87,
    93–94
Huxley, Henrietta, 198–99
Huxley, Thomas Henry, 187, 191–94,
    198–99, 213–16, 220, 226

Lamarck, Jean-Baptiste, 76
Lewes, George, 214, 215
Lincoln, Abraham, 18
Linnaean Society, 172, 174–78
Linnaeus, Carl, 128
Litchfield, Henrietta Darwin (Etty),
    29, 39, 45, 91, 122, 127–28, 130,
    135–36, 160, 163–64, 174, 199,
    205, 212
  and Annie's illness and death,
    137–39, 142–45, 151, 154–56, 190
  birth of, 120

and Charles's death, 225, 226
and criticism of *The Origin of Species*, 189–90
at Crystal Palace exhibition, 153
education of, 135–36, 203
during Emma's last pregnancy, 167
Emma's letters to, 209–10, 218, 219, 231–33
Emma's letters edited by, 235
illness of, 168–71, 177–78, 197–98
marriage of, 209
religious upbringing of, 162–63
at séance, 214–16
Litchfield, Richard, 209, 214
London Zoo, 47–48, 153
Lubbock, John, 115, 118, 166, 193, 226
Lyell, Charles, 7, 75, 102, 122, 167, 191, 192, 226
and Charles and Emma's engagement, 60, 61
death of, 220
geological theories of, 10, 123
religious views of, 78, 112, 197
and Wallace paper, 170–72, 175
Lyell, Mary Horner, 7, 61, 75, 196

Malthus, Thomas Robert, 42, 49–51, 78, 79, 169, 175
Martineau, Harriet, 6, 15, 85, 94
Martineau, James, 94
Mendel, Gregor, 184
Milton, John, 38
Murray, John, 126, 187

Natural History Museum (London), 229
Newman, Francis, 141–42
Newton, Isaac, 226

Origin of Species, The (Darwin), 1–3, 174, 166–71, 178–95, 198, 206, 207, 226, 234
Owen, Fanny, 29, 32–34
Owen, Richard, 192, 193
Owen, Sarah, 32
Oxford University, 76, 192–94

Paley, William, 23, 50, 181
Parliament, 226, 235
Parslow, Joseph, 110, 139, 141, 162, 168, 190, 227
Paxton, Joseph, 84

Raverat, Gwen Darwin, 229, 235–36
Royal Society, 88

Sedgwick, Adam, 10, 124, 182, 190
Sismondi, J. C. de, 40, 62, 75, 81, 115, 159, 161
Sismondi, Jessie de, 37, 45, 56, 57, 67, 68, 81, 101–103, 105, 108–111, 234
and Charles and Emma's engagement, 61–63
death of, 160–61
Emma in Switzerland with, 40–41
marriage of, 62, 115
religious views of, 115, 156, 159
Smellie, William, 84
Smith, Adam, 76
Society for the Prevention of Cruelty to Animals, 203
Stevenson, Robert Louis, 231
Stonehenge, 219
Swift, Jonathan, 217

Thoreau, Henry David, 179
Tollet, Ellen, 66

University College London, 76, 80, 141

Ussher, Archbishop James, 11

Vestiges of the Natural History of Creation (Chambers), 123–26, 188

Victoria, Queen, 138

Voyage of the Beagle, *The* (originally *Journal of Researches*; Darwin), 73, 95, 101–104, 125, 126, 150–51, 229

Wallace, Alfred Russell, 169–75, 177, 178

Wedgwood, Bessy (mother), 25, 29, 37, 40, 73, 88–89, 105, 116
  and Charles and Emma's engagement, 57
  child-rearing philosophy of, 30
  death of, 129
  Emma's correspondence with, 90, 93, 94
  illness of, 57, 64, 72, 88, 115, 126
  and Fanny's illness and death, 42, 44–45

Wedgwood, Caroline Darwin (Charles's sister), 8, 19, 32, 33, 41, 44–45, 56, 61, 63, 85, 89, 97, 102, 130, 230

Wedgwood, Charlotte (sister), 37, 41, 43, 61–62, 168, 178

Wedgwood, Elizabeth (sister), 31, 34–37, 93, 102–103, 111, 112, 162, 168, 178, 220
  and Annie's death, 152, 153
  at birth of Emma's first child, 105
  Emma's letters to, 40–41, 91, 92, 94
  and Charles and Emma's engagement, 56, 57, 64
  and Fanny's illness and death, 42–45

Wedgwood, Emma, *see* Darwin, Emma Wedgwood

Wedgwood, Erny (nephew), 119

Wedgwood, Fanny (sister), 32, 36–46, 55, 70, 72, 78, 96, 145, 154, 159, 200

Wedgwood, Fanny (Hensleigh's wife), 54, 57, 80, 85, 92, 94, 95, 103, 116–17, 119, 133–34, 145–48, 151, 190, 214

Wedgwood, Frank (brother), 37

Wedgwood, Harry (brother), 37

Wedgwood, Hensleigh (brother), 6, 30–31, 37, 54, 61, 80, 92, 95, 102, 103, 122, 190
  and Annie's death, 151
  and Charles and Emma's engagement, 57
  illness of, 119
  marriage and family of, 8–9
  religious views of, 78
  at séance, 213–15

Wedgwood, James (nephew), 119

Wedgwood, John Allen, 73

Wedgwood, Josiah (brother), 37, 56, 61, 89

Wedgwood, Josiah (father), 24–26, 29, 37, 42, 44, 57, 102, 105, 116
  and Charles and Emma's engagement, 56, 58, 133
  child-rearing philosophy of, 30
  death of, 120
  illness of, 64, 115

Wedgwood, Josiah (grandfather), 18, 71

Wedgwood, Julia (Snow; niece), 119, 190, 214

Westminster Abbey, 220, 226

Wilberforce, Bishop Samuel, 193–94

Wordsworth, William, 15